The German Pointer:
Shorthaired and Wirehaired

ANNA KATHERINE NICHOLAS

Title page photo: This handsome headstudy is of the famous Best in Show winner Ch. Nock's Chocolate Chip bred by K. Little and owned by Sherri and Jack Nock, Nock's Chocolate Shorthairs, Jupiter, Florida.

ISBN 0-86622-150-6

Distributed in the UNITED STATES by T.F.H. Publications, Inc., 211 West Sylvania Avenue, Neptune City, NJ 07753; in CANADA by H & L Pet Supplies Inc., 27 Kingston Crescent, Kitchener, Ontario N2B 2T6; Rolf C. Hagen Ltd., 3225 Sartelon Street, Montreal 382 Quebec; in ENGLAND by T.F.H. Publications Limited, 4 Kier Park, Ascot, Berkshire SL5 7DS; in AUSTRALIA AND THE SOUTH PACIFIC by T.F.H. (Australia) Pty. Ltd., Box 149, Brookvale 2100 N.S.W., Australia; in NEW ZEALAND by Ross Haines & Son, Ltd., 18 Monmouth Street, Grey Lynn, Auckland 2 New Zealand; in SINGAPORE AND MALAYSIA by MPH Distributors (S) Pte., Ltd., 601 Sims Drive, # 03/07/21, Singapore 1438; in the PHILIPPINES by Bio-Research, 5 Lippay Street, San Lorenzo Village, Makati Rizal; in SOUTH AFRICA by Multipet Pty. Ltd., 30 Turners Avenue, Durban 4001. Published by T.F.H. Publications Inc. Manufactured in the United States of America by T.F.H. Publications, Inc.

Contents

About the Author

Since early childhood, Anna Katherine Nicholas has been involved with dogs. Her first pets were a Boston Terrier, an Airedale, and a German Shepherd Dog. Then, in 1925, came the first Pekingese, a gift from a family friend who raised them. Now her home is shared with a Miniature Poodle and a dozen or so Beagles, including her noted Best in Show and National Specialty winner, Champion Rockaplenty's Wild Oats, an internationally famous Beagle sire, who as a show dog was top Beagle in the nation in 1973. She also owns Champion Foyscroft True Blue Lou and, in co-ownership with Marcia Foy who lives with her, Champion Foyscroft Triple Mitey Migit.

Miss Nicholas is best known in the dog fancy as a writer and as a judge. Her first magazine articles were about Pekingese, published in *Dog News* magazine about 1930. This was followed by a widely acclaimed breed column, "Peeking at the Pekingese," which appeared continuously for at least two decades, originally in *Dogdom* and, when that magazine ceased to exist, in *Popular Dogs*.

During the 1940s she was Boxer columnist for the American Kennel Club *Gazette* and a featured East Coast representative for *Boxer Briefs*. More recently, many of her articles of general interest to the dog fancy have appeared in *Popular Dogs, Pure-Bred Dogs/American Kennel Gazette,* and *Show Dogs*. She is presently a featured columnist for *Dog World, Canine Chronicle,* and *Kennel Review* in the United States and *Dog Fancier* in Canada. Her *Dog World* column, "Here, There and Everywhere," was the Dog Writers Association of America selection for Best Series in a dog magazine which was awarded her for 1979. And for 1981 her feature article, "Faster Is Not Better," published in the *Canine Chronicle,* was one of four nominated for the Best Feature Article Award from the Dog Writers Association. She also has been a columnist for *World of the Working Dog*.

It was during the 1930s that Miss Nicholas' first book, *The Pekingese,* was published by the Judy Publishing Company. This book completely sold out two editions and is now an eagerly sought-after collector's item, as is her *The Skye Terrier Book,* published through the Skye Terrier Club of America during the early 1960s.

Miss Nicholas won the Dog Writers Association of America award in 1970 for the Best Technical Book of the Year with her *Nicholas Guide to Dog Judging*. Then in 1979 the revision of this book again won the Dog Writers Association of America Best Technical Book Award, the first

Ch. Nock's Chocolate Morsel winning Best of Breed, under the author as the judge, in Texas K.C. in March 1983. George Heitzman handled for breeder-owner Jack Nock.

time ever that a revision has been so honored by this association.

In the early 1970's Miss Nicholas co-authored with Joan Brearley five breed books for T.F.H. Publications. These were *This is the Bichon Frise, The Wonderful World of Beagles and Beagling, The Book of the Pekingese, This is the Skye Terrier,* and *The Book of the Boxer. The Wonderful World of Beagles and Beagling* won a Dog Writers Association of America Honorable Mention Award the year that it was published.

All of Miss Nicholas' recent releases from T.F.H. have been received with enthusiasm and acclaim; these include *Successful Dog Show Exhibiting, The Book of the Rottweiler, The Book of the Poodle, The Book of the Labrador Retriever, The Book of the English Springer Spaniel, The Book of the Golden Retriever, The Book of the German Shepherd Dog* and *The Book of the Shetland Sheepdog.* In the same series with the one you are now reading, Miss Nicholas has finished *The Maltese, The Chow Chow, The Keeshond, The Poodle,* and *The Boxer.* Two other recent books of Miss Nicholas, co-authored with Marcia A. Foy, are *The Beagle* and *The Basset Hound.* In the T.F.H. "KW" series, she has done *Rottweilers, Weimaraners* and *Norwegian Elkhounds.* She has also supplied the American chapters for two English publications, imported by T.F.H. *The Staffordshire Bull Terrier* and *The Jack Russell Terrier.*

Miss Nicholas, in addition to her four Dog Writers Association of America awards, has on two occasions been honored with the *Kennel Review* "Winkie" as Dog Writer of the Year; and in both 1977 and 1982 she was recipient of the Gaines "Fido" award as Journalist of the Year in Dogs.

Her judging career began in 1934 at the First Company Governors' Foot Guard in Hartford, Connecticut, drawing the largest Pekingese entry ever assembled to date at this event. Presently she is approved to judge all Hounds, Terriers, Toys, and Non-Sporting Dogs; all Pointers, English and Gordon Setters, Vizslas, Weimaraners and Wire-haired Pointing Griffons in Sporting breeds and, in Working Group, Boxers and Doberman Pinschers. In 1970 she became the third woman in history to judge Best in Show at the prestigious Westminster Kennel Club Dog Show, where she has officiated on some sixteen other occasions through the years. In addition to her numerous Westminster assignments, Miss Nicholas has judged at such other outstandingly important events as Santa Barbara, Trenton, Chicago International, the Sportsmans in Canada, the Metropolitan in Canada, and Specialty Shows in several dozen breeds both in the United States and in Canada. She has judged in almost every one of the mainland United States and in four Canadian provinces, and her services are constantly sought in other countries.

Ch. Robin Creek Captain Blaze taking Best of Breed German Shorthair at Rock Creek in 1967. Owned by breeders, Rita and John Remondi. Handled by Mr. Remondi.

Chapter 1

History of the German Pointers

Sportsmen owe a tremendous debt of gratitude to the early German breeders, as, indeed, does everyone who loves the sporting dogs, for the development of two of our most adaptable, useful, intelligent and versatile breeds, the German Shorthaired Pointer and the German Wirehaired Pointer.

Both of these breeds provide the rare combination of a pointing bird dog, an excellent duck dog, and a dog who retrieves easily and skillfully on land or in water.

Both are handsome breeds; both make excellent companions and "family dogs." Either one will bring you many hours of pleasure in the field; or, if formal competition is your "thing," in field trials, obedience, and conformation shows in which the dogs are judged for their physical adherence to the breed standard.

The German Shorthaired Pointer and the German Wirehaired Pointer are two different and distinct breeds of dog; they are NOT two varieties of the same breed, although they have some mutual characteristics. It is said that the Shorthaired is the result of early interbreeding between the descendants of English Foxhounds, early Spanish Pointers, and some of the German tracking hounds, the latter also known as the St. Hubert's Hounds, which are credited with having brought trailing ability to the Shorthairs.

It was in the 1870 era, we have read, when Prince Albrecht zu Solms-Bauenfels of the House of Hanover decreed that "form should follow ability" in these dogs. Christian Bode of Altenau and Herr Mehlich of Buckow are other names we have read in connection with

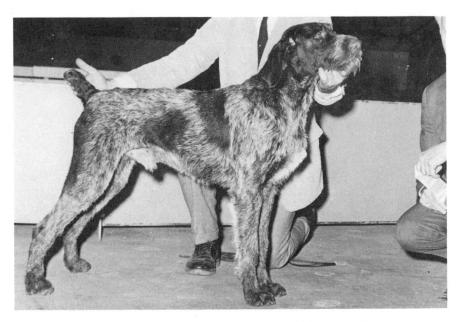

Ch. Jagersbo Mill Dietrichsteid, a famed German Wirehaired Pointer, photographed April 1967. Photo courtesy of Erik Bergishagen, Birmingham, Michigan.

The German Shorthaired Pointer Ch. Ricefields Jon, by Ch. Beaver of Hollabird ex Ch. Ricefields Brown Bomber (dam of four champions), was the top winning solid liver Shorthair in 1959. Jon had 85 Bests of Breed and over 25 Group placements. Owned by Miss Camilla Lyman, Ricefields Kennels, Westwood, MA.

Shorthair development. Christian Bode is credited with having crossed in English Pointers, bringing more style and more keen nose.

It was in 1883 when a Shorthair named Nero distinguished himself by performing notably against Pointers and Setters at Buckow. This splendid dog, owned by Herr Julius Mehlich of Berlin, tied with Treff, another German Shorthair, for the German Derby that year. It is these two dogs, Nero and Treff, who are given credit as being the two great foundation dogs of the Shorthair breed. And it was a daughter of Nero, named Flora, who produced three pups who became highly successful and influential foundation dogs. These were Hertha, Waldin and Waldo. Early in the following decade, Nero's granddaughter, a bitch named Erra Hoppenrade, gained fame as a field trial winner.

The German Wirehaired Pointer, or Deutsch Drahthaar, was developed through crossings of the rough coated early Griffon and the German Stichelhaar (Germany's early rough-coated dogs—which, in the minds of German owners, fell far short of the requirements of the 1870's for their sporting dogs) with the Pudelpointer (a cross between the Poodle and the English Pointer) and the German Shorthaired Pointer. The desire was to produce a skilled and versatile rough-coated hunting dog, equally at home pointing or retrieving, on land or in the water. Much emphasis was placed on the coat, intended to serve as protection to the dog against tough ground cover and bad weather, so that in 1902 the membership of the Drahthaar Club stated that "The breeding of the correct wire coat is the most important feature."

When the Verein Deutsch Drahthaar was founded in 1902, it was for the specific purpose of breeding the perfect rough-haired sporting dog for all sorts of sporting use. That they succeeded well is self-evident! Verein Deutsch Drahtraar's primary goal was perfection in sporting abilities, which was quickly reached. Then came emphasis on a good, strong and suitable build, to equip the dog well for his work. These were followed by beauty of appearance, which was slower in coming but has certainly long since been attained, as one can quickly note in the records of this breed in multi-breed competition at the dog shows.

In keeping with the stern rules covering registration in the German Stud Book, or Stammbuch Deutsch, Drahthaars were only eligible for listing and entry therein after they had reached the age of one year (this later became seven months) and their coat and conformation had been approved. Dogs not approved for the stud book could not be used for breeding.

BEST of BREED (Variety)

Ch. Robin Crest Kajobar von Stoneybrook owned by Robin Crest Kennels, Rita and John Remondi, Armonk, New York. The youngest Dual Champion in the history of the breed and the youngest Dual to win the breed at Westminster in Shorthairs.

Chapter 2

German Pointers in the United States

Shorthairs

German Shorthaired Pointers would seem to have first appeared in the United States around the mid-1920's, when a gentleman from Missoula, Montana, imported a bitch from Austria. Her name was Senta von Hohenbruck, and she had been bred prior to shipping, whelping her litter in the United States on July 4th 1925. Dr. Thornton was an avid upland game hunter, and it was agreed by him and his friends that in the Shorthairs they had discovered a truly exceptional breed of dog. Subsequently Dr. Thornton imported at least several more bred bitches from Europe, with eager future owners for the pups among his friends.

The German Shorthaired Pointer Club of America was organized during the late 1920's, with the breed admitted to the American Kennel Club Stud Book in March of 1930. The first National Specialty was held by the Club on March 29th and 30th, 1941, in conjunction with the International Kennel Club of Chicago All-Breed event.

It is interesting to note that at the Westminster Kennel Club in 1937 there were three Shorthairs entered. Two, shown as a brace and separately in the appropriate classes, were owned by George M.L. La Branche of Hillsdale, New York and were littermates, born April 21st 1936. They were Rex of High Holt and Hilda of High Holt. They were bred by their owner and Mrs. Pauline V. Rogers, and they were by Fox Tremonia ex Scholze's Elli. The third entry, an American-bred bitch, was Heidi, bred by Bargee Kennels, owned by Bailey Balken, and sired by Nimrod v. Gottorp ex Bargee Princess Bella. Colin A. MacFarlane was listed as handler.

Wirehairs

German Wirehaired Pointers, then known as German Drahthaars, first made their appearance in the United States around 1920. At that time they did not really create too much excitement; but following World War II all that changed, and the acceptance and appreciation of these grand dogs here has been widespread.

It was in the Midwest where Wirehairs first became popular, due to the outstanding versatility and quality of their work in the field. In 1959 official recognition was granted by the American Kennel Club, and but two short years later a member of the breed won the National German Pointing Breeds Field Trial Championship. This breed was the 114th to be recognized by the American Kennel Club (A.K.C.). A Specialty Club had been formed back in May 1953 which was originally called the German Drahthaar Pointer Club of America, and Al Gallagher was the first to serve as President. The American Kennel Club chose to Anglicize the name of the breed prior to its recognition, and so it became, and remains, the German Wirehaired Pointer Club of America.

During the first ten years of their recognition, German Wirehaired Pointers competed successfully in field trials, obedience trials and dog shows. At the end of this period the breed had seven Dual Champions, three Field Champions, 69 Show Champions, and in Obedience one U.D. was earned as well as three C.D.X. and fourteen C.D. titles.

The German Wirehaired Pointer Club of America held its first Specialty Show in conjunction with the International Kennel Club of Chicago in April 1962.

Kennel Names

A kennel name is important to a breeder, and should be selected and used from the time of one's first homebred litter. Kennel names are chosen in many different ways. Some people select for them the name of the street on which they live. Others will use a form of their own name, such as Pat Laurans has done with "Laurwyn," or a coined combination of the names of members of their family. Some will name the kennel for a child, or children, who may be especially enthusiastic over the dogs, as you will note the Remondis have done when you read their kennel story. Many use the names of the foundation dogs behind a breeding program, either the proper names or call names of these dogs. Whatever strikes your fancy is appropriate, and not burdensome or infringing on another person's rights is fine, and will identify you

A famous Wirehair from the past. Ch. Talbach's Gremlin owned by Harold Sanderson winning at Chicago International in 1961 under judge Alva Rosenberg.

15

and your German Pointers down through the generations—especially important in those you yourself have bred.

A kennel name can be registered with the American Kennel Club, which gives the registrant the exclusive right to that name in registering dogs, and no other breeder or owner may include it in the registered name of one of their dogs without written permission of the registrant during the period in which the registration is effective. Detailed information regarding the type of name eligible for registration is available by contacting the American Kennel Club, 51 Madison Avenue, New York, N.Y. 10010. There are specific requirements regarding the type of name eligible for registration, and a fee is to be paid if one chooses this course.

Ch. Hilltop Tina's Honey, *on the left*, taking Best of Breed; Ch. Hilltop Honey's Beau Brummel, *on the right*, Best of Opposite Sex. Breeder-owners, Charles and Betty Stroh, Suffield, CT. Photo taken in 1970. Handled by Richard L. Bauer and Michael Pawasarat.

Ch. P.W.'s Challenger von Fieldcrest owned by Larry Berg, Woodhaven, NY.

To be of greatest value, kennel names should be applied to all dogs bred by your kennel, as then it immediately identifies your dog and its background. A good way is to work out a system by which your home-breds will bear names *beginning* with the name of your kennel while dogs purchased from others and already bearing *one* name will have that of your kennel added at the *end*. Or whatever other system appeals to you as a way to indicate whether the dog was actually *bred by you*, or was purchased.

We take very special pride in our kennel stories for this book, for their wide range and the many prominent and successful breeders represented. We feel that they bring you the history of German Pointers as it has unfolded in America in a complete, interesting and authoritative manner. We hope that you will agree, and find these chapters and their many illustrations as enlightening and representative as they seem to us.

Generally speaking, the kennel stories are presented in alphabetical order with each breed identified under its heading. The one exception will be Desert Mills, as the owner of this establishment, Helen B. Shelley, has been tremendously active in *both* the Shorthaireds and the Wirehaireds; since this kennel history is our only one featuring the two breeds, we feel it belongs right up front.

Desert Kennels

Desert Kennels, owned by Helen B. Shelley, consist of both German Shorthaired and German Wirehaired Pointers, who divide their time between Roanoke, Texas (November-May) and Eagan, Minnesota (May-November).

Mrs. Shelley started breeding the Shorthairs mostly for hunting; she had been a farm wife whose one vacation annually was a month or more spent duck, goose, and upland game hunting in the Midwest and in Canada. She and her husband became friends with Jack Shattuck, and acquired a pup sired by the first German Shorthaired Pointer Dual Champion, Rusty von Schwarenberg. Mrs. Shelley soon became interested in Field Trialing and bought Champion Waldwinkel's Painted lady, finished by Don Sandberg for Ernie Christiansen. Loral Delaney, a professional handler, and Helen Shelley made her a Dual Champion as well. To date Helen Shelley has owned and trialed four Field Champions and two Dual Champions.

The first of the show dogs was Champion Sky Hawk of Kaposia, the only dog to win the Veterans Class at the National Specialty on three occasions. Later she purchased Champion Kaposia's Waupon II. This dog, "Deuce," was born in 1966 and died in 1978. He was the only German Shorthair to win the National Specialty three times. He was retired in 1972, age six years, after his third victory there and winning the Minneapolis Specialty the following day.

Deuce was bred by Don and Betty Sandberg of Kaposia Kennels, by Champion Kaposia's Otsego ex Champion Kaposia's Blue Chinook. This splendid dog epitomized the finest in Shorthair type. Good topline, well angulated, with a classic head, noble carriage and driving gait. Temperamentally, he was the perfect combination of show dog, companion, and hunting dog—the true dual-purpose family dog a Shorthair should be!

It is interesting to note that the year following Deuce's retirement, it was his son, Champion Kaposia's Tucumcar, who carried on the family tradition of winning the National Specialty.

The breeding program at Desert Kennels concentrates only on Dual type in both its German Shorthairs and its German Wirehaired Pointers. Mrs. Shelley has shot over all her champions, and hunted many of them. She is the person who initiated "Dual Day" for German Shorthairs, which comes on the final day of the yearly National Specialty Memorial Day weekend, a four day affair for the breed, and the highlight of the year for Shorthairs. Dual Day features a field test

Ch. Mueller Mill's Valentino II, "Willy" to his friends, taking Best of Breed at Westminster in 1971, the judge Louis Murr, handled by Roy L. Murray for Helen B. Shelley. An all-breed Best in Show winner, twice a Specialty Best of Breed winner, this handsome dog has 250 Bests of Breed to his credit along with 30 times First in Group and 70 Group placements. The sire and grandsire of Best in Show winners.

and conformation evaluation for each dog, and is rewarded by a certificate attesting to Dual potential for those dogs who merit it.

Helen Shelley is a Lifetime Honorary Member of the German Shorthaired Pointer Club of America and of the Lone Star German Shorthaired Pointer Club. She is the only person who has attended all twenty of the Nationals, she tells us, and the only woman G.S.P.C.A. member who is a pointing breed Field Trial judge as well as an A.K.C. judge of all Sporting breeds. She notes that Virginia Hardin is her counterpart in Irish Setters.

Interest in German Wirehaired Pointers soon followed upon the Shorthairs at Desert Kennels. Champion Mueller Mill's Valentino, 1962-1976, made a stunning record for Mrs. Shelley importantly both as a show dog and as a sire. Bred by Kurt W. Mueller, handled by Roy L. Murray, "Rudy" was unbeaten as a special throughout his career. He finished his title in 1963, won the National Specialty in 1963 and 1965. Between 1966 and 1970 he gained seven all-breed Bests in Show, won the Sporting Group on 88 occasions; had a total of 132 Group placements, and 300 times was Best of Breed.

A son of Champion Oldmill's Casanova ex Mueller's Ina, Rudy thus was sired by the first German Wirehaired Pointer to win an all-breed Best in Show. "Rudy" himself was soon following in his sire's footsteps as a Best in Show, all-breeds, winner; while *his* son, Champion Mueller Mill's Valentino II, also took a Best in Show, siring a multiple Best in Show winner in Champion Desert Mill's Lon Chaney who in his turn sired the multiple Best in Show winning Champion Winter Hawk Snow Owl. Quoting Mrs. Shelley, she notes that the "Old Mill's, Mueller Mills, Desert Mills line is the only one in the United States with a direct father-son Best in Show record." Particularly notable is the fact that this has been through five generations.

Mrs. Shelley's German Wirehair breeding program has been based principally on the Kurt Mueller line. She also has used Champion Brewmaster of Brookside, of whom she was for a while co-owner, and strengthened the field quality with two German import bitches, Champion Ella v d Hohenroth and Britta von Landhaus. Ella was the dam of Mexican and American Champion Mueller Mill's Valentino II. Britta, bred to Valentino II for two litters produced champions who are the sires and dams of Mrs. Shelley's present Wirehaired stock.

Valentino II, known as "Willy," carried on in the show ring for Mrs. Shelley where his sire left off. Born in 1967, he lived to be thirteen years of age. He became a champion in 1968, and gained a total

20

The German Shorthaired Pointer Champion Kaposia's Waupon II, at four years of age. Mrs. Helen B. Shelley, owner, Desert Kennels, Texas and Minnesota.

show record which included an all-breed Best in Show, two Specialty Bests of Breed, 30 times first in the Sporting Group, 70 Group placements, and 250 times Best of Breed. A worthy son of Valentino and Ella, the sire of numerous champions including Champion Desert Mills Lon Chaney, multiple Group and Best in Show winner who in his turn sired the multiple Best in Show winning Champion Winter Hawk Snow Owl.

Champion Desert Mill's Medow Rok Willy, current stud at Mrs. Shelley's, is the only finished champion Wirehair who is double Willy —Rudy bred. One of his sons from Champion Desert Mill's Tilly v Landhaus, named Desert Mill's Henry Tickencote, is the first German Wirehaired Pointer exported to England from the United States, who in his first year out of quarantine, qualified for Crufts and has won and placed in several pointing breed trials.

Mrs. Shelley is a member of the German Wirehaired Pointer Club of America, which she has served as a director.

21

Ch. Weidenbach Bridget, a Top Ten winner among German Shorthaired Pointers of the 1970's, is by Weidenbach Umber Mick ex Weidenbach Bo's Calypso. Owned by Mildred L. Revell, Cotati, California.

Weidenbach-Weidenhugel

It appears that Weidenbach Kennels are now placing greatest emphasis on their German Wirehaired Pointers; but Shorthairs, too, have been very much in the picture at this establishment over a goodly number of years as among the pictures they have sent us are those of Champion Weidenbach Bridget, a Top Ten winner among Shorthairs of the 1970's, whom we note has at least four generations behind her which include Weidenbach Shorthairs. Bridget herself is by Weidenbach Umber Mich (Dual Champion Kamiak Desert Sand—Weidenbach Lisa J) from Weidenbach Bo's Calypso (Field Champion Bo Boy —Champion Weidenbach Miss Mischief, the latter a daughter of Champion Weidenbach Yankee Chief).

However, it is mostly about the Weidenhugel Wirehaireds that owner Mildred P. Revell of Cotati, California, has sent information. And they are indeed an impressive representation.

Champion Weidenhugel Aramis v Beau has especially distinguished himself as a sire, his progeny including twelve show champions; two obedience title dogs; two perfect score NAVHDA National Ability Dogs; and a 1983 Deutscher Bundessieger.

Champion Weidenhugel Moonraker, Deutscher Bundessieger 1983 won at Dortmund, West Germany 1983 German Republic National Championship Show. The title awarded to each Best of Breed dog is Deutscher Bundessieger, provided that the dog is also given the Vorzuglich (superior) rating. The title is always listed, once having been won.

Moonraker, an Aramis son from Heidi von Hohenzollern, was bred in the United States and after completing his championship here went to Europe for only two shows. He won Best of Breed and third in a 35 dog Sporting Group at the Arnhem and Omstreken Kennel Club in Holland in June 1984.

Champion Livewyres I'm A Shocker, C.D. and Weidenhugel Achates, C.D. are Aramis's two obedience degree holders. The two perfect score NAVHDA Natural Ability Dogs are Livewyres Sudden Storm, Prize 1, who earned the first *perfect score* in the state of California, and Champion Weidenhugel Drahtmore Polka, Prize 1.

Aramis's son, Champion Weidenhugel Drahtmore Kurt, won a NAVHDA Prize 2 Utility Dog.

The twelve bench show champions sired by Aramis out of seven different bitches are Champions Weidenhugel Top Gunnar, Top Flyte, Drahtmores Polka, Quincy v Aramis, Quena v Aramis, Solita, Drahtmore Kurt, Autumn Splendor, Moonraker, Rex v Soyen, Champions Livewyres Atom Smasher, and I'm A Shocker.

The Aramis son, Top Gunnar, would seem to be following in his sire's pawprints. To date he has eight champions to his credit. These are Champions Geronimos Anacharis, A Son of A Gun, Aachen v Galeon, A Floating Feather; Champions Weidenhugel Capucine, Calliope and O'Kim v Gunnar; and Champion Livewires I'm A Shocker, C.D.X.

Shorthair Kennels

Coat of Arms

Coat of Arms German Shorthaired Pointers belong to Karen and David Beddow and are located at Dallas, Texas.

Top Dog here is Champion Lowenbrau's Ben Von Greif, who headed for the 1982 Houston Astro World Series of Dog Shows and returned with three 5-point majors and his championship, all in one great weekend—certainly a brilliant start for a very excellent young dog.

The following month at the Dallas Cluster Shows, this young champion logged in his first Specialty Best of Breed win at the Lone Star German Shorthaired Pointer Club event judged by Otto Walzel. That same weekend he chalked up his first Group placement. On October 17th 1982, at the Sooner State Kennel Club in Enid, Oklahoma, Champion Lowenbrau's Ben Von Greif won his first Sporting Group under Tom Rainey. In only three months, Ben had completed his championship, doing so at one of the country's most prestigious and keenly contested dog show weekends, and had become a Group and Specialty Show winner, all while still a year old.

3-day-old German Shorthair puppies by Ch. Lowenbrau's Ben Von Greif ex Hillhaven's Penny's From Heaven. Owned by Karen B. Beddow, Dallas, Texas.

By the end of 1983, Ben's record included 66 times Best of Breed, 24 Group placements, including four Firsts, and two Specialty Best of Breed wins, bringing him to No. 3 ranking in the German Shorthaired Pointer National Systems.

Moving into 1984, from January through April Ben added 26 Bests of Breed, seven Group placements (three of them First), and another Specialty Best of Breed.

The first litter sired by Ben was whelped in February 1984, the dam being Hillhaven's Penny's From Heaven. At three months of age, many of the puppies look quite promising, and should hit the show rings for this year's Astro World Series at Houston, two years after their father. Needless to say, hopes are high for these babies.

Ben was bred by Becky Wood of Houston, Texas and is owned by Karen B. and David G. Beddow of Dallas. From the beginning he has been conditioned, trained and handled by Shirlee Murray at Frisco, Texas.

Ben has just won his first Best in Show at the Kennel Club of Texarkana in June of 1984. As always Shirlee Murray handled him.

Donavin

Donavin German Shorthaired Pointers, at Stanton, California, belong to Christopher and Donna Gillian Saris and have earned themselves a position of respect and distinction by their very notable accomplishments.

This is the home of the magnificent Champion Donavin's Sir Ivanhoe, who, at four years of age, claims a record of eight all-breed Bests in Show, first in 62 Sporting Groups, Best of Breed at 16 Specialties, 261 Bests of Breed, and 171 Group placements all of which have made him the Nation's No. 1 Shorthair for 1979, 1980, and 1981, Phillips System, the Nation's No. 4 Sporting Dog for 1980, the Nation's No. 2 Sporting Dog for 1981, and the German Shorthaired Pointer Club of America's "Show Dog of the Year" for two years. Ivanhoe was the youngest recipient ever of this award when he gained it for the first time at only 26 months of age, having completed his championship in May 1979, then in only six months raced to the top of the charts and ended the year with his first "German Shorthair of the Year Award" and No. 1 Shorthair at the 1982 National Specialty, owner-handled.

Ivanhoe holds the all-time record for Shorthairs for Specialty and Best of Breed wins. He is second in the all-time records of his breed for number of Sporting Group Firsts, and third for the number of Best in Show wins. Both the second and third positions are to his own famous

Ch. Geezee's Super Chief making one of his many important wins, this time under Mrs. Winifred Heckman. Owned by Donavin Kennels. The sire of Ch. Donavin's Sire Ivanhoe. This famed father and son Best in Show winning pair are both alive and well as this is written. Handled by Ric Bryd.

great-grandsire, Champion Gretchenhof Columbia River, and his great-great-grandsire, Champion Gretchenhof Moonshine.

Ivanhoe is the sire of an impressive number of champions, both American and Canadian, including those with Group placements despite their extreme youth. He comes from a litter, sired by his own kennel's Champion Geezee Super Chief, that produced four champions, three of which became Sporting Group winners. His littermates are Champion Donavin's Gusto, a multi-Group winner who died during air transit at 2½ years age, already then ranking among the Top Ten Shorthairs; Champion Donavin's Magic Mischief, a Group winning Top Ranking bitch; and Champion Donavin's Gold Dust.

Champion Geezee Super Chief, who sired the above, was the Nation's No. 2 German Shorthaired Pointer in 1975 and 1976 (both times No. 1 on the West Coast). He was an all-breed Best in Show winner with first in ten Sporting Groups, eight Specialties, 116 Bests

Ch. Donavin's Chocolate Confetti, by Ch. Donavin's Sir Ivanhoe ex Ch. Gretchen Donavin Le Beau, born April 1982. This bitch is a double granddaughter of Ch. Geezee Super Chief. Mary Ann Pavack, owner, Milpitas, California.

of Breed and 42 Group placements. Chief is the sire of 17 champions, thus is ranked among the Top Ten All-Time Shorthair Producers. As Ivanhoe's sire, Chief, became one of the very few Best in Show Shorthairs to have sired a Best in Show son, and both of them are alive and well as this book goes to press. Geezee Super Chief has many multi Best of Breed and Specialty winners among his progeny, plus several Top Ten ranking Shorthairs including a son, preceding Ivanhoe, who was on the Top Ten list along with him, as well as winners from both National Specialties and Westminster.

With the photos she submitted for this book, Mrs. Saris has included one of special interest of Ivanhoe with Miss Valerie Nunes, who is winning Best Junior Handler at Westminster with this famous dog in 1981. Valerie was for awhile co-owner of Ivanhoe, and it is interesting that Donna Saris bought her first German Shorthair as a pet from this young lady's parents when Valerie was only six years old.

Among other noted winners at Donavin, sired by either Chief or Ivanhoe, are Champion Crista von Brandenburg, Champion Donavin's Fabulous Feather, Champion Gretchen Donavin Le Beau, Champion Donavin's Auerbach Ready Maid, Champion Donavin's Chocolate Confetti, Champion Placer Country's Cinderella, and Champion Placer Country King Bleugras. Also Champion J.R.'s Genie, who was ranked the Nation's No. 1 German Shorthaired Pointer Bitch for 1978, having to her credit the following wins: first in two Sporting Groups, two Specialty Bests of Breed, 32 additional Bests of Breed, plus 11 Group placements, and champion progeny to her credit.

Fieldfines

It was in the middle of the 1950's that Dorothea Vooris and her family first became involved with German Shorthairs, when Kara von Lictenwood was purchased for son Allen as a replacement for his German Shepherd which had to be put to sleep due to hip dysplasia. Kara was bred to Blue Chips Count Bangabird, and thus the Fieldfines Shorthairs were under way, located at Ronkonkoma, New York.

The Kara-Bangabird litter produced the Vooris's first pointed show dog, Fieldfines The Charger, who was later bred back to his mother in an attempt to solidify the strong points of the earlier breeding. This litter produced five bitches, one of which was kept and the other four sold to hunting homes. This bitch was named Fieldfines Tasha, and she went on to become famous as one of the Top Ten Producing bitches in the breed. Tasha was also the dam of American and Canadian Champion Fieldfines Count Rambard, the No. 2 Sire of Show Champions in German Shorthaired Pointer history. Rambard was the Top Sire for six years, and one year tied for the honor. Recently this splendid dog was the recipient of a silver and of a gold certificate, presented to him by Schlintz Publications as the sire of 25 champions (silver) and fifty champions (gold).

As a show dog, Rambard was handled by his breeder-owner, Dorothea Vooris. He was the first champion at Fieldfines—what a way to start, with so super a dog! At his first two shows, Rambard won back-to-back five point majors. In his first Specialty Show he was Best of Breed, then went on to second in the Sporting Group. He was on the Top Ten Shorthairs list for four years.

Rambard was a Canadian champion and one point short of his title in Bermuda. He was a multiple Sporting Group winner in the United

Kara Von Lichtenwood, foundation bitch of Fieldfines Kennels, shown with R.E. Vooris, Jr.

Ch. Fieldfines Ribbons, owned by Joyce Oesch and Kathleen Plotts, with her good friend and handler Dot Vooris.

States and in Bermuda. He received two important Bests of Breed from the Veterans' Dog Class. He was then retired.

Rambard was brought out for his final dog show at the 1983 National in the Parade of Champions where he received a standing ovation, the greatest honor that could be bestowed on a dog who had been so tremendous an asset to his breed.

Rambard died two days following his 11th birthday. A sad loss not only to the Shorthair breed but to Dot Vooris and her family, for Rambard truly was part of that family.

As a sire, Rambard has more than 60 champions to his credit with a goodly number more who are on the way to finishing. He was, in addition to being so successful a sire of show dogs, the No. 9 All-time Shorthair Obedience sire, five of his get having earned C.D. degrees.

Rambard was bred to Shaas River Risque, which produced seven champions, among them American and Canadian Champion Fieldfines River Shannon. She was bred to Rambard's half brother, Champion Fieldfines Rocky Run (Ch. Rocky Run Stoney-Ch. Fieldfines Tasha). This breeding produced Champion Fieldfines Ribbons, Top

Winning German Shorthaired Pointer 1983 and the No. 3 Sporting Dog. Ribbons is a multiple Best in Show winner. She won seven Specialties in one year, and was Best of Opposite Sex at the 1981 National and Best of Winners at the 1980 National. Ribbons is owned by Joyce Oesche and Kathleen Bowser and was handled throughout her career by Dot Vooris. Her total record to date includes two all-breed Bests in Show, 110 times Best of Breed (including Westminster in 1982), and she has won 29 Sporting Groups.

Two interesting facts about Ribbons are that she won the very first Group in which she and Dot Vooris competed. And it was she who whelped the last litter born sired by her grandfather, Champion Field-fines Count Rambard.

Fieldfines, from the beginning, has been a family project, and right to the present time three of the five Vooris children still show dogs. Dot comments, "It has done so much for them in teaching them that anything in life that you work for hard enough can be successful".

Am. and Can. Ch. Fieldfines Count Rambard, a truly great Shorthair owned by Dorothea and Robert Vooris, Ronkonkoma, NY.

Gretchenhof

Gretchenhof Kennels were established in 1955 with Joyce B. Shellenbarger's acquisition of Champion Columbia River Jill, by Champion Columbia River Chief ex Helga von Krawford; and Champion Columbia River Thundercloud. At about this same time, Champion Columbia River Lady, by Champion Columbia River Lightning ex Champion Hunter's Moon Jemimah, was added. In their one breeding, Thundercloud and Lady Jane produced Champion Gretchenhof Santana, multiple Specialty winner; and Champion Gretchenhof Chinook, dam of Champion Gretchenhof Lightning, multiple Group and Specialty winner. Lightning appears four times in the pedigree of the latest German Shorthaired Pointer Club of Southern California Specialty winner as we go to press.

In two breedings to Thundercloud, Jill produced Champion Gretchenhof Moonshine, the winner of 15 all-breed Bests in Show and 50 Group firsts, the dam of champions; Champion Gretchenhof White Frost, multiple all-breed Best in Show winner; Champion Gretchenhof Cinnabar, C.D.X., dam of the only Dual Champion U.D.T. in the history of the breed (Dual Champion Frie of Klarbruk, U.D.T.) in addition to two other Champion U.D.T.'s, a bench champion, and another U.D.T.; Champion Gretchenhof Cimmaron, multiple Group winner; Champion Gretchenhof Tradewind, dam of a Dual Champion and additional bench show champions; Champion Gretchenhof Snowflake, dam of four champions including a Group winner; Champion Gretchenhof Thunderbird, a Group winner; Champion Gretchenhof Stormy Weather; Gretchenhof Thunderbolt; and Gretchenhof Tally Ho, dam of 14 champions including two National Specialty Show winners, multiple Group winners, and a total of more than 100 champion grandchildren and great grandchildren!

Champion Gretchenhof Moonshine, bred back to her sire, Thundercloud, produced Champions Gretchenhof Blue Moon and New Moon, multiple Group and Specialty winners. Blue Moon bred to Dual Champion Baron Fritz v. Hohen Taan (heavy in the Pheasant Lane lines behind the old Columbia River stock) produced Champion Gretchenhof Moonsong, multiple Group and Best in Show winner; Champion Gretchenhof Moondance, Group winner; Champion Gretchenhof Moon Fire; and Champion Gretchenhof Moon Frost, sire of Champion Gretchenhof Columbia River.

Champion Gretchenhof Moon Dance, bred to Champion Lightning, produced what Joyce Shellenbarger refers to as "probably the

The famous German Shorthaired Pointer Ch. Gretchenhof White Frost. Joyce Shellenbarger, Huntington Beach, California.

most beautiful of all the Gretchenhof dogs or bitches," Champion Gretchenhof Moon Walk, a Group winner, Westminster breed winner, dam of multiple champions. An additional champion from this breeding was Gretchenhof Kaluah.

Champion Gretchenhof Moonsong, bred to Champion Gretchenhof Columbia River, produced Champion Gretchenhof Fredericus Rex, Champion Gretchenhof Windjammer (multiple Group winner), Champion Gretchenhof Westminster (Group winner, sire of 20 champions, named "Westminster" as he was born on the day his sire won Best in Show there).

Unquestionably the most famous dog to carry the Gretchenhof prefix, and one of America's greatest show dogs of any breed, must be Champion Gretchenhof Columbia River, known as "Traveler"—the winner of 30 all-breed Bests in Show, 102 times Best Sporting Dog, and multiple Specialty Bests of Breed including the National from the

Ch. Gretchenhof Columbia River, the winner of 30 all-breed Bests in Show, 102 Group Firsts, multiple Specialties including the National from the Veterans Class, the only German Shorthaired Pointer ever to win Best in Show at Westminster. Jo Shellenbarger, owner, Gretchenhof Kennels, Huntington Beach, CA.

Veterans' Class. This magnificent dog is the only German Shorthaired Pointer ever to have won Best in Show at Westminster, which he did in 1974. His Bests in Show also include such prestigious ones as Golden Gate, Westchester, Somerset Hills, and Texas Kennel Club.

"Traveler" was sired by Gretchenhof Moon Frost ex Columbia River Della (she sired by Champion Columbia River Chief, the sire of Champion Columbia River Jill, thus back to basics). He in turn sired 46 champions, including Group and Specialty winners. An amusing and interesting side-note on how "Traveler" was so named is that after grading the litter and selecting her pup, Jo Shellenbarger sneaked him on the plane and carried him home in her tote bag. An unforgettable, incomparable dog!

Gretchenhof Kennels averaged about one litter every two years. In some cases no puppies were retained, so the term "kennels" is perhaps deceiving. At no time were more than six adults maintained, with four the normal number.

Gunhill

Gunhill Kennels, owned by P. Carl Tuttle, are situated at Hague, Virginia. Carl Tuttle has been closely associated with German Short-haired Pointers over a goodly period of time, and between 1953 and about 1979 he raised more than 200 of them.

After that he became active in Field Spaniels, Pointers, then Whippets, finishing champions in each of these breeds. Now it is good to hear that he plans on returning to Shorthairs with a puppy coming to him shortly from Pat Crowley at Saybrook, Connecticut.

Among the noted Shorthairs which have brought fame to Gunhill Kennels one finds such dogs as Champion Gunhill's Gallant Knight, Canadian and American Champion Tasso Fran Hallum, Champion Gunhill's Mesa Maverick, Champion Gunhill's Maid of Iron, Champion Calvados Aleda, Champion Gunhill's Flying Dutchman, Champion Ledernacken's Fleck, Champion Maverick of Dobroyed Hall, and Champion Cede Mein Chat Nuga Chu Chu.

Mesa Maverick, of course, was Gunhill's top winner. Sired by American and Canadian Champion Tasso Fran Hallum from Manchap's Alaska, Maverick represented the well established and admired early bloodlines of Ross Chapman, the breeder from Albany, New York, who was one of the true pillars of German Shorthairs in the United States and whose dog, Champion Graf von Windhausen (by Champion Rex von Windhausen), was considered by many to be one of the ideal members of the breed.

Mesa Maverick was a direct descendant of Graf, who surely proudly carried on the line! As a show dog, Mesa Maverick was the winner of four all-breed Bests in Show, numerous Specialties, including the National in both 1965 and 1966 along with a number of local events, had first prize in 27 Sporting Groups, plus 90 Group placements, and a total of 175 times Best of Breed. He was the Top Show Dog in German Shorthairs for 1964 and 1965.

Carl Tuttle's first bitch was one called Bonnie of Millbrook.

Canadian and American Champion Tasso Fran Hallum, the sire of Maverick, was by Baron Treff from Penny Fran Hallum. Hollis Wilson had finished this dog in Canada and the United States; then the owner came East and Carl Tuttle took over the handling of Tasso in this part of the country over a period of about a year and a half. The owner gave Tasso to Carl at the close of his show career, and Carl used him for breeding to Manchaps Alaskan, who was granddaughter to the above-mentioned Graf, thus producing Maverick.

Can. and Am. Ch. Tasso Fran Hallem in 1959. Handled by Carl Tuttle, to whom he eventually belonged. This was the sire of Ch. Gunhill's Mesa Maverick.

Among other honors, Tasso won the Eastern German Shorthaired Pointer Club Specialty in 1960 judged by Jerry Rich.

Champion Chat Nuga Chu Chu, by American and Canadian Champion Cede Brass Badge ex the Moonwatcher daughter, American and Canadian Champion Cede Mein Gadabout, C.D., was a big winner for C.D. Lawrence in the Seattle, Washington, area. This dog was leased to Carl for stud purposes, and exhibited by him here, in the East, during 1974 and 1975. He was a very special dog, Carl tells us, personality plus. He won the National Specialty in Florida in 1976.

Champion Gunhill's Flying Dutchman was another quick champion for Carl, but unfortunately was short-lived.

Carl Tuttle is the fancier who was put in charge, by the Parent Club, of rewording the Shorthair Standard, and the one presently in use is the result of eight years' hard work put in by Mr. Tuttle and his committee—work which has proven well worthwhile one cannot help thinking as one reads and seriously considers the Standard which these knowledgeable and dedicated people produced!

Mr. Tuttle comments on and laments the fact that, as in so many sporting breeds, there has been a widening gulf between Field Trial owners and the breeders of show dogs. This is indeed a pity! And the breed as a whole can only suffer as the result.

Hawkeye

American and Canadian Champion Dee Tee Fan Cede v Greif, C.D. was the foundation on which John R. and Sandra Trotter built their Hawkeye Shorthairs at Cedar Falls, Iowa.

Fancy was the "runt" of the first repeat breeding of the now famous Mac-Dolly progeny, these coming from Dual Champion Oxton Minado von Brunz ex Dual Champion Cede Mein Dolly der Orrian. The breeder was D.W. Tidrick. The Trotters saw her at only three days of age, looking like a tiny mouse beside her strapping brothers and sisters. At eight weeks Fancy adopted the Trotters. Their cat gave her the food bowl competition she missed in the litter box, and she became a "chow-hound" for the rest of her life from then on.

Sandra Trotter says that to the best of her knowledge, Fancy was the only Mac-Dolly dog to earn a companion dog title, which she did with

Ch. Lowenbrau's Yahtzee von Greif, by Ch. Schatzi's Greif der Ripper ex Ch. Dee Tee's Fan Cede v Greif, C.D. Bred by Sandra and John R. Trotter. Owner Mrs. Robert Wood. A First Futurity Winner, also Best of Opposite Sex in 1978 National Sweepstakes and Best of Winners to finish at 13 months next day at Minnesota Specialty.

ease. Her first litter was whelped in 1976, three puppies which included Hawkeye's Zane von Adolph, C.D., who was major pointed and had two legs towards his C.D.X. when a fall from a bridge to frozen ground ended his show career. He was owned by Lyle Kurtenbach of Dallas, Texas.

The following year Fancy had a litter of nine, among them the first National Specialty Futurity winner, Champion Lowenbrau's Yahtzee v Greif, C.D., who is owned by Mrs. Robert Wood, at Sugarland, Texas. Littermates included Champion Hawkeyes Yea Taylfuer v Greif, C.D.; Champion Hawkeyes Dan Sir von Greif; and Canadian Champion Short's Happy Birthday owned by Earl Wallace. Regina, Sask, Canada.

Kaposia

Kaposia Kennels were founded in 1952, with Don and Betty Sandburg's purchase of a solid liver German Shorthaired Pointer male puppy from the well-known Oak-Crest Kennels of South St. Paul, Minnesota. The owners, Joe and Maggie Deiss, came from Germany, bringing with them some of the true foundations of the breed in the United States; thus the Sandbergs considered themselves most fortunate, in retrospect, to have lucked into the excellent strain owned by the Deisses on which to base their own Kaposia breeding program.

These dogs were the well-known and respected producing Winterhauch-Schwarenburg strain which was tightly linebred on the true foundation German Shorthairs in Germany. Down through the following 32 years, the Sandbergs kept within this line, producing sound, substantial dogs with excellent temperaments; kindly, smart, biddable, eager to learn and easy to work with, possessing lots of natural pointing and retrieving instincts, thus easy for the average novice owner-handler to hunt over.

This original solid liver dog puppy became Field Champion Kaposia Chief of Oak-Crest, C.D. When he had reached about two years of age, the Sandbergs purchased a puppy bitch from the same lines whom they named Kaposia's Firebird. She was a prodigy, to quote Betty Sandberg, "a true natural." By the time she had reached three years old, Firebird had become a Dual Champion, being campaigned concurrently in field and conformation. She completed her field title on one weekend, her show championship the following weekend, at two years and ten months of age.

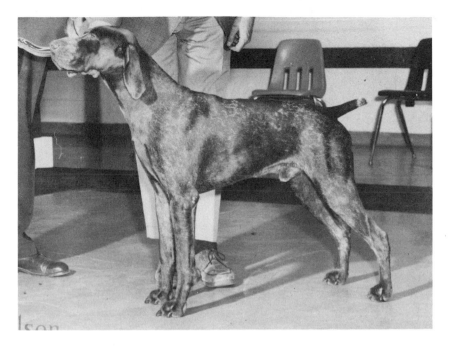

Ch. Kaposia's Oconto, by Ch. Kaposia's War Lance ex Ch. Kaposia's Star Dancer, here is going Best of Breed at the German Shorthaired Pointer Club of Minnesota Specialty, Oct. 1967. Bred, owned, and handled by Don and Betty Sandberg, St. Paul, MN.

Am. and Can. Ch. Kaposia's Apache Maiden, U.D., by Am. and Can. Ch. Kaposia's Wildfire ex Ch. Star Dust of Kaposia, the first bench champion to have become a Utility Degree dog. One of the many famous Shorthairs from Kaposia Kennels of Don and Betty Sandberg, St. Paul, MN.

Firebird was a busy lady, having also had three litters during the time she was campaigning in field and conformation. Her first litter was sired by Chief and produced three champions. These were American and Canadian Champion Kaposia's Wildfire, who was kept by the Sandbergs; Champion Kaposia's Black Hawk, a solid liver which figured in some of the early breeding of the Erdenreich Kennels belonging to Irene Pauly in California; and Champion Kaposia's Sweet Sioux, one of two foundation bitches which went from the Sandbergs to the Johelsie Kennels owned by Joseph Siemion in Indiana, the other having been Champion Cherokee Star of Kaposia, a Wildfire daughter.

One of Chief's first breedings was to an "early Minnesota bloodline" bitch named Prince's Pat, going back to the same strong bloodlines as his own. From this litter the Sandbergs took a bitch they named Star Dust of Kaposia, who finished her title at an early age.

Chief, Wildfire, Firebird and Star are behind ALL Kaposia dogs of the present day.

The Sandbergs take pride in the fact that many top producing Shorthair kennels over the years have used Kaposia dogs in order to consolidate their strong attributes in the breeding programs of their own kennels. They are also proud of having several of the breed's top producers, including Champion Kaposia's Wildfire, Champion Kaposia's War Lance, Champion Kaposia's Oconto, Champion Kaposia's Star Dancer, Champion Kaposia's Dancing Wind, and that many of the descendants of these great Shorthairs have also become top producers in the breed.

Champion Kaposia's Waupun, II, owned by Helen Shelley, had an especially illustrious show career, winning the National Specialty in 1969, 1970 and 1972. He was a Group winner and a Best in Show dog. Following his retirement from the show ring, he lived for awhile with the Sandbergs, and provided some splendid pheasant hunting for Don, prior to going to California to Mrs. Shelley's daughter and her family, where he joined kennelmate Champion Sky Hawk of Kaposia as his hunting partner until his death at a ripe old age.

Waupun sired Champion Kaposia's Tucumcari, bred and owned by the Sandbergs, who won the National Specialty in California in 1973. This lovely dog sired an imposing number of champions. His loss, of cancer, at only seven years was hard, indeed.

Another of the Sandbergs' "greats" was Champion Kaposia's Oconto, by War Lance from Star Dancer. He was Winners Dog and Best of

Winners at the 1966 National Specialty in Salinas, California, his very first time in the show ring, going on to become a Group, Specialty, and all-breed Best in Show winner. He was also a dominant producer, and one of his sons was Champion Ashbrook's Papageno, one of the breed's Top Sires.

Kaposia dogs are to be found the length and breadth of the United States, as well as in South America and in Canada. The Sandbergs are pleased that many of their puppies are sold to "repeaters"—i.e., people who got their first Kaposia dogs back in the 1950's and 1960's, and that when the old dog died, came back for another. Some of their "family," which they truly have become, are on their fourth dog purchased from the Sandbergs. By far the greatest majority of dogs they sell are hunting dogs. Many of these are shown and become top producers. But what this breed is all about are *gun dogs*, and so the Sandbergs are happy that so many of their dogs are used exactly that way—as loved family companions and bird dogs.

Dual Ch. Kaposia's Firebird, one of the four Shorthairs to be found behind all of the Kaposia dogs to this day. Don and Betty Sandberg, owners, St. Paul, MN.

Kingswood

Kingswood German Shorthaired Pointers came into being with the acquisition, by James and June Burns of Cuddebackville, New York, of the lovely bitch who became American and Canadian Champion Wentworth's Happy Wanderer, C.D., who is now nine and a half years old, a solid liver although beginning to turn a bit gray in the face, and still Jim Burns's favorite hunting companion.

Through Happy Wanderer, the Burns met a whole new world and a modicum of fame though not much fortune, to quote June. Wanderer is now the No. 3 All Time Top Producing Dam among Shorthairs, with 15 champions to her credit. The Burns have two more on the way to their titles which they hope to finish, which would make it a tie for Happy Wanderer for second place.

Happy Wanderer was one of the first bitches to be bred to the great American and Canadian Champion Fieldfines Count Rambard. Nine of her champions are sired by him! Additionally she has five champions by Champion Nock's Chocolate Chip, and one by American and Canadian Champion Kingswood's Windsong. As frosting on the cake, Happy Wanderer's children are carrying on her producing success, giving her as of now 12 champion grandchildren with, again, more pointed and on their way.

One of Happy Wanderer's offspring which June Burns mentions with special pride is her daughter by Windsong. This bitch, Champion Kingswood's Miss Chiff, attended her first National Specialty, in California, when only 14 months of age. By the end of the judging, she had been awarded Winners Bitch, Best in Sweepstakes and Best in Futurity. In 1983 at the National in Connecticut, with the largest entry ever for German Shorthairs, she went Best of Breed. Quite a record! It even topped that of her half-brother, Champion Kingswood's Night Rider, who in 1979 took Best of Winners, Best in Sweepstakes, and Best of Opposite Sex in Futurity.

At that same 1979 Specialty, Night Rider's sister, Champion Kingswood's Gilda, took Reserve Winners Bitch and Best of Opposite Sex in the Sweepstakes. These two are solid livers, which prompts Mrs. Burns to comment, "We feel almost like pioneers in getting solid livers accepted in the show ring here in the East. We were told when we started with our first liver how difficult it was to finish a solid liver, and since then 11 liver children and grandchildren of hers have done so."

The Burns's male, American and Canadian Champion Kingswood's Windsong, was the No. 3 German Shorthair Pointer in 1978, and still

Ch. Kingswood's Encore, dam of two champions, a daughter of Ch. Nock's Chocolate Chip ex Am. and Can. Ch. Wentworth's Happy Wanderer, C.D., bred and owned by James M. and June D. Burns, Cuddebackville, New York.

is an All Time Top Producer with 15 champions to his credit. He is the sire of the abovementioned Miss Chiff, as well as of many other Specialty winners including a half-brother and sister who took Winners Dog and Winners bitch at the National in 1981, along with many more pointed progeny.

Lenape

Lenape Kennels takes its name after an Indian tribe that was located in the Pennsylvania-Delaware area. This tribe was noted for exceptional abilities in hunting and stalking game, thus the identification seemed appropriate for the breed of dog to be raised here—the German Shorthaired Pointer.

The kennel, which has become a large and successful boarding-grooming establishment as well as for breeding Shorthairs, is operated by Patricia S. Mullin and Judith L. Sener, both Shorthair fanciers. Pat Mullin has been active in breeding, grooming, showing, and training dogs since 1962, and was employed by a veterinarian and a professional dog handler prior to opening her own kennel in 1966. She is currently a member of the German Shorthaired Pointer Club of America, the Dauphin Dog Training Club, the Harrisburg Kennel Club and the Professional Handlers Association.

Judith Sener has been actively involved with many aspects of the canine world since 1975, having shown her own Shetland Sheepdogs and now German Shorthairs to championship and being active as well in obedience. Champion Rocky Run's Tobert is one of her current dogs.

Lieblinghaus

Lieblinghaus Kennels, at Philadelphia, Pennsylvania, was established in 1969 when Dennis G. and Ruth Ann Ricci acquired their first German Shorthair. Following a divorce in 1984, Mrs. Ricci, now known as Ruth Ann Freer Ricci, continues the breeding of outstanding Shorthairs.

The Shorthair who started this enormously successful kennel was a bitch, Champion Mein Liebchen v. Werner, C.D., who was sired by Champion Grouse Manor Windstorm from Champion Harkins' Heide Ho, 1968 Dam of the Year. Liebchen was bred to Champion Whispering Pines Ranger (Champion Adam v. Fuehrenheim ex Gretchenhof Tally Ho) and in that litter produced the greatly admired and highly successful bitch, Champion Lieblinghaus Snowstorm (1971-1984). Stormy was certainly a breeder's dream come true! She was No. 1 Shorthair Show Bitch in the Country for 1976; in the Top Ten among *all* Shorthairs that year; and was the winner more than 50 times of Best of Breed plus multiple Group wins and placements, as well as Best of Breed at the 1975 Westminster. As a producer, she contributed well to her breed! She was Dam of the Year 1982, No. 5 All Time Top Producing Dam; had 14 champions, and eight additional pointed get to her

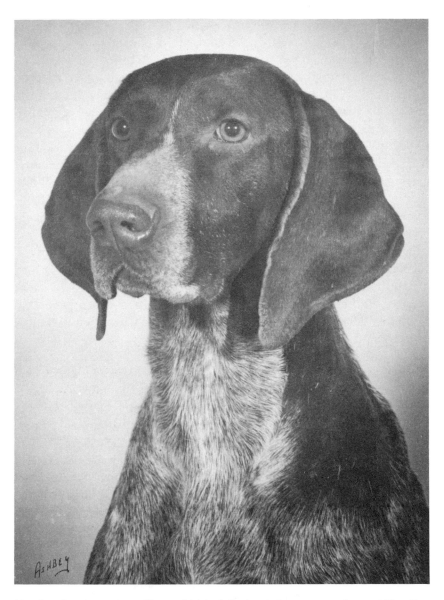

Headstudy of the magnificent Ch. Lieblinghaus Snowstorm, famous Top Ten Shorthair and an outstanding producer, bred and owned by Lieblinghaus Kennels, Dennis and Ruth Ann Ricci, Vincentown, New Jersey.

credit, from four litters which had totalled 31 puppies. Thus close to 75% of her children were either champions or pointed.

Bred to Champion Whispering Pines Patos, Snowstorm produced Champion Lieblinghaus Starshine and Champion Lieblinghaus Storm Trooper. By Champion Gretchenhof Columbia River, Snowstorm produced Champion Lieblinghaus April Snow, Champion Lieblinghaus Storm Hawk, C.D. and Canadian Champion Lieblinghaus Lynda v. Deister, who had points in the United States. In two litters sired by Champion Gretchenhof Westminster, Snowstorm produced Champion Lieblinghaus Retaliation, Champion Lieblinghaus Interceptor, Champion Lieblinghaus Deja Vu, Champion Lieblinghaus Lucky Lady, Champion Lieblinghaus W.A. West Storm, Champion Lieblinghaus Cisco's Liebchen, Champion Lieblinghaus Dust Storm, Champion Lieblinghaus v. Sonnenschein, Champion Windsong's Lieblinghaus, and Champion Lieblinghaus Olympian.

Returning for a moment to the original bitch, Champion Mein Liebchen v. Werner, C.D., in addition to Snowstorn, she also produced Champion Daisy Lane's Lieblinghaus, C.D. and Champion Lieblinghaus Upland Streak'r.

The real success of the Lieblinghaus breeding program has come through linebreeding the old Whispering Pines bloodline with Gretchenhof/Columbia River bloodlines. At this point Lieblinghaus have bred or co-bred 29 champions, five Group winners, Top Ten winners, Futurity winners, Specialty winners, and about 40 additional Shorthairs with points— all of these from a total of only 15 litters.

Another especially valuable dog owned by Lieblinghaus was American and Canadian Champion Hungerhausen's Dreimal Adam, May 1972-August 1980, who was by Champion Adam v. Fuehrenheim ex Hungerhausen's Debe. Interestingly, this dog was the result of taking an Adam daughter and for three generations breeding her back to her sire. Thus Dreimal Adam was a son, grandson and great grandson of the noted Champion Adam v. Fuehrenheim. He was an extremely impressive showdog, we are told, exhibiting tremendous style and quality, along with being somewhat of a "ham" who enjoyed "pointing" judges, photographers, etc. "Pache," as he was known, was in the Top Ten Shorthairs in 1974 and 1975, the latter year having been No. 1 with first in 10 Sporting Groups, Best of Breed 54 times, and as frosting on the cake, owner-handled he defeated more than 10,000 Sporting Dogs to become No. 20 in the Group for the same year. He also won the breed at Westminster in 1976, and had Specialties to his credit.

Am. and Can. Ch. Hungerhausen's Dreimal Adam, 1975 German Shorthaired Pointer Show Dog of the Year, bred by Wolfgang H. Hunger, sired by Ch. Adam v. Fuehrerheim ex Hungerhausen's Debe. Owned by Dennis G. and Ruth Ann Ricci, Vincentown, NJ.

Along with being a fantastic show dog, Pache was a fully trained field dog over whom each fall hundreds of pheasants and quail were shot. Mrs. Ricci comments, "Pache pointed with style and enthusiasm. He was a very rare dog—a once in a lifetime dog. Pache could do it all—and with style."

Pache died in 1980 in an unfortunate accident while out hunting. The one consolation for this sad event is the fact that it happened while he was doing what he most enjoyed—finding birds!

Some other especially distinguished Shorthairs which Lieblinghaus has produced or owned include Champion Lieblinghaus Storm Hawk, C.D., from Columbia River and Snowstorm, who is the youngest German Shorthair ever to have finished championship, Mrs. Ricci tells us,

Ch. Lieblinghaus Starshine, by Ch. Whispering Pines Patos ex Ch. Lieblinghaus Snowstorm, finished in August 1976 at Talbot Kennel Club. Bred, owned and handled by Dennis G. and Ruth Ann Ricci, Vincentown, New Jersey.

having done so in January 1978 three days before reaching nine months of age. From there he went on to become a multiple Best of Breed winner and Group placing dog.

Champion Lieblinghaus April Snow is co-owned by her breeders, the Riccis, with Debbie Pugsley Jackson, and is also from the Columbia River—Snowstorm litter. She is following in her dam's pawprints as a Top Producer, with six champions putting her on the 1983 Top Producer's list, and five others with points in her only two litters to date. Bred to Champion Columbia River Superstar, April Snow produced Champion Liebmeister Lieblinghaus Riker, a multiple Group winner and on the Top Ten for 1983 and 1984; Champion Mangis Autumn River Exactly, winner of Bests of Breed and Group placements; and Champion Liebmeister Edelweiss.

For her second litter, April Snow was bred to Champion Indian Country Columbia Moon, producing Champion Lieblinghaus Flagstaff (Best of Breed and Group placing dog), Champion Liebmeister Lieblinghaus Abagab (also Best of Breed and placing in Groups), and Champion Lieblinghaus Misty Moonglow.

Champion Lieblinghaus Starshine, from Champion Whispering Pines Patos ex Snowstorm, won the Sweepstakes at the Mason and Dixon Specialty in 1976, and finished title almost entirely from the Bred by Exhibitor Class. She went from Winners Bitch to Best of Breed at the Western New York Specialty in 1976 at the age of thirteen months over five "specials"! From her only litter, by Champion Gretchenhof Westminster, she produced American and Canadian Champion Bleugrass Lieblinghaus U.S.A. (Top Ten 1982), Champion Lieblinghaus Miss Liberty (Group Winner), Champion Lieblinghaus Liberty Bell, and two others with points.

Champion Lieblinghaus Storm Trooper (Patos-Snowstorm) was Best in Sweepstakes at the Eastern Specialty 1976, and Best of Winners at the National Specialty in 1977.

Champion Lieblinghaus Miss Liberty (Westminster-Starshine) finished at Westminster in 1983 with her third major, having been Winners Bitch under the author at Philadelphia in 1982. During 1984, Misty won 12 Bests of Breed, a Group, and multiple Group placements, to become No. 5 Shorthair Bitch in the Country. She is co-owned by Mrs. Ricci with Stephen and Doreen Urbanczyk, Freehold, N.J.

Champion Lieblinghaus Flagstaff, another well-known winner owned by the Riccis, finished his title with four majors, from where he, too, has become a consistent breed and Group placing dog.

Robert H. McKowen

We do not find a kennel name listed for Robert H. McKowen, who is surely one of the leading figures in the world of German Pointers through his ownership of the great and famed Shorthair sire, Champion Adam v. Fuehrenheim. This fantastic dog was bred by Charles L. Jordan, 1V and owned by Mr. McKowen who resides at Leola, Pennsylvania.

Adam was born in April 1962 and lived to be 12 years old. He was a son of International Champion Adam, a Swedish import, from Tessa von Fuehrenheim, and he is the all-time leading sire of German Shorthaired Pointer Champions. Officially listed at 115 champions, his owner lists the total as 128 dual, show and field champions all told. Adam stands No. 7 in the all-time sires of all breeds! He is, as well, the second leading sire of German Shorthaired Pointer obedience degree winners.

Adam's special honors include having been No. 1 sire, all breeds, in 1970, No. 1 sire, Sporting breeds, 1971, sire of the leading German Shorthair Sire in the United Kingdom, grandsire of the second leading Shorthair sire in the United States, sire of the seventh leading Shorthair sire in the United States.

The great Ch. Adam V. Fuehrerheim, all-time leading sire of German Shorthaired Pointer Champions; second leading sire of German Shorthair Obedience Degree holders. Owned by Robert L. McKowen, Laola, Pennsylvania.

Robert H. McKowen owns Ch. Adam's Happy Warrior, by Ch. Adam V. Fuehrerheim ex Gretchenhof Tally Ho (litter sister to Ch. Gretchenhof Moonshine). Shown winning under Mrs. Bede Maxwell during her first German Shorthair judging assignment in the United States, in 1968.

Winner of 60 Bests of Breed, including the German Shorthaired Pointer Club of America National Specialty and 11 other Specialty Shows, Adam was also the winner of 54 field trial placements, including firsts in All Age, Gun Dog, Amateur Gun Dog and Puppy Stakes. It hardly seems necessary to add that he was a member of the German Shorthaired Pointer Club of America Hall of Fame.

Another famous Shorthair owned by Mr. McKowen is Champion Adam's Happy Warrior, by Champion Adam V. Fuehrenheim ex Gretchenhof Tally Ho. Winner of a four point major the first time shown, Happy was one of six champions from the same litter, and equally at home in the field as in the show ring. His dam is a full sister to the all-time winning bitch in Shorthair history, Champion Gretchenhof's Moonshine.

Nock's Chocolate Shorthairs

Two very famous winning Shorthairs have carried the banner high for Sherri and Jack Nock, owners of Nock's Chocolate Shorthairs which are located at Jupiter, Florida.

The first of these is the great Champion Nock's Chocolate Chip, the sire, who is now more than 12 years old. Bred by K. Lytle, Chips was born January 13th 1972 from a litter sired by Champion Baron Marquis of Ashbrook (Champion Kaposia's War Lance ex Champion Sieglinde of Ashbrook) from Wild Winds Mitzi (Champion Gunner V. Hackenschmidt ex Megary's Dasher).

Chips completed his championship in 1974, going Winners Dog at the National Specialty. In 1975 he became No. 3 German Shorthair for that year on breed points. His wins included a Specialty Best in Show (Chagrin Falls) and six times first in Sporting Groups. 1976 found him No. 7 Shorthair on breed points; No. 4 on Phillips System points, No. 3 Kennel Review System, a Best in Show winner and a multiple Group winner.

In 1977, Chips was No. 1 German Shorthaired Pointer on both Phillips System and Kennel Review System, plus No. 6 in breed points. He also gained three Bests in Show that year.

He finished out the 1970's still winning Groups and on the Top Shorthair lists. 1982 saw him again among the Top Shorthairs and a Group winner. And in 1983 he achieved the very notable victory of Best in the Veteran Dog Class at the National Specialty and a Best in Show All Breeds at 11½ years of age, which his owners understand to be a breed record.

Champion Nock's Chocolate Chip has sired 14 champions to his owners' knowledge as we go to press. The most notable is the No. 1 German Shorthaired Pointer for 1983, American, Bermudian and Bahamian Champion Nock's Chocolate Morsel. His progeny have won futurities, sweepstakes, and important victories at prestigious Specialty events. In 1982 he was No. 13 Top Producing Shorthair.

Chip's son, Champion Nock's Chocolate Morsel, was bred by the Nocks. His dam is Champion Kejan's Independence, by Champion Krauss V. Franzel ex Fraulein Ginger Snap (Champion Strauss's Happy Go Lucky—Champion Riegeland's Pepper). Making his show debut in 1980, he was Reserve Winners Dog at the National that year, completing his title and achieving No. 10 German Shorthaired Pointer on breed points in 1981. The following year found him No. 2 Shorthair on the Phillips System, #3 in breed points, and the winner of six

Two very famous Shorthairs at the Nutmeg Specialty Show in Connecticut in 1983 with judge Herb Rolling. *On the left*, Ch. Nock's Chocolate Chip winning the Veterans and Stud Dog Classes. *On the right*, his son, Ch. Nock's Chocolate Morsel, taking Best in Show. Chip belongs to Sherri and Jack Nock, Jupiter, Florida; Morsel to Ashlyn Cannon, Charlotte, NC.

Sporting Groups. By 1983 he was No. 1 Shorthair both Phillips System and breed points; had a Best in Show that year to his credit, three Specialties, and a dozen additional Groups, to become No. 10 Sporting Dog, *Canine Chronicle*.

Morsel is carrying on in his own sire's tradition as a stud dog, having six champions already to his credit.

Paladen

Paladen German Shorthaired Pointers are owned by Paul and Karen Detterich, located at Riverside, California.

Paladen began with the purchase of a puppy intended to be a gun dog, later to become Champion Wil-Lyn's Sienna Gold, C.D., by Dual Champion Erick von Enzstrand ex Champion Clsambra's Gold Mein. Her breeders, Jerry and Andrea Ammel, encouraged the Detterichs to try her in the show ring, and it was Sienna's early wins, including a Specialty Best in Sweepstakes, that hooked them on conformation competition. Unfortunately, Sienna does not share the Detterichs' enthusiasm for showing, and only gives her all when in the field.

The Detterichs' next purchase, later to become Champion Wil-Lyn's Wild Bear Cody (Champion Baron Erik von Austin, C.D., ex Champion Geezee Cinderella von Clsambra), went to the other end of the scale, loving to show but being a lot for his novice owner to handle. He finished quickly at 17 months with a major Specialty win and Best of Breed over specials. Following his second birthday he started

Four-week-old puppies by Ch. Wil-Lyn's Wild Bear Cody ex Can. and Am. Ch. Clearsky Answer to Cedarpark. Owned by Karen Detterich, Paladen Shorthairs, Riverside, California.

out on a specials career, from which he emerged No. 6 German Short-haired Pointer in the United States for 1982, and No. 5 in 1983. His victories include more than 75 times Best of Breed, multiple Specialty Bests in Show, Group wins and placements. He is one of four champion littermates, with another "pointed" sister headed towards the title. Cody is three quarters of the way towards a Mexican championship, which should be completed by the time you are reading this book.

Few newcomers to the sport are so fortunate as to get an exceptional dog at once, without suffering through years of trial and error. The Detterichs had the good luck to find that special combination of show-manship and correct conformation in Cody, traits which he now is passing along to his progeny. At Paladen Kennels, the preference is to breed selectively, trying for high quality and consistency in a few lit-ters rather than a large number of sole champions from different dams. By leasing quality linebred bitches instead of by "starting from scratch," it has been possible for the Detterichs to improve on their strain within a relatively short time. Their favorite bloodlines are from Columbia River, Gretchenhof, Cede Mein and Whispering Pines, all tracing back to many of the same outstanding foundation dogs.

Paladen is a new kennel, their oldest litter just having turned two years in mid-1984. In this litter, by Cody ex Sienna, are Paladen's Son of a Gun (major Specialty reserve placements), Paladen's Most Wanted (minor points and Futurity placements), Paladen's High Sierra Ranger (minor points and Futurity placements), and Paladen's Showgirl of Enelrad (major points, Best of Breed and Group place-ments from the classes, plus Field Trial placements). Then there is Paladen's Brat Balou, a Specialty Show winner now close to the title, a very exciting "young hopeful" from a different litter.

Robin Crest

Robin Crest is a unique and outstanding Shorthair Kennel which was founded by Rita and John Remondi of Armonk, New York, 33 years ago when, in 1951, they purchased a bitch who had been bred in Germany and sold to a doctor in Canada. The Remondis bought this puppy, named Montreal Belle, a daughter of Champion Sleben von Graferhorst ex Bay Shore Lady, and it was she who became the foun-dation of the Robin Crest line.

When she was three years old, the Remondis bred Belle, who by then had become an American Champion, to Champion Alnor's Brown Mike. And in that very first litter they had the puppy who was

Dual Ch. Robin Crest Chip, C.D., T.D., and American, Canadian and Bermudian Champion, winning at Troy Kennel Club in 1963 under judge Maxwell Riddle. Bred and owned by Rita and John Remondi, Robin Crest Kennels, Armonk, NY. Handled by John Remondi.

to become Dual Champion Robin Crest Chip, C.D., T.D., an American, Canadian and Bermudian Champion. Chip went on to become the Greatest Winning German Shorthair of all time, Rita Remondi tells us, as she lists his record: six All Breed Bests in Show; more than 200 Best of Breed wins; 12 Specialty Show wins; best of Breed at Westminster; Field Trial Champion; Obedience Champion; Tracking Champion; Certified Water Trial; Winner of the American Pointer Club Trial; both a Bench Show and Obedience Championship in Canada and Bermuda. In June 1984, Chip was accepted into the German Shorthaired Pointer Hall of Fame. Very deservedly, we might add.

It is the practice at Robin Crest to breed from only top quality champion bitches, with few exceptions, the Remondis feeling that this is the only way to measure a bitch's quality. Any bitch with a glaring fault is unacceptable. And it has worked out well for them, as in 31 years of breeding they have had only quality pups of which they have been proud.

Ch. Robin Crest Ringo Riant winning under judge Horward Tyler at Windham County May 1966. Handled by John Remondi, owned by Rita and John Remondi, Armonk, NY

The Robin Crest kennel name was registered with the A.K.C. two years after the purchase of the first German Shorthaired Pointer. It was named after the Remondis' daughter, Robin, who was a big influence in the development of the line, as all obedience work was done by her at the Portchester Dog Obedience Classes in Westchester. The showing, field trialing, and water trials were done by John Remondi. The co-ordinating and book work was done by Rita Remondi.

Chip appeared in many publications, and the Remondis called him Cover Boy. He adorned the front cover of the *German Shorthaired Pointer News* twice. He made *Sports Illustrated* when they did a piece on Westchester. And twice he appeared on the cover of *Popular Dogs*.

Not only has Chip himself been a Westminster Best of Breed winner, but carrying on for him there in the family tradition have been Dual Champion Kajobar von Stoneybrook, Champion Robin Crest Achilles, and Champion Robin Crest Little John, the latter in 1984.

Champion Bama Bell Scotch 'n Soda has just been named Brood Bitch of the Year with one litter sired by Robin Crest Duke of Ireland. Six champions gained her the award, and since then still another has finished, bringing the total to seven.

The thinking at Robin Crest is not how many champions you can make or how many times you can use your dogs at stud, or records of how many. It is concentration on quality, and erasing faults. And never, ever breeding a shy, vicious, ill tempered bitch.

Some of the other famous dogs from Robin Crest are Champion Kajobar von Stoney Brook, the youngest Dual Champion in the history of the breed. The youngest Dual to win Best of Breed at the Garden. Champion Garden Crest Achilles, also a Garden (Westminster) winner, a Specialty winner. Best in Show winner, and a Canadian Champion. Champion Robin Crest Ringo Riant, also a Canadian Champion, who has been extremely influential in the line. And Champion Robin Crest Kaptan Blaze, a big winner in his time with over a hundred Bests of Breed and many Group placements.

There have been numerous other champions as well, but these either were not shown as extensively as the above, or held back in favor of them.

Rocky Run

Rocky Run Kennels had their start in 1953 when the Robert Arnolds purchased their first Shorthair bitch, strictly as a hunting dog. She was Arnold's Lady Hedi. She was bred for two litters to Crissy's Treth Fuehrenheim, the puppies selling so fast the first time that the Arnolds did not even get to keep one for themselves. After that the Arnolds moved to their present location, at Boothwyn, Pennsylvania, settling there in 1956, and naming it Rocky Run after a stream which is filled with large rocks or boulders that runs around the kennel. Hedi's second litter was born there, and this time the Arnolds did keep one, a dog puppy which Bob selected right off, and put aside refusing to sell this one. He became Champion Rocky Run's Rascal, the Arnolds' first champion. He was hunted for two years before ever getting to a dog show. Then the Arnolds entered him in the Open Class for Westminster 1958 (that class was chosen as it was the only one Bob could remember). A complete novice at the time, Bob was not aware that whiskers should be trimmed and dogs gaited to the left of the handler. But the judge was Alva Rosenberg, and he carried Rascal clear on through to Best of Opposite Sex. After the judging, he called Bob Ar-

Ch. Rocky Run's Firebrand, November 1965, by Ch. Adam of Fuehrerheim ex Rocky Run's Gretchen, bred, owned and handled by Bob Arnold. Firebrand won 30 Bests of Breed and three Specialty Shows.

nold back into the ring (as Alva has so often done during his career as a great judge) and said, "Young man, you have a very nice dog there. You should either learn how to handle him or hire a handler." The second time out Rascal placed fourth in the Sporting Group.

The Rocky Run dogs are primarily of the Fuehrenheim bloodlines. Rascal was bred to Deda V Fuehrenheim and from this litter Bob took two bitches. Both of these were eventually bred to Champion Adam V Fuehrenheim. Champion Rocky Run's Poldi produced seven champions and Rocky Run's Gretchen produced two.

Poldi's most famous son was Champion Rocky Run's Stoney who won 105 Bests of Breed and five Specialty Shows and was an all-breed Best in Show winner. He was also elected to the German Shorthaired Pointer Hall of Fame.

Ch. Rocky Run's Poldi, by Ch. Rocky Run's Rascal ex Deda V. Fuehrerheim. Breeder, Harold G. Fuehrer. Owner Bob Arnold, Rocky Run Kennels, for whom Poldi has produced seven champions including a Hall of Fame dog, all by Ch. Adam of Fuehrerheim.

Stoney is the sire of Bob Arnold's Champion Fieldfines Rocky Run. Rocky in turn is the sire of the noted Champion Fieldfines Ribbons, the Top Shorthair in the United States for 1982.

The Arnolds like to hold the kennel to around ten dogs as they try to hunt all of them and it is difficult to get them all field time. All of the Rocky Run dogs are trained by Bob Arnold's hunting partner, Bill Shilling of Claymont, Delaware.

The Rocky Run dogs are all sold as hunting dogs, but the Arnolds are pleased when they are shown as well.

Serakraut

The owners of Serakraut German Shorthaired Pointers, Ann and Margie Serak at Sturtevant, Wisconsin, have much in which to take pride as they survey the stunning accomplishments of their various dogs, so many of which are homebred.

Serakraut was fortunate in the acquisition of its foundation dog, Champion Strauss's Happy Go Lucky, bred by the Del Glodowskis and representing the finest of their Strauss's line. Happy Go Lucky became the No. 1 Shorthair in the United States for 1968, 1969, and 1970; won four all-breed Bests in Show; won 13 Specialty Shows; won 28 Sporting Groups. He won Best of Breed 185 times, including Westminster in 1969. All of this is simply frosting on the cake when one

The German Shorthair, Ch. Strauss's Happy Go Lucky, bred by Del and Val Glodowski, owned by Ann Serak is the foundation dog for Serakraut Kennels, Ann and Margie Serak, Sturtevant, Wisconsin. Pictured in New Orleans 1968, judged by Vincent Perry and handled by Larry Downey.

considers his real contribution to the breed and   Serakraut *as a stud dog.* He is the all-time Top Obedience Sire, and the sire of 47 show champions including a Best in Show son and several Group winners, as well as a Best in Show grandson.

Lucky's offspring have competed, and won, in all sections of the United States. In keeping with the character of his breed, Lucky is a true all purpose dog, and he and his pups are very keen in the field, both in trials and as personal hunting dogs.

Serakraut Kennels, located on 72 acres, have produced many champions who have distinguished themselves well not just with gaining bare titles but with truly important wins as well. Among those deserving extra-special mention are Champion Serakraut's Stardust, who is the dam of ten champions including Champion Serakraut's Bravo (sired by Champion Serakraut's Tailor Made, who is an all-breed Best in Show winner, multiple Specialty winner, and multiple Group winner during the early 1980's) and Champion Serakraut's Exactly, by Champion Serakraut's Rocky Mountain, the only German Shorthaired Pointer to date who has won a Sporting Group at the Chicago International, plus other Group Firsts, multiple Specialties, and a place among the Top Ten Shorthairs for 1979 and 1980.

Returning to the beginning, the Seraks founded their kennel, as we have mentioned, on the Strauss line. In 1964 they selected their foundation bitch, Strauss's Jodi, and it was the following year that the eight-week-old puppy who was to grow up to become Champion Strauss's Happy Go Lucky came to them. The Seraks linebred, going out a little occasionally, then returning to the original line.

The original foundation bitch, Jodi, produced five champions; Champions Serakraut's Ramblin Rose, Robinhood's Lucky Chips, Happy Go Lucky's Crazy Legs, and the Group winning brothers, Serakraut's Lucky Buck and Hot Shot.

Since the Serakraut Shorthairs are based on the Strauss line, this would seem an appropriate place to tell you a bit more about the dogs involved. Champion Strauss's Happy Go Lucky and Strauss's Jodi between them have brought to their progeny the quality of such admired early Shorthairs as Dual Champion Baron v Strauss, Dual Champion Hans v Eldredge, C.D., Dual Champion Esso v Enzstrand (imported from Germany), Strauss's Viktor (1963 National Futurity winner), Champion Strauss's Josilde Winterhauch, C.D.; Field Champion Greta v Ahornstrasse, Champion Otto v Strauss, Champion Thaldback Waldwinkel Hans, and others.

A true Dual Purpose Shorthair! Ch. Serakraut's Exactly, noted show winner, is equally at home in the field. Ann and Margie Serak, owners, Sturtevant, Wisconsin.

Serakraut is a mother-daughter project. Ann, who is Mother, and Margie, her daughter, did most of the showing of their dogs, traveling as far as Texas, Louisiana, Florida, New York, New Jersey, Pennsylvania, Iowa, Minnesota, Indiana, Michigan, Kentucky, Illinois, and wherever else an interesting Shorthair event might be scheduled to take place. Also they did a lot of hunting with their dogs, and bred for good nose, conformation and disposition.

Ch. Tabor's Orion, C.D., by Ch. Bruiser v. Fuehrerheim ex Euwina V. Esserschling, one of the German Shorthairs owned by J. and J. Tabor, Upper Montclair, NJ.

Tabor

Mr. and Mrs. J. Tabor of Upper Montclair, New Jersey, are fanciers who have met with some exciting and rewarding success as breeder-owners of German Shorthaired Pointers.

At the top of their list is American and Canadian Champion Tabor's Zephyr of Orion, by Champion Tabor's Orion, C.D. ex Champion Arawak Blue Angel, who won the Futurity Class at the 1979 National

Ch. Tabor's Zeus, C.D., German Shorthair by Ch. Tabor's Zephyr of Orion ex Ch. Conrad's Liberty Bell, at eight weeks of age. Breeder, J. and J. Tabor. Owners Paula Downey and Joan Tabor.

Specialty and then in 1980 returned to the National to take Winners Dog there in an entry of 94. Since then this splendid dog has brought home more than 135 Best of Breed awards in keenest Eastern competition, more than 50 Group placements and wins, plus three all-breed Bests in Show. At Westminster he was a Best of Breed winner in 1983, and he has Specialty Show top awards as well. Owner-handled to his championship, he was then turned over to Raymond E. Scott who campaigned him as a special.

Champion Tabor's Orion, C.D., the sire of Zephyr, was sired by Champion Bruiser v. Fuehrenheim ex Euwina V. Esserschling. Orion as a sire has produced two dogs who have been Winners at National Specialties. He was bred by J. Damon, is owned by J. and J. Tabor, and handled by John Horan.

Champion Arawak Blue Angel, by Champion Conrad's Brid ex Champion Traveler V. Waldtaler, was bred by Robert and Sandy Abel and is owned by the Tabors.

Champion Tabor's Zeus, C.D. is by Champion Tabor's Zephyr of Orion ex Champion Conrad's Liberty Bell, bred by the Tabors, owned by P. Downey and J. Tabor.

Champion Tabor's Banner of Hidden Acre, by Orion ex Liberty Bell, bred by the Tabors and co-owned with De Rafferty, was Best in Sweepstakes at the Greater Pittsburgh Specialty in 1982, Best of Winners at the National Specialty that same year, and at the Schuylkill Specialty as well; bred by the Tabors, owned and handled by De Rafferty.

Then there is Champion Tabor's Twice As Spicey, by Zephyr from Artemis, who was Best of Opposite Sex at the Sweepstakes and Best of Opposite Sex in the Futurity at the 1981 National Specialty. She was also Reserve Winners Bitch at the Eastern German Shorthaired Pointer Club Specialty in 1981 (from the puppy class over an entry of 50), and again over an entry of 50 in 1982. She is co-owned by De Rafferty with her breeders, the Tabors.

von Franzel

Walter and Betty Franzel, Land O'Lakes, Florida, have been working hard establishing their own von Franzel strain based on the most excellent of foundation stock.

Champion Sprenkle von Franzel, C.D.X., V.B. is a son of the foundation stud owned by the Franzels, Adam von Hollenberg, who sad to say was stolen when four and a half years old—truly a loss to his owners personally, and to their breeding program for which he was producing so well.

Adam was a son of Strauss's Happy Go Lucky from Champion Strauss's Miss High Society. Sprenkle's dam, Fraulein von Franzel, C.D., was by Champion Baron De Ville, C.D. ex Arlene von Unterfurberg. Fraulein was the foundation dam owned by the Franzels.

von Franzel dogs are to be found in the pedigrees of many current winners.

Ch. Sprenkle von Franzel, C.D.X., V.B., going Best of Breed. Ch. Von Franzel Nock Sherwood, C.D., his daughter, going Best of Opposite Sex. Owned by Mr. and Mrs. Walter Franzel, Von Franzel Shorthairs, Land O'Lakes, Florida.

von Thurber

It was in 1960 that the first of their German Shorthairs came into the lives of Dr. Robert and Jeri Leach at Birmingham, Michigan, with the arrival of a Shorthair puppy, a gift from a friend. Jeri Leach comments, "In retrospect, we *know* we received the better bargain because of the many years of pleasure our dogs have given us." The puppy bitch, Cindy, was registered Sieglinda Thurber because she reminded Dr. and Mrs. Leach of the drawings of James Thurber's dogs. When they started breeding, they added "von" to Thurber to lend a German touch, and thus the von Thurber Shorthairs were established.

67

In comparing their puppy to the breed Standard, the Leaches were sure they had the perfect Shorthair. On a whim, Jeri entered her at the Progressive Dog Club of Wayne County Show, in those years a benched event. It was a long day, as benched shows are, but the Leaches left there firmly committed to a future of showing dogs, for not only had their puppy won her class, but Alva Rosenberg had selected her for Reserve Winners in a sizable bitch entry.

Dr. Leach has been supportive, but owing to his limited leisure time, the breeding and showing has been Mrs. Leach's project and responsibility. It did not take long for these new fanciers to learn that

Am. and Can. Ch. Galileo von Thurber in the field. This famous show winning son of Ch. Ashbrook Papagano ex Lori von Thurber was bred and is owned by Robert B. Leach, M.D., of Birmingham, Michigan, and handled in the show ring by James Berger.

Juliet von Thurber winning the Sporting Group at Northeastern Michigan under judge Marg Patterson. Breeder-owner, Robert B. Leach, M.D., Birmingham, Michigan. Handler, James Berger.

while *good*, Cindy was of course not perfect. On her sire's side was Field Champion Dixon's Skid-do and her dam was out of Dual Champion Wendenheim's Fritz. She was a typey little bitch within the desired 21-23 inches, but shown at a time when preference seemed to lean toward the bigger bitches. Jeri Leach's first choice for a stud to whom to breed her was Dual Champion Biff Bangabird, and from the litter they kept the one that was to become their first champion, Abigail von Thurber. From her litter by Champion Adam von Fuehrenheim came Lori von Thurber who was subsequently linebred to Champion Ashbrook's Papageno, and the Leaches' fourth generation homebred "star" was born, American and Canadian Champion Galileo von Thurber. Mrs. Leach comments that at this point she felt that the "effort and time spent poring over pedigrees for studs to complement her bitches had been in the right direction." With Galileo as the backbone of her breeding program, Mrs. Leach was beginning to attain the type and soundness for which she had been working.

From a litter sired by Galileo came a bitch who is now American and Canadian Champion Katrina von Thurber. She was first bred to her grandsire, Champion Ashbrook's Papageno, which produced one A.K.C. champion, two others needing one major apiece, one Canadian Champion, two needing just two more Canadian points, plus one pointed puppy who was sold to a new owner in Bogota, Colombia, who has finished there.

Katrina next was bred to Galileo, from which came the dog, American and Canadian Champion James von Thurber and a female, American and Canadian Champion Juliet von Thurber. Two others from the litter are pointed with one bitch needing only a major here while another has her ten Canadian points but due to having won them at two 5-point shows needs a win under a third judge to complete title.

Looking to the future, Mrs. Leach has recently acquired a male puppy who will bring the Kaposia breeding back into her bloodlines. At five months, predictions are difficult, but right now he looks like a promising addition to von Thurber's program.

Recognizing the dual purpose of the German Shorthaired Pointer, Mrs. Leach has maintained the field instinct and all of the von Thurber dogs have loved working with their owners in the field. Show homes have not always been found for them, but Mrs. Leach has never placed a puppy that did not do well in the field. At present American and Canadian Champion Juliet von Thurber is back for further field training with Lee Sienkowski, Sr., because her style, speed, range and bird work indicate field-trial potential.

The breeding program at von Thurber has never been on a large scale, averaging one litter over a one to two year period. Quantity has not been the aim, but the maintenance of quality is of utmost importance to these fanciers.

American and Canadian Champion Galileo von Thurber was No. 2 German Shorthaired Pointer in 1979 and 1980, and No. 3 in 1981 even though he died in July of that year. His death was the result of drowning—a tragic accident when this marvelous dog was right at the height of his career and starting to have impact as a sire.

Galileo won Best of Breed on more than 165 occasions, including three Specialty wins; had more than 65 Group placements including many firsts. In addition to his success in the States, he was No. 3 Canadian Shorthair in 1979 with limited showing. He produced four American-Canadian Champions, three Canadian Champions, two needing only a major to finish, and several pointed who hopefully will finish in the future.

Regarding Galileo's death, Mrs. Leach wishes to correct an impression which has gone around that the dog had a seizure. To quote her, "Knowing that rumors abound and multiply, I had Dr. Mostosky of Michigan State Veterinary Hospital do an autopsy, and it was the consensus of the heads of all the departments, including cardiology, that he was in top physical condition. It was a case of simple drowning."

Wirehair Kennels

Arkayem

Arkayem German Wirehaired Pointers are owned by Bob and Kathy Marks, at Dundee, Illinois. This is the home of two very distinguished winners, Champion Spindrifter's Chip of Laurwyn, C.D. and Champion Spindrifter's Bang of Laurwyn, both of whom have distinguished themselves in the field, in obedience and in the show ring.

The dog, Chip, completed his championship on October 12th 1980, finishing with four majors at the International. He was next started in obedience, and at his first trial, the German Wirehaired Pointer National Specialty in 1981 at New Hope, Pennsylvania, went High in Trial as the first leg of his C.D. title. Chip achieved his three legs in three consecutive shows, scoring in the 190s. each time. Chip, now deceased, was owned by Robert and Kathleen Marks and Jack Writer.

Ch. Spindrift's Chip of Laurwyn and Ch. Spindrift's Bang of Laurwyn winning Best Brace in Sporting Group at Oshkosh, Wisconsin. These fine German Wirehaired Pointers belong to Arkayem Kennels, Robert J. Marks, Dundee, Illinois.

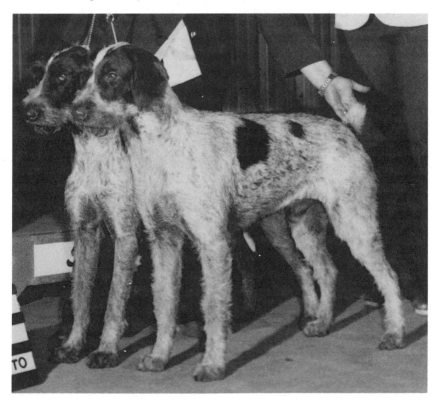

Ch. Spindrifter's Chip of Laurwyn, C.D., was another Wirehaired "star" from the Arkayem Kennels of Bob and Kathy Marks, Dundee, Illinois. Here making one of his numerous wins.

The bitch, Bang, completed her championship on January 18th 1981 at the Gold Coast Kennel Club Dog Show. She earned her three legs for her C.D. title in only four shows, and she was only the second German Wirehaired Pointer to pass the American Temperament Testing Certification. Bang loves to hunt, and does so quite well, once again proving the German Wirehaired Pointer to be a versatile gun dog. Bang was bred by Patricia Laurans, and is a daughter of Champion Laurwyn's Cheeseburger (American and Canadian Champion Winterhawk's Snow Owl-American and Canadian Champion Hilltop's S.S. Cheese Cake) from American and Canadian Champion Laurwyn's Barbed Wire (Champion Hilltop's Bradshaw ex Champion Laurwyn's Cream Cheese).

Bang whelped a splendid litter of nine puppies late in 1982. Her son, Arkayem's Bootleg Hooch, took his first show points with a four-point major at seven months of age.

Dual and Amateur Fld. Ch. Lutz Zur Cadenberg, C.D. completing his T.D. Silke Alberts, owner, Vallejo, California.

Cadenberg

The Cadenberg German Wirehaired Pointers are owned by Silke Alberts who lives at Vallejo, California. Top Dog here without a doubt is the very famous and handsome Dual Champion and Amateur Field Champion Lutz Zur Cadenberg, C.D., T.D., a German import bred by Fritz Butt, born May 3rd 1972.

Lutz has been bred to many good bitches, but most frequently to his owner's Champion Weiden Hugel Cappucine, C.D., T.D. So far he has produced 25 American show champions, a Dual Champion, two Amateur Field Champions, and one Open and Amateur Field Champion. Interestingly, he has produced over 30 NAVHDA Tested Dogs (for *N*atural *A*bility and *V*ersatility). Also obedience and tracking dogs, as his progeny seem to be as versatile as he is himself! Like their sire, Lutz puppies have all matured into wonderful companions and dependable good hunting dogs for their owners. Lutz is a real "people lover" himself along with being a tough dog who loves to hunt, and his children decidedly seem to inherit these traits from him.

Then there is the lovely bitch, Champion Weidenhugel Capuccine, C.D., T.D., born November 1974, bred by Mildred Revell. All of Cina's puppies have been by Lutz, the only dog to whom she was ever bred, and they include eight show champions, one Amateur Field Champion, 15 NAVHDA NA Dogs (12 of which have been Prize 1), one NAUHDA Utility Dog, and four Griffon Intermediate Hunting Tests Winners (sponsored by the Wirehaired Pointing Griffon Club of America). Cina has to her credit a NAVHDA Utility Prize III, earned with 163 points. She is described by her owner as a wonderful hunting dog with a great passion for water.

Champion Cadenberg Goetz v. Lutz, T.D., was born in July 1982. He is an A.K.C. show champion; a First Prize WPGC NA winner; a First Prize NAVHDA NA winner; an A.K.C. Tracking Dog, and a First Prize Wirehaired Pointing Griffon Club Intermediate Hunting Dog winner. This dog is exhibiting a good deal of natural talent for his age, and is becoming an excellent worker.

Cadenberg Filou v. Lutz, T.D. is also an A.K.C. Tracking Dog and a First Prize NAVHDA NA dog. She is an exciting, stylish bitch in the field. Her first litter, by a Danish import, has recently been born. She is bred and owned by Silke Alberts.

Hilltop Farm

The purchase of a hunting companion from the Haar Baron Kennel was made in 1965, thus starting off Mr. and Mrs. Charles Stroh of Suffield, Connecticut, on a hobby which has surely been one filled with pleasure for these highly successful breeders. The original hunting companion was soon to become Champion Hilltop Tina's Honey, as she started out placing in the Sporting Group from the puppy classes, and she became the foundation bitch for one of America's most widely admired Wirehaired bloodlines.

A daughter of Champion Talbach's Gremlin Rennie ex Dual Champion Haar Baron's Tina, C.D., young Honey maintained a breed standing of No. 1 German Wirehaired Pointer bitch over a three year period. Her overall breed standing also included No. 3 German Wirehair in 1966, No. 5 in 1969 and 1970. While Champion Hilltop Tina's Honey continued her limited showing, she was also producing seven champions and two Top Producers: a daughter from the 1966 litter, Champion Hilltop Honey's Sugar and Spice and a son from the 1968 litter, Champion Hilltop Honey's Beau Brummel.

As a winning brace in 1968 in the Westminster Sporting Group, Ch. Hilltop Tina's Honey (on right) and Ch. Hilltop Honey's Sugar and Spice, owned and bred by Charles and Betty Stroh, Hilltop Farm. Handled by Jimmy Mitchell and Richard L. Bauer.

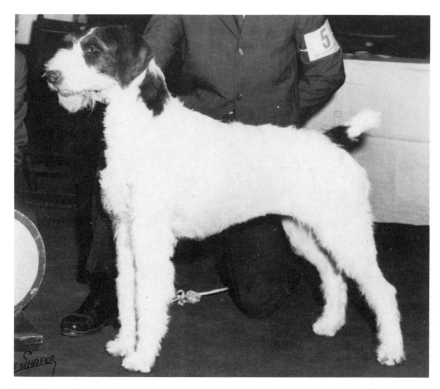

Ch. Hilltop Honey's Misty Lady, sister to Sugar and Spice, dam of multiple champions. By Ch. Talbach's Gremlin Rennie ex Ch. Hilltop Tina's Honey. Mrs. Charles Stroh, breeder-owner, Hilltop Farm, Suffield, CT.

Champion Hilltop Tina's Honey and Champion Hilltop Honey's Sugar and Spice made breed history as a brace, having been shown for this competition twice and winning Best Sporting Group Brace both times—on no less auspicious occasions than Detroit in 1967 and Westminster in 1968.

The August 1966 litter, by Champion Talbach's Gremlin Rennie ex Champion Hilltop Tina's Honey, produced three champions. These were Top Producer Champion Hilltop Honey's Sugar and Spice; Champion Hilltop Honey's Misty Lady; and Champion Hilltop Honey's September Morn. In 1968 Honey was bred to Champion Tordenballes Nico, a Danish import. This litter produced Top Producer Champion Hilltop Honey's Beau Brummel and Champion Hilltop Honey's Charlemagne. Honey's last litter was whelped in 1971 and included Champion Hilltop Honey's Peche Melba and Champion Hilltop's Chocolate Chip.

Seven champions were the result when Champion Hilltop Honey's Sugar and Spice was bred to Champion Hilltop Honey's Beau Brummel, among these the great and magnificent Champion Hilltop's S.S. Cheese Cake, the only Best in Show German Wirehaired bitch in history, and the all-time top winning Wirehair bitch.

Champion Hilltop Honey's Beau Brummel is the sire of 22 bench champions, including two Best in Show winners, and at least one Canadian Champion and an obedience champion. Beau is the grandsire of more than 62 bench champions plus two additional Best in Show winners.

When Champion Hilltop Honey's Beau Brummel and Champion Hilltop Honey's Misty Lady were bred, three more champions were added to this kennel's roster. One of these, Champion Hilltop's Bradshaw, was No. 6 German Wirehaired Pointer in 1976, and Top Producer for the years 1977 and 1978. Bradshaw sired only two litters, producing 15 bench champions, one of them a Best in Show winner.

With 19 homebred Hilltop Farm champions, number 20 is only a single point from joining them as this is written.

Ch. Hilltop Honey's Sugar and Spice, the famous Top Producing dam of Ch. Hilltop's S.S. Cheese Cake and numberous other champions, winning here handled by Richard L. Bauer for breeders-owners Charles and Betty Stroh, Hilltop Farm, Suffield, CT.

Jagersbo

Jagersbo Kennels, now famous in the world of German Wirehaired Pointers, were originally established and registered with the American Kennel Club back in 1928, having been at that time primarily a Pointer and Setter kennel until Erik Bergishagen, Sr., purchased his first Labrador in 1946.

It was Erik Bergishagen, Jr., who brought German Wirehaired Pointers to Jagersbo, when he received one as a gift from his wife, Jane. This was Champion Oldemill Cinnabar, who came from the Oldemill Kennels belonging to Newton Compere, one of the "Founding Fathers" of Wirehairs in the United States, to whom Jane Bergishagen's sister was married. Of this lovely Wirehair Mr. Bergishagen tells us "Cindy was perhaps the best field dog I have ever had. She hunted grouse, woodcock, pheasant, and hit the water after ducks harder than any of my Labradors." Previous to owning Cindy, Mr. Bergishagen had had some experience with Wirehaired dogs, particularly two of the breed who had come to him for training, and at

Ch. Oldemill Cinnabar was the first German Wirehaired Pointer owned by Erik Bergishagen, Jr., purchased from Newt Compere in 1961. Jagersbo Kennels, Birmingham, Michigan.

Jagersbo Mill Stig at Westminster in 1965 where, handled by Dick Cooper, he took Best of Breed over specials. One of the great German Wirehaired Pointers of the 1960's, he was owned by Erik Bergishagen, Jr., Jagersbo, Birmingham, Michigan.

that time he was impressed with how smart and how quick they were. The senior Mr. Bergishagen also had admired the working abilities of the breed, which he had come to respect on hunting trips with Lauritz Melchior, the world-famous operatic tenor who was a Wirehaired owner and whose dog they frequently used.

Mr. Bergishagen comments on three of the German Wirehaired Pointer dogs which he had especially liked of all the ones he's had. These were Champion Mueller Mill's Valentino, which was sold to Helen Shelley. Then a dog named Champion Jagersbo Mills Stig, who was by Valentino from Cinnabar, and Champion Jagersbo Friar Tuck who was by Stig from a bitch called Oldemill Flower. Both Stig and Friar Tuck were important winners, first one, then the other, being second to Valentino for awhile in the ratings.

Another dog Mr. Bergishagen mentions is one he calls "Luke," named officially Champion Jagersbo Mill Dietrichstein. This he describes as a somewhat different type of Wirehair than the others, of leggier build and with a coat of the quality that requires "little upkeep", which he later succeeded in putting on Champion Jagersbo Flying Mallard and Champion Jagersbo Wild Turkey whom he still has. All these dogs were excellent "meat dogs," as well as have been their get.

Mr. Bergishagen is a very knowledgeable fancier of the Wirehairs whose association with the breed over the years has, as one can see, included some of the greatest and most representative of its members.

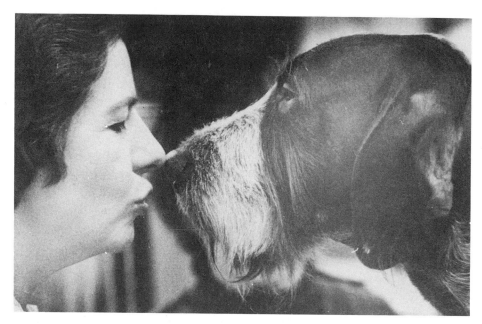

Mutual admiration! Ch. Laurwyn's Banner with friend and handler Joy S. Brewster after going Best of Breed at Westminster.

Laurwyn

It was Fate, and American and Canadian Champion Hilltop's S.S. Cheese Cake, C.D. that combined to start Patricia W. Laurans off with what were to become the Laurwyn German Wirehaired Pointers.

In August of 1969, Pat was in a very serious automobile accident. Up until that time she had owned, raised and shown Doberman Pinschers, and been a licensed assistant to J. Monroe Stebbins, Jr.

A year after the accident, when Pat had been released from the hospital and physical therapy, she and several of her dogs went to stay with Joy Brewster, a well-known Eastern handler. While Pat was there recuperating, a client of Joy's asked her to find an exceptional dog of any breed that she could campaign for him. Having just seen their first German Wirehair "up close," Hilltop's S. S. Funny Girl, owned by another "Doberman person," the breed came to mind as one with group entry potential. Funny Girl herself seemed like a fine young bitch. So Pat called her breeder, Betty Stroh. She learned that there were several four-month-old pups still available from a repeat breeding of Funny Girl's parents. On November 24th 1970, Joy, her client, and

Pat went to Hilltop Farm to look at the litter. Pat was immediately attracted to one of the pups, and said, "I don't know anything about German Wirehaired Pointers, but if she was a Doberman she'd be a Best in Show bitch. If you don't buy her I will." Joy also felt that the pup seemed to be unusually good, so her client bought Cheese Cake and took her home. Two weeks later he called to say that she was too active and spirited for him, and since Pat had said she would buy her, she should do so. Pat's first thought was that an offhand comment was coming back to haunt her, as she really wasn't prepared for another dog, let alone another breed. However, since she *had* said she would buy Cheese Cake she *did*. And it changed and influenced her life tremendously.

Cheese Cake, or "Racket" as Pat and Joy called her, turned out to be everything one could dream of in the way of a dog. Handled in the show ring by Joy, she became a multi Best in Show and Specialty winner, and is the Top Winning German Wirehaired Pointer of all time, all point systems. As a brood, she is the Top Producing dam of all time with 22 champions among her offspring. A side note is that all of Cheese Cake's puppies were given the word "cheese" as part of their names. They made a very impressive group indeed.

Cheese Cake was the perfect combination, a superbly constructed bitch, full of breed type and outstanding showmanship, who was herself tightly linebred—a prepotent bitch without any major faults. As Pat is quick to say "We were so lucky."

The Laurwyn breeding program had a wonderful foundation. Cheese Cake combined the wealth of knowledge and outstanding mental attributes of the Hillside and Haar Baron bloodlines and brought in some Mueller Mills and Desert Mills. One of the keystones of the Laurwyn breeding program was when Cheese Cake was bred to her outstanding grandson, Champion Winterhawks Snow Owl. This breeding produced Champion Laurwyn's Cheeseburger, a two-time National Specialty winner and himself a Top Producer. Pat Laurans comments, "our most recent litter is perhaps the most exciting, the first from a Cheese Cake son ex a Cheese Cake daughter, with the participants being Cheeseburger and his litter sister, Champion Laurwyn's Cheese Twist—a totally inbred litter." The pups are just over a year old. Five are already finished and have been winning in breed competition. These youngsters are exceptional and should prove to be totally prepotent. "Happily, even when we bred this close, we produced pups with wonderful temperament and exceptional structure," continues Pat, "and the problems that cropped up were not any more

A youthful picture of Ch. Laurwyn's Shore Point Gis Tweed owned by Marcia Wolkerstorfer, a Wirehair puppy who went on to win Best in Sweepstakes and Winner Bitch at the National Specialty.

noticeable or severe than in less tightly bred litters." Pat cautions, "I am not advocating breeding this close unless one is totally aware of their breeding problems and potential, and unless one is able to keep track and stay somewhat in control of all pups in the litter until almost a year old."

Another notable Laurwyn German Wirehaired Pointer is Champion Laurwyn's Banner. He, too, is a Best in Show and National Specialty winner, and one of the top producing sires of the breed. His litter sister, Champion Laurwyn's Barbed Wire is the No. 2 Producing Dam of champion offspring.

In 14 years, Laurwyn has owned and/or produced more than 66 champions. Two of them are Best in Show dogs. Five are Specialty winners. Nine have Groups to their credit. In addition, numerous Laurwyn dogs have earned Obedience and NAVDHA ratings.

Pat Laurans is proud of what Laurwyn dogs have accomplished, and of what is being produced by their offspring. She feels most fortunate that the people who have purchased dogs from Laurwyn Kennels are carrying on the fine record and tradition that started with Cheese Cake.

Lieben-Wald

Lieben-wald Wirehaired Pointers are owned by Diana Leigh Nordrum and located at Maple Valley, Washington. The foundation bitch here was a most beautiful daughter of American and Canadian Champion Brewmeister of Brookside ex Champion Desert Mill's Elke v Britta, bred by Helen B. Shelley and Esther I. Lyddon. She is Champion Desert Mill's Ilda V Landhaus, and she is co-owned by Diana Nordrum and Robert L. Calentine.

In addition to being a typical Wirehair, super in temperament, great in the field and a very nice show bitch, "Tish," as she is known, has proven herself a truly excellent producer. She has whelped three litters to date, one only ten months old as this is written, and her progeny are surely making their presence felt in a most admirable manner.

One of Tish's sons is Champion Brewster Von Liebenwald, C.D., sired by American and Canadian Champion Windhaven's Stutzer Stumper, now owned by Larry B. and Nancy Mason, Auburn, Washington.

At the Wisconsin Specialty Show in 1982, Brewster was Best in Sweepstakes. At the National that same year he was Reserve Winners Dog, eight months of age at the time. And by 16 months old he was a champion, and also had won a Group 2nd from the classes en route to his title.

Ch. Brewster Von Lieben-wald, C.D., "The Fisherman" at three months old. Photo by Robert Calentine, who won a Certificate of Merit in the A.K.C. photo contest in 1983. Brewster owned by Larry and Nancy Mason, Auburn, Washington.

Brewster participated in the North American Versatile Hunting Dog Association's natural ability test, a well-known and widely recognized gun dog test, distinguishing himself by first prize and a perfect score, 112 points. In obedience, he gained his C.D. in three consecutive shows, going Highest Scoring Wirehair in Trial at the 1983 Sea-Tac Specialty and placing second at the 1983 German Wirehaired Pointer Club of America National in Novice B. His average score, 192. He ranked No. 8 among Novice Wirehairs for 1983, and No. 11 in all obedience classes for 1983. Also he ranked No. 18 for Top Twenty German Wire show dogs in 1983.

Tish has produced two champions to date, one of them the above-mentioned Brewster, plus two others who are pointed and on their way with both majors, one of whom was Best of Breed over specials from the 6-9 month puppy class for a 5-point major at the 1984 Illinois Specialty Show. In obedience, three of the Top Ten German Wirehaired Pointers for 1983 are from Tish (including No. 3, a C.D.X. and T.D. as well as pointed in conformation), and in Novice standings Tish progeny are No. 5 and No. 8. Also four of her offspring have earned the North American Versatile Hunting Dog' Association Natural Ability prize, two taking First Prize (perfect score) and two taking Second.

From Tish's most recent litter, ten months old, one of the major pointed puppies has just placed second among ten dogs in Open Puppy Stake at the Sea-Tac German Wirehaired Pointer Club Field Trial, the puppy's only field trial to date.

Ripsnorter

Ripsnorter German Wirehaired Pointers are owned by Jeffrey and Helen George at Mt. Vernon, Ohio.

This kennel is the home of one of the breed "greats," American, Canadian, and Bahamian Champion Windhaven's Stutzer Stumper, known as "Duff," who is the top winning *owner handled* German Wirehaired Pointer in breed history. This famous dog has five Best in Show wins to his credit in the United States, plus one in Canada and one in the Bahamas (on the latter occasion handled by Tom Glassford and in winning it he became the only Shorthair ever to have gained this honor there). He was No. 3 among German Wirehaired show dogs in 1980; No. 1 in 1981 (German Wirehaired Pointer Club of America and Canine Chronicle Systems), No. 1 in both the United States and Canada in 1982; and No. 2 in 1982.

At Illinois German Wirehaired Pointer Specialty 1981, Chicago International. Best of Breed, the sire, Ch. Windhaven's Stutzer Stumper; Best of Opposite Sex, the dam, Ch. Briarpatch Jaleska Wanda; Winners Bitch and Best of Winners, daughter, Ch. Briarpatch Ripsnorter Gal; Winners Dog, son, Ch. Briarpatch Ripsnorter Rip, and the Best of Breed went on to 2nd in Sporting Group. Judge was Fred Young.

Duff has won five Specialty Bests of Breed, and his 115 Sporting Group placements include his having won first on 24 occasions.

A son of Champion Brewmeister of Brookside ex the Danish import Champion Fevus, Duff was bred by Robert S. Furlong.

As a sire, Duff also has distinguished himself, having 17 champions to his credit as we go to press, including Group winners and placers, C.D. titlists, and NAVHDA qualified pups.

Ripsnorter is also the home of the lovely bitch, Champion Briarpatch Ripsnorter Gal, a daughter of Duff's from Champion Briarpatch Valeska Wanda, bred by Gail and Richard Hutchinson. She finished undefeated for the points in six shows, including the 1982 National and the 1982 Illinois Specialties, completing her title at age 14 months. Her litter brother, Champion Briarpatch Ripsnorter Rip, was Winners Dog at the two above-mentioned Specialties.

An interesting note on Duff is that he had been hit by a car ten days earlier resulting in a fractured jaw and his leg shaved for I.V. But it did not hurt his super movement nor his showmanship, and he went in to be part of the family "clean sweep" pictured at the Illinois Specialty in 1982, then on to second in the Sporting Group that day.

85

Walker's

Walker's German Wirehaired Pointers are owned by Phil and Jean Walker and located at Eagle, Wisconsin. The Walkers are noted for some very outstanding field dogs who have distinguished themselves with many honors.

Field Champion and Amateur Field Champion Madchen, sired by Haar Baron's Revel ex Pat's Pfann Kuchen Gretel, started out winning a second place in her very first field trial in the fall of 1970. She had nine placements and Derby points by two years of age. At just over three years she became a field champion—the 16th of this breed. In the fall of 1973 she became the first Amateur Field Champion German Wirehaired Pointer, going on from there to become one of the breed's biggest winning field trial contending bitches. She was retired at the close of the 1976 trial season having accumulated 54 trial placements and having defeated 792 dogs during her trial career. Madchen produced four extremely competitive field dogs who have become winners of 82 field placements and two field championship titles.

Walker's High Time Holly, by Dual Champion and Amateur Field Champion Graf Bowser from Madchen was from Field Champion and Amateur Field Champion Madchen's first litter. She placed 12 times with six firsts out of 15 starts. Unfortunately, she was killed in 1976 at the age of two and a half.

Walker's Rip Off, son of Field Champion and Amateur Field Champion Madchen by Walker's Tanglefoot, was a very consistent field dog, with 15 placements and 214 dogs defeated by the age of 22 months. He won the 1977 Pheasant Futurity and has proven a most consistent sire, to date having sired one American Field Amateur Champion, three American Kennel Club Field Champions, two American Kennel Club Amateur Field Champions, and three Futurity winners, along with four show champions.

Then there is Field Champion and Amateur Field Champion Walker's Summer Wind, from Madchen by Tanglefoot. This dog placed nine times as a puppy and derby, with points in both stakes. She was No. 3 in the 1977 Pheasant Futurity; became a Field Champion in 1980 and received her Amateur Field Championship in 1981. Windy accumulated 39 field placements. She was the No. 1 German Wirehaired Pointer in the field during 1981 after having accumulated 25 field placements. She acquired 320 Top Ten Points and defeated 465 dogs. She was also Runner-up Illinois Shooting Dog for 1981 and 1982. She died in the fall of 1982. A truly remarkable dog!

F.C. and A.F.C. Walker's Summer Wind, by Walker's Tangelfoot ex F.C. and A.F.C. Madchen, outstanding performer bred and owned by Phil Walker, Eagle, Wisconsin.

The German Wirehaired Pointer Walker's Rip Off, by Walker's Tangelfoot ex Field Ch. and Amateur Field Ch. Madchen. Bred and owned by Phil Walker, Eagle, Wisconsin.

Ch. Moruada Liebe Ziggy and Ch. Wildheart Gratin, a well-known Australian Short-hair Brace as well as individual winners in their own right. Owned by Mrs. S.H. Wright, Liverpool, New South Wales, Australia.

Chapter 3

German Pointers in Australia

We in the United States are becoming steadily and increasingly aware of the successful activities of our friends "down under"; of the enthusiasm existing among Australian dog breeders; and of their sincere desire to not only *own* dogs of highest quality but also to *breed* them. So well are they succeeding that in numerous breeds dogs are being exported from New Zealand and Australian breeders to the United States, Canada and the United Kingdom. Despite the long and stringent period of quarantine, when the Australian breeders feel that they can improve their stock by importations, they have never hesitated to do so.

Many Americans have judged there during the past few years, and they return home with glowing accounts of the really *good* Australian dogs as well as of the enthusiasm and energy displayed by their owners. This country is becoming a strong force in the world of pure-bred dogs. Their shows are not only huge in numbers but also filled with superb quality. Competition is no cinch here. In order to win, one must present dogs of *excellence*, and this is exactly what is taking place, from all reports.

Shorthair vs. Wirehair Activity

German Shorthaired Pointers have attracted some very sincere and talented Australian breeders who are bringing forth truly lovely dogs. You will read about these dogs on the following pages. Regretfully, we do not find the same enthusiasm there for the Wirehairs, possibly because the Australian fanciers so far are not well acquainted with them. We hope that sometime in the future, when we may do a new

The German Short-hair dog Aust. Ch. Ausdauer Fahnden, C.D., born October 1977, photo taken Jan. 1983. An Australian-bred Shorthair of imported ancestry owned by W.W. Davies, Carlingford, New South Wales.

edition of this book, there will be lots of Australian Wirehairs whom we may have the pleasure of including, too.

One owner of some very high quality German Shorthaired Pointers in the New South Wales section of Australia is Mr. W.W. Davies from Carlingford, who has submitted photos of two of his champions.

The dog is Australian Champion Ausdauer Fahnden, C.D., an Australian-bred dog of imported ancestry. Born in 1977, he is an Australian Champion show dog with obedience qualifications, having also earned his C.D. degree. At one particular show he was the Best Gundog Exhibit for three years running, under three different judges, and on the first and third of these occasions he was runner-up to Best in Show.

Mr. Davies' other Shorthair is an imported bitch who came to him from England. She is Australian Champion Trolanda Arctic Tern, C.D., now an Australian Champion and holder of the Companion Dog obedience degree. Both of Tern's parents are full English Champions, which means that they are working dogs who have passed working tests. Otherwise they would be called "English Show Champions" were they titled for conformation only. Additionally the parents are Field Trial Champions. It is interesting that in 30 years of Shorthairs in England, only four of the breed have become Dual Champions, two of which are the parents of this bitch. The other two are dead.

Mr. Davies is about to start his dogs in field trial work as this book is written.

Shorthair Kennels

Burnbrook

The involvement of Georgina and Michael Byrne from Helena Valley, Western Australia which led eventually to the founding of the Burnbrook German Shorthaired Pointers began with their introduction to Shorthairs while living in Boston, Massachusetts over a five year period. When they returned home to Australia, they visited the local animal shelter and purchased the dog who was to become their first show champion. It took almost a year for Mrs. Byrne to track down his breeder and registration papers, but he won the first time they showed him despite the handicap of being four years old then and, as was his handler, a complete novice, plus the fact that he was solid liver colored. This dog became the first solid liver Shorthair champion in Western Australia!

Am. Ch., Eng. Show Ch., and Aust. Ch. Adam's Hagen von Waldenburg, a group winner imported from the U.S.A. Owned by Burnbrook German Shorthaired Pointers, Georgina and Michael Byrne, Helena Valley, West Australia. This dog is the only American Champion in Australia and the only German Shorthair Pointer in the world with those three titles.

The first black and white Shorthair dog out of Germany since the early 1950's, Vasall vom Niestetal, by W.S. Ciro vom Bichtelwald (black and white) from Lara vom Niestetal (black and white). Owned by Burnbrook German Shorthaired Pointers, West Australia.

Next the Byrnes purchased an English-bred bitch from the leading sire in the United Kingdom, Champion Wiltekind Gregory. This bitch they bred to the original Shorthair, to whom Mrs. Byrne refers as "old Pluto," and thus obtained their prepotent pair, Atlas and Aphrodite. These are behind all but one of the 20 German Shorthaired Pointer champions the Byrnes since have bred during the past seven years. Burnbrook dogs are now in all states of Australia, New Zealand, Singapore, Hong Kong, and there are two in Hawaii, one of them a highly successful drug detection dog with the Hawaiian Police Force— Hawaii KG.

Old Pluto was more than just a handsome face as it turned out. His sire, the first solid liver import into Australia, Arko von der Feldkampen (imported from Germany) was linebred to the dam of the famous stud Axel vom Wasserschling. Pluto won and placed in numerous retrieving trials against top class Labrador and Golden Retrievers. There are no field trials held in Western Australia, and the distance is so great from there to the other states that there is little opportunity to travel to field trials elsewhere, so the people from Western Australia compete with their Shorthairs in retrieving. Pluto's son and grandson, both highly successful show dogs, have won retrieving trials, too. Atlas is the top producing Western Australian-bred sire.

Following their success with the solid livers, the Byrnes introduced into their part of the world the black and white Vasall vom Niestetal, imported from Germany, who came to them through Mrs. Ann Spoors of the United Kingdom who had imported him from Germany, the first black and white dog brought into England since the early 1950's. The dog is by W.S. Ciro vom Bichtelwald, who is currently the leading sire in Germany, in spite of the handicap of his color (Germans still prefer the livers). Vasall has three champions so far: Australian Champion Burnbrook Quest (black and white), New Zealand Champion Burnbrook Tigris (black and white), and New Zealand Champion Burnbrook Tavy (liver and white). The Byrnes's own Quintessence lacks only one Challenge for her title.

At the same time as they obtained Vasall, the Byrnes had the good fortune to find and purchase the amazing American-bred American, English Show and Australian Champion Adam's Hagen von Waldenburg. He was promptly purchased for his bloodlines—a son of the great Adam—despite the fact that he was six years old when he left the U.S.A. and nearly seven years old when he left the U.K. quarantine. He was shown "for fun" and won a challenge certificate, which is no easy feat in England as German Shorthair entries at championship shows there are usually in the 90's with few absentees. He went on to gain another two and finish at the age of seven plus. During that period he sired four litters.

The Byrnes rested Hagen for awhile after he came out of quarantine in Australia. He had a kennel accident which set him back, but he looked so good a year or so later that again he was shown "just for fun." He finished his Australian championship six months later at the age of nine years, once more beating all comers and picking up a couple of Group firsts along the way.

Hagen was declared U.K. 1983 Stud Dog of the Year in the breed, and as we write is well on the way to being 1983-84 Stud Dog of the Year in Western Australia, despite having only five litters in Australia. He now has champions in the U.S.A., the U.K. and Australia and five Group 1st winners in two countries.

The Byrnes also own one of Australia's top producing imported sires in Champion Axel of Kenstaff Wittekind, a U.K. import.

The Byrnes are both all-breed judges at open shows and Championship Sporting Group judges. Mr. Byrnes is also a retrieving trial judge. As Georgina Byrne adds, "all from one old brown dog in a cage at the 'Dog's Home'."

Canawindra

The Canawindra German Shorthaired Pointers are owned by M.J. and F.L. Park who are located at Strathewen, Victoria, Australia.

The Parks own some exceptionally handsome members of this breed who have distinguished themselves in the show ring, obedience and the field.

For example, there is Australian Dual Champion Deddick Tarshish, a daughter of Australian Field Trial Champion Dunfriu Kaiser ex Vorstehhund Eve (imported from New Zealand) who was bred by Mr. and Mrs. D. Hall. Tarshish, a notable producer of quality Shorthairs, in 1981, 1982 and 1983 was Dam of the Year in Victoria, in addition in 1982 Dam of the Year in Western Australia. Her progeny includes three Australian and two New Zealand Champions, two who have earned C.D. titles, and one with C.D.X. She has 14 placings in Retriever Trials, four in Field Trials, and many Group specials to her credit.

Australian and New Zealand Champion Canawindra Winara, owned by G. and R. Stewart, was bred by the Parks. A multiple specials winner, in 1980 Winara took the Challenge at the Melbourne Royal Show, also doing so at the 1981 New Zealand Tux National.

Aust. Ch. Canawindra Warreen, by Aust. Ch. Canawindra Audipi, C.D. ex Aust. Dual Ch. Deddick Tarshish, is one of the handsome Shorthairs owned by Canawindra Kennels, M.J. and F.L. Park, Strathewen, Victoria.

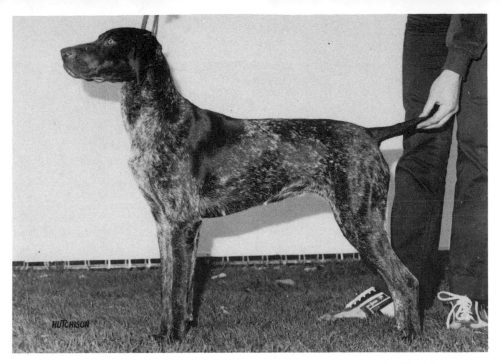

Canawindra Roamba, on the way to her title, sired by Aust. Field Trial Ch. Robcardi Redlich ex Aust. Dual Ch. Deddick Tarshish. Bred and owned by M.J. and F.L. Park, Canawindra Kennels, Strathewen, Australia.

Australian Champion Canawindra Nandrena, by Australian Champion Bergen Shatten ex Australian Champion Shannondowns Fantail is among the most distinguished of the Parks's Shorthairs. She has won Challenges at Brisbane Royal 1980, Canberra Royal 1981, Perth Royal 1981, and Reserve Challenge at the Melbourne Royal in 1982, plus numerous Group awards. She has a Qualifying Certificate in Field Trials; was the 1982 Top Show Bitch in Western Australia; and the 1983 Top Show German Shorthair Pointer in Victoria.

Australian Champion Canawindra Audipi, C.D. is a son of Australian Champion Adrem Jason (imported from the U.K.) ex Australian Champion Kurpfalz Eva. A homebred, this splendid dog is the sire of five Australian Champions and one New Zealand Champion; was 1982 Top Obedience Dog in Western Australia and Top Dog All Types Western Australia.

A star for the future, Canawindra Teera, by Audipi from Tarshish, was bred by the Parks and is now owned by W. and H. Stone. This Shorthair has Challenge Points and is well on the way to championship—Best Opposite Sex in Show at the Victorian Gundog Club Open Parade in 1983.

Australia's All Time Top Winning German Shorthaired Pointer, Aust. Ch. Jinfrau Jubal, Q.C., by Ruvalan Jacob ex Aust. Ch. Oakspur Jindi, owned by Jim and Colleen Sawers, Frohjager Shorthairs, Queensland, Australia.

Frohjager

Jim and Colleen Sawers at Brisbane have the honor of owning Australia's all time top show winning German Shorthaired Pointer, Australian Champion Jinfrau Jubal, Q.C., a son of Ruvalon Jacob ex Australian Champion Oakspur Jindi. This dog, combining some of the best show and working lines in Australia, has won 12 all-breed Bests in Show, 38 times Best Exhibit in Group, and over 2,000 Challenge Points. Six times he has been Best of Breed, and three times Reserve, at Australian Royal National Shows. He was Best Gundog exhibit, PAL Champagne 1000, in 1979. He was Queensland's German Shorthaired Pointer Show Dog of the Year for 1978-79; 1979-80; 1981-82; and Runner Up Show Dog 1982-83, beaten only by his daughter, Liesel. Jubal has won every class in Group from Baby Puppy to Veteran. He was awarded Q.C. First Run at a Non-Slip Retriever Trial. He is the sire of champions who include Royal Challenge and Royal Group winners.

Jubal's record includes more Bests in Show, Bests in Group, and Challenge Points than any other German Shorthaired Pointer has recorded since the breed first came to Australia around 1962, according to his owner's figures.

The Sawers also own Jubal's great daughter, the above-mentioned Australian Champion Gastfrei Liesel (her dam is Litzeveldt Xena), who at eight and three quarter months became one of the youngest dogs to achieve Australian championship. She, too, is a multiple All Breed Best in Show winner; has been Best Exhibit, Runner Up and Opposite Sex at breed Specialties; and her exciting wins also include Best Gundog Puppy and Reserve Challenge at 1981 Brisbane Royal; Challenge Bitch at 1982 Brisbane Royal; Best Opposite Sex in Group and Challenge Bitch, 1983 Brisbane Royal; Reserve Challenge Bitch, 1984 Sydney Royal; and Best Exhibit in Group and Best of Breed, 1984 Toowoomba Royal. These successes have made her German Shorthaired Pointer Puppy of the Year in Queensland for 1981-82, and German Shorthaired Pointer Show Dog of the Year in 1982-83, and 1983-84.

Frohjager Shorthairs combine some of the finest show and working bloodlines in Australia. Among them Ruvalan, owned by Westy Morris in Victoria; Dunfriu, owned by Jack Thompson, Victoria; Linstan, also in Victoria, and Jinfrau owned by Bernie Campbell in Queensland.

Gillbrae

Gillbrae German Shorthaired Pointers, belonging to Alex and Olga Gillies at Wallacia, New South Wales, base their success on their foundation bitch, Klugerhund Siegi, imported from the United Kingdom. This bitch has proven an outstanding producer for them, having given her owners champion progeny who have gone on to reproduce their own quality in later generations.

Australian Champion Gillbrae Nice 'N Easy is a son of Siegi by Australian Champion Wildheart Nennen, C.D. He is a Best Exhibit in Group winner, with multi "in Show" and "in Group" awards to his credit, plus being an excellent hunting dog. "Sandy" is producing top winning puppies, and is the sire of Australian Champion Moruada Major Viktori.

Aust. Ch. Gillbrae Play'n Our Song, by Aust. Ch. Moruada Wotta Krakka ex Kluger-hund Siegi (bred in U.K.) was whelped March 1983. Runner-up to Best Exhibit in Gundog Group at six and a half months of age; Best Exhibit in Gundog Group at 12½ months old. This lovely bitch gained her title in only seven challenges within 4½ months of showing. Has multiple "in Group" and "in Show" awards. Alex and Olga Gillies, owners, Wallacia, New South Wales, Australia.

Australian Champions Gillbrae Mi Masquerade, Moonshine, Bit of a Skite, and Greatest Hit are others who have done prestigious winning. Siegi's sixth to finish, Australian Champion Gillbrae Play 'N Our Song, has lately done so with some notable wins along the way, including Runner Up to Best Exhibit in Group at six and a half months of age.

The latest addition to Gillbrae Kennels is Heiderst Sir Torre, a liver and white male of superb conformation and temperament by Australian Champion Moruada Major Viktori. This one out of Heiderst Mi Minnesota, daughter of American, English Show Champion and Australian Champion Adam's Hagen von Waldenburg, imported from the United States.

Jabring

When Steve Rudd and Raina Burke decided to own Shorthairs, they selected a most promising ten-week-old puppy who more than fulfilled their hopes for him when he grew up to become Australian Champion Limburgia Chockdaw, C.D., one of the most distinguished Shorthairs in Australia. This was their first Shorthair, purchased after deciding that they would like to own a member of this breed as a hunting dog and as a pet. Both of this dog's parents were hunting dogs who had never been shown.

Chockdaw, or "James" as he is more informally known, was shown six times as a puppy. But his real show career began when he was 12 months old, and three months later he became an Australian champion.

When James was retired at four years of age he had won Best Exhibit in Show ten times, runner up to Best Exhibit in Show nine times, 25 times Best Gundog in Show, and hundreds of other Group and Show placements. His owners tell us that he was German Shorthaired Pointer Show Dog of the Year 1979-80 and 81, and won the Paul Lowe Perpetual Trophy in those three years, this trophy awarded by the New South Wales German Shorthaired Pointer Society to the Shorthair who has proven outstanding.

James was never unplaced at an all-breed show, including eight Royal Shows, at which he was four times awarded Best of Breed. Additionally he has won Best in Show at Shorthair Specialties and at Gundog Specialties. Twice he was awarded the LIK LIK Trophy by the A.C.T. Gundog Society for being the most consistent Gundog.

Illustrating splendid form, Aust. Ch. Limburgia Crookdaw, C.D. heads for the water. Steve Rudd and Raina Burke, owners, Jabring Shorthairs, Canberra, Australia.

New Zealand and Australian Ch. Jabring King Quail went to N.Z. as a pup, quickly gaining his title. Sired by Aust. Ch. Limburgia Chockdaw, C.D.

More than 1500 Challenge Points have been awarded to this splendid dog, who has won major awards in New South Wales, Queensland, South Australia, Victoria, and in the Australian Capital Territory, and under leading judges from local, interstate and overseas areas.

Making his show career seem all the more impressive is the fact that James was temporarily out of shows for eight months right at the peak of his career due to an accidental breaking of a front leg while out hunting, but came right back to consistent winning, returning with a Best of Breed at the 1980 Sydney Royal. During the time when he was out of the show ring, James qualified for and was awarded his Companion Dog title. He then went on to become the first German Shorthair to win a Dunbar Medal, awarded by the Canberra Kennel Association for excellence in obedience as well as in the show ring.

As a stud dog, as of June 1984, James has nine titled progeny with many more on the way. Two of his youngsters are Australian and New Zealand Champion Jabring King Quail and Australian Champion Jabring Chestnut Teal. King Quail went to New Zealand as a puppy, gaining his title before he was a year old. He is a Best Gundog in Show winner as well as a Shorthair Specialty winner. In 1982 he was awarded German Shorthaired Pointer of the Year. As for Teal, she is based in Melbourne, where she has proven herself to be an outstanding show dog, too. She is a multiple in Group and in Show winner and was Best of Opposite Sex at the Gundog exhibit and a Best of Breed Specialty winner.

James also has progeny doing well in the obedience ring and in the field. One of these is Bullamalita Baron C.D. and C.D.X., who has placements in obedience and in Retrieving Trials, and is also a Reserve Challenge winner at a Royal.

100

The Australian dog, Klugerhund Starbuck, age ten months, by Aust. Ch. Kazia Lord Nelson ex Aust. Ch. Gillbrae Moonshine, is one of the splendid Shorthairs owned by J.R. Maxwell, Klugerhund, Werombi, New South Wales, Australia.

Klugerhund

One of Australia's smallest, yet most successful Shorthair kennels, Klugerhund, owned by Mr. and Mrs. J. Maxwell at Sydney, New South Wales, began with the breed in 1972.

The Maxwells are owner-handlers of Australian Champion Birdacre Maximilliam. C.D., Australia's first Shorthair to gain one thousand challenge points, or ten times the number required for a championship title.

Through Shaydorn Brown Mouse, the Maxwells introduced English bloodlines, and after a mating with English Champion Wittekind Igor, a Best Gundog Exhibit at Crufts and consistent winner throughout the United Kingdom, they imported her in whelp to Australia. With loss through problems from infection in quarantine, only two puppies remained to reach their Australian owners, Klugerhund Von Igor and Klugerhund Siegi. Von Igor was mated to Australian Champion Birdacre Kara, C.D., producing the only direct line grandson of Wittekind Igor in Australia, Australian Champion Kazia

The German Shorthair, Aust. Ch. Klugerhund Mein Asher, by Charle● O'Hanlon of Cheshire (U.K. import) ex Aust. Ch. Gillbrae Mi-Masquerade. Owned by Klugerhund Shorthairs, J.R. Maxwell, Werombi, New South Wales, Australia.

Lord Nelson, owned by Mr. and Mrs. R. Butler of Sydney, New South Wales.

Nelson has become one of Australia's most successful Shorthairs in the show ring. New South Wales' German Shorthaired Pointer Showdog of the Year 1981 to 1983, he became a Multiple Best in Show, multiple Best in Group, multiple Royal and Spring Fair winner, and at the age of six years has never been unplaced throughout his show career.

Siegi went to the Butlers, where she became foundation bitch of their Gillbrae Kennels. Mated to Australian Champion Wildheart Nennen, C.D. she produced Australian Champion Gillbrae Moonshine and Australian Champion Gillbrae Mi Masquerade, both owned by Mr. and Mrs. Maxwell and both consistent winners in their own right.

Moonshine bred to Lord Nelson has produced Klugerhund Starbuck, and at only 11 months of age he already is a multiple all breeds Sweepstakes winner, multiple age "in Group" and challenge winner, and multiple "in Show" winner.

From Mi Masquerade mated to Charles O' Hanlon of Cheshire came Australian Champion Klugerhund Mein Asher, Australian Champion Klugerhund Mein Aana, and Australian Champion Klugerhund Mein Astrid. Mein Asher and Mein Aana were both Specialty show winners in 1983; also New South Wales Best German Shorthair Puppy and Runner-Up Best Puppy in 1982 and 1983. Mein Asher also won Challenge at Sydney Royal in 1984, and is a multi Best in Show and multi Best in Group winner. Asher's grandsire is English Field Trial Champion Wish-Ton-Wish Sampson and Asher's sire's brother is still in the United Kingdom where he is a Show Champion.

Moruada

A kennel of great prominence in Liverpool, New South Wales, Australia, is known as Moruada German Shorthaired Pointers, and this establishment is owned by Mrs. S.H. Wright.

Among the Shorthairs who have brought fame to this kennel is Australian Champion Wildheart Gratin, born in 1977, who was German Shorthaired Pointer Show Bitch of the Year in 1979, 1980, 1981, 1982 and 1983. The winner of more than 1900 Challenge Points (100 Challenge Points are the necessary number to attain Australian Championship), this bitch has the unique record of being the only bitch in Australia to have earned so great a number, plus being the only Shorthair to have won Show Bitch Award *five times* and in successive years! Her show wins include 13 Best in Gundog Group awards; Best of Breed at the 1983 Sydney Royal Show; Challenges and Runner Up Best in Show at two Shorthair Specialties; and Best Champion in German Shorthair Pointer Parades on five successive occasions. She is a daughter of Australian Champion Wildheart Namisch ex Australian Champion Wildheart Gerda.

Australian Champion Moruada Liebe Ziggy, born in 1978, is another famous Shorthair belonging to Mrs. Wright. Ziggy was Best Exhibit in Show at the German Shorthaired Pointer Parade in 1979, is a multiple "In Show" and "In Group" winner, and, with Gratin, has been part of the Best Brace in Show at the German Shorthair Championship Specialty four times in succession. Ziggy was sired by Australian Champion Wildheart Namisch from Australian Champion Wildheart Gratin.

Australian Champion Moruada Wotta Krakka, born in 1980, was Reserve Challenge Dog at the German Shorthaired Pointer Society Championship Show in 1983. A multiple "in Show" and "in Group"

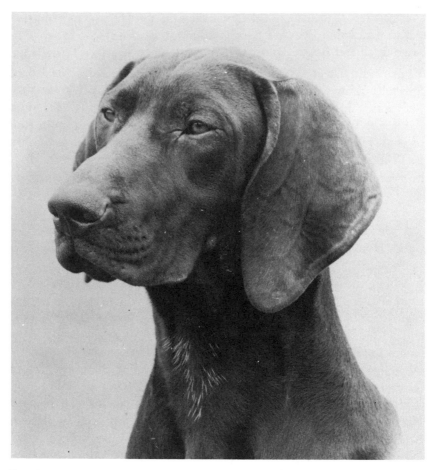

The German Shorthaired Pointer Aust. Ch. Moruada Liebe Ziggy, by Aust. Ch. Wildheart Namisch ex Aust. Ch. Wildheart Grafin. Owned and bred by Mrs. S.H. Wright, Liverpool, New South Wales, Australia.

winner, this dog is sire of a Best in Group winner and German Short-haired Pointer Society Parade Best in Show winner for 1984, plus one champion and one with 60 points towards title. He is a son of Australian Champion Wildheart Nennen, C.D. from Australian Champion Benanee Bongaree, a U.K. import.

Australian Champion Moruada Major Viktor, born January 1982, is a multiple Best in Show and in Group winner, who was Runner Up Top Showing German Shorthaired Pointer male in South Australia 1983—a son of Australian Champion Gillbrae Nice N' Easy from Australian Champion Moruada Liebe Ziggy.

Then there is Australian Champion Moruada Wish Me Well, by Australian Champion Benanee Bongaree (imported U.K.) who took Challenge Bitch and Best of Breed 1984 at the Sydney Royal and Challenge Bitch and Runner Up Best of Breed at the 1983 Spring Fair Dog Show, where the judge was Mrs. Robert S. Forsyth from the United States. This multiple "in Show" and "in Group" winner at the German Shorthaired Pointer Society Championship Show in 1982 was Best Junior in Show, and at the 1982 Parade was Best Minor in Show.

For the future, Mrs. Wright is looking forward to a good career with the puppy bitch, Gillbrae Wotta Scandal, a year old daughter of Australian Champion Moruada Wotta Krakka from Klugerhund Seici (U.K. import). Already she has 60 points toward her title, and has a Parade Best in Show, plus "in Show," "in Group," Sweepstakes awards and Challenge Bests of Breed.

Aust. Ch. Wildheart Gratin, bred by Wildheart Kennels, owned by Mrs. S.H. Wright, Liverpool, New South Wales, Australia. "Show Bitch of the Year" 1979, 1980, 1981, 1982 and 1983.

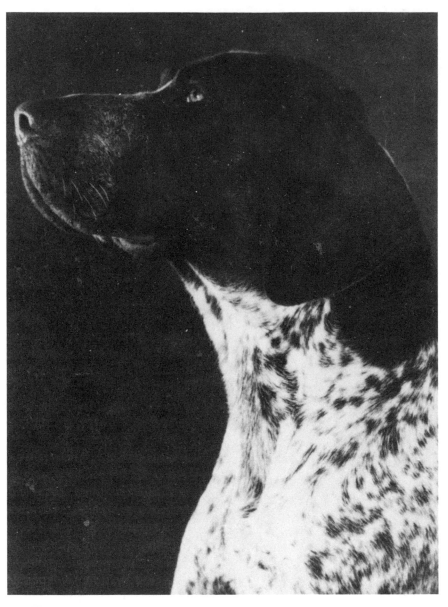

Can. Ch. Jaegershund's Firefox Quester, Can. C.D. is owned by Jerry and Sharon Freeman, Alton, Ontario, Canada.

Chapter 4

German Pointers in Canada

Shorthair vs. Wirehair Interest

Sporting dogs are extremely popular with Canadian fanciers, and to this the German Pointers are no exception. We have many references to them, as you will note, in our United States Kennel stories, as there is a steady traveling back and forth to show dogs between here and there. Also we have some photos and kennel stories of some of the Canadian-owned Shorthairs for you. Regretfully, although we know that there are some very notable Wirehairs in Canada, too, we are not able to bring those to you.

We do want to pay tribute to the German Wirehaired, American and Canadian Champion Laurwyn's Bonfire, who is owned by Elaine MacDonald, popular Poodle breeder and professional handler, and her family. I believe that this lovely dog actually belongs to Elaine's daughter, for whom he became an important winner and producer. He is a littermate to American Champion Laurwyn's Banner and American Champion Laurwyn's Barbed Wire.

Also some folks named Richardson have owned good ones over quite a period, so there is very definite Wirehair interest, although to a lesser degree than in Shorthairs, among our Canadian friends.

Shorthair Kennels

Cordova

Cordova German Shorthaired Pointers were started in the early 1970's when Jerry and Marlyn Kennedy became interested in showing and field trialing. Since that time this couple has traveled with the dogs across Canada and through most of the upper United States, achieving considerable success and some very exciting records.

The Cordova Shorthairs are all solid liver in color. Glenmajors Dunka's Top Boss is a direct German import from the Seigar line. He is a Canadian Dual Champion by N.F. C. Uodibar's Bossman ex Champion Seigar's Farina, C.D.X. Top Boss, or "Tyr" as he is known at home (pronounced "tear" as in teardrop) was 1979's No. 1 Shooting Dog in Canada. He has seven points toward Open Field Championship and seven points toward Amateur Field Championship for U.S.A. Field Trial Championship. He was Canada's first Dual Champion German Shorthaired Pointer, and is the sire of both Dual Champions and Show Champions.

Another famous Canadian Dual Champion from this kennel is Kingsacres Cordova Keri, by Tyr from Smithfield's Chip Off The Boss. Keri, too, is a Top Canadian Field Trial Dog.

German Shorthair puppies relaxing after busy day. Owned by Marlyn Kennedy, Streetsville, Ontario, Canada.

German Shorthaired Pointer puppy owned by Mrs. Maryln Kennedy, Streetsville, Ontario, Canada.

Firefox

The Firefox German Shorthaired Pointers live at Shelburne, Ontario, Canada, having just moved there from Alton, also in Ontario, with their owners, Jerry and Sharon Freeman.

This kennel is a small one, but includes two splendid Shorthairs in whom their owners take special pride. These are the dog, Canadian Champion Jaegershund's Firefox Quester, Canadian C.D., who is by Champion Royal Flush C.D. ex Champion Shasha, was bred by P. and G. Jordan, and carries Wasseschling and Enztrand bloodlines. Quester, who has just completed his C.D. as we are going to press, with scores of 189½, 192 and 194, is used in hunting, and finished his conformation championship at Markham in August 1983 with Best of Breed and five points from the classes. His owners are anxious, now, to add C.D.X., F.D., and T.D. to his titles, so it is on those he will be working in the immediate future.

Then there is a lovely bitch, Whirlwynds Flame at Firefox, bred by Rod and Madelyn Webb, a daughter of American Champion Chances Are B.W. Crackerjack ex Champion Whirlwynds Winter Edition who goes back to Fuehrenheim and Columbia River lines. Born in October 1983, she is just on the threshold of her career and is considered to be a fine show and working prospect.

The noted Shorthair, Ch. Thomashenry's Top Mark, by Adam Von Ducham ex Ch. Rockly Run's Wildflower. This royally bred young dog is a famed show and field dog. Owned by Tom and Dorothy Alexander, Thomashenry Kennels, Ste. Anne's, Manitoba, Canada.

Ch. Rugerheim's Electric Lady, sired by Ch. Rugerheim's Autumn Wynde ex Adam's Heller von Waldenburg. Bred by Terry and Janet Chandler, owned by Tom and Dorothy Alexander, Thomashenry Shorthairs, Manitoba, Canada.

The Shorthair, Kruger's Heart of Gold, sired by Ch. Fieldfine's Count Rambard ex Ch. Fieldfines Ribbons. The last naturally sired litter from Rambard and the only litter produced from Ribbons, pictured at five months. Bred by Joyce Oesch and Kathleen Plotts, owned by Tom and Dorothy Alexander, Thomashenry Kennels, Manitoba.

Thomas Henry

Located at St. Anne's, Manitoba, Canada, the Thomas Henry Kennels are owned by Tom and Dorothy Alexander who concentrate on the breeding of German Shorthaired Pointers and English Springer Spaniels.

Their Shorthairs, which are the breed concerning us here, are of truly excellent quality and background. The Alexanders have the good fortune to own, as their foundation bitch in Shorthairs, the Group-placing Champion Rocky Run's Wildfire, who was bred by Bob Arnold in the United States and is a daughter of Champion Fieldfines Rocky Run ex Champion Rocky Run's Shati. Wildfire has been a good producer for them, and among her sons is the very excellent and admired dog Champion Thomashenry's Top Mark, sired by Champion Adam Von Ducham. Along with being a top show dog, Mark is a professional field dog well known for the excellence of his ability.

The bright young hopeful for the future at this kennel is Kruger's Heart of Gold, who has the distinction of being from the last naturally sired litter by the great Champion Fieldfines Count Rambard ex the famous winning bitch Champion Fieldfines Ribbons. With a heritage such as this to be lived up to, the future seems bright for this most beautiful youngster who it is expected should make a meaningful contribution to Canadian Shorthairs during the 1980's. Heart of Gold was bred by Joyce Oesch and Kathleen Plotts.

Champion Rugerheim's Electric Lady is another highly valued Shorthair at this kennel; she is a daughter of Champion Rugerheim's Autumn Wynde ex Adams Heller von Waldenburg.

Eng. Ch. Bellandowa Cirio owned by Mrs. Barbara Wood, Bellandowa Shorthairs, Shoreham, Sussex, England.

Chapter 5

German Pointers in Great Britain

Shorthairs

The first recorded entry of German Shorthaired Pointers in a British dog show took place, the historians tell us, at the Barn Elms in 1887. A single appearance which, from any records I've been able to find was not repeated until late in the 1940's when the breed made a re-appearance in the world of British bench show competition.

In 1951 the German Shorthaired Pointer Club in England was formed. Field trials for the German breeds were gradually introduced, and the Shorthairs' abilities in the field, as a family companion, and as a show dog gained steady recognition and supporters from that time onward.

Now the Shorthair classes at British dog shows are well filled, and one notes many "Champions" and "Show Champions" being in competition. In Great Britain, the title "Champion" means, when applied to a sporting dog, that this dog has completed certain working requirements as well as earned the required number of Challenge Certificates for a Show Championship. The latter title is the one used when only the *show* requirements have been fulfilled.

Shorthair entries at championship dog shows in Great Britain now average well above the 100 dog area. For example, the big National Dog Show at Birmingham in May 1984 had 120 Shorthairs entered, representing a wide variety of breeders.

In Shorthairs, as in Wirehaireds, the Wittekind Kennels owned by Mrs. W.H. Mills De Hoog has earned a position of tremendous prestige. The lovely bitch, Champion Wittekind Erica, is one of the noted

Waldburg Cara of Bellandowa winning the C.C. at Bournemouth Championship Show in 1979 at age 15 months. Owned by Bellandowa Shorthairs, Mrs. Barbara Wood, Shoreham, Sussex, England.

Shorthairs from here. Field Trial Champion Sky High Jonny and his son, Christopher of Wittekind, are representative members of this kennel's quality, too. Wittekind Donner, born in 1981, made his presence felt when he won two novice field trials within six days, and now is ready for the open stakes. He has as well some early show wins, too, plus puppies which are showing good promise. He is a son of Jonny.

Then there is Jagerheim, from where Show Champion Christingham Azalea Mist not long ago gained title. This bitch is proving an excellent producer for her owner, Elaine Boeree at Sittingbourne, Kent, with puppies in the field and show ring, and more expected soon. The young dog, Jagerheim Anatole, holds a Junior Warrant with five Best Puppy awards and five Best of Breeds in show competition, with some working test wins also among his credits.

Mr. R. Wren, at Nottingham, owns the dog, Champion Midlander Sumatra, born in 1979, by Inchmario Ballyragget ex Midlander Oriental Ranee, bred by Mrs. Layton. Mr. and Mrs. J. Rusk at South Humberside have several Shorthairs currently in competition, including Show Champion Galahad of Booton, by Show Champion Wittekind Happy Harpo ex Anna of Earlescote and two young sons of this dog, Hillanhi Fleider of Booton (from Show Champion Hillanhi Hjordis) and Booton Einar (from Wittekind Lovely Velvet). I.E.T. Sladden, Inchmarlo Kennels at Doncaster, has a dog, Inchmarlo Felix, and two littermates, bitches, Inchmarlo Carolina and Inchmarlo Georgia, the latter two homebreds by English and American Champion Adams Hagen von Waldenburg ex Show Champion Inchmarlo Cammus o'May.

Aust. Ch. Moruada Wotta Krakka, by Aust. Ch. Wildheart Nennen, C.D. ex Aust. Ch. Benanee Bongaree, U.K. import. Owned and bred by Mrs. S.H. Wright, Liverpool, New South Wales, Australia.

Mr. and Mrs. J. Park-Pearson, Gillingham, Kent, have littermates in competition, Booton Torgils of Perpoint and Booton Nanook of Perpoint; these are a dog and a bitch bred by Mr. and Mrs. Rusk, sired by Show Champion Galahad of Booton and from Wittekind Lovely Velvet, thus littermates to the Einar dog with whom the Rusks themselves are competing. As we write the Park-Pearsons are also currently showing Perpoint Amethyst, by Champion Newsirs Paddock ex Booton Nanook of Perpoint, who is a homebred bitch, and Bellandowa Bacardi of Perpoint, by Field Trial Champion Sky High Johnny ex Champion Bellandowa Cirio, bred by Barbara Wood whose kennel story closes this chapter.

Mrs. M. Simons, Bicester, Oxon, owns Champion Geramers Cromarty of Swifthouse, a daughter of Dual Champion Swifthouse Tufty ex Champion Isara Kurzhaar Alpe, born in 1981, and her full-sister from the same breeding but a later litter (born 1983), Geramers Victriss of Swifthouse.

In looking through entry lists, and other current reading matter, we note the frequency with which several dogs in particular are obviously being used successfully at stud. These include Field Trial Champion Swifthouse Tufty, Show Champion and American Champion Adams Hagen von Waldenburg, Champion Sky High Jonny of Wittekind, Show Champion Galahad of Booton, Champion Geramer's Sea Venom, Show Champion Wittekind Inca Zortowski, Show Champion Isara Kurzhaar Viper, Show Champion Inchmarlo Coramor, Show Champion Newsirs Paddock, Champion Wittekind Happy Harpo, to name a few that seem especially prominent.

The Bellandowa German Shorthaired Pointers are owned by Mrs. Barbara Wood of Shoreham-by-Sea in Sussex. There are some very excellent Shorthairs here who have distinguished themselves in all phases of Pointer activity.

English Champion Bellandowa Cirio, a daughter of Wittekind Zeppelin from Kalpugin Anastasia, obtained her title at 22 months and boasts seven Challenge Certificates plus a Reserve Challenge Certificate to her credit. She is the winner of two Gundog Groups and two Reserve Bests in Show at Open Shows, plus having participated in field trials which on at least two occasions have brought her Certificates of Merit. Between times she has been busy with maternal duties, and is the dam, among others, of the beautiful and exciting Bellandowa Ballarina, C.D.X., at 18 months a Junior Warrant winner. Following a successful show career while a puppy, in 1982 Ballarina

116

An English Shorthair Obedience "Star", Bellandowa Ballarina, C.D.X., owned by Mrs. Barbara Wood, Shoreham, Sussex.

started out by winning the juniors at Crufts, going on as a Junior and as a Post Graduate to Best of Breed under Mr. Harry Jordan and a Reserve Challenge Certificate under specialist judge Mrs. Mieneke Mills de Hoog, enabling her to obtain her Junior Warrant.

Ballarina is described by her owner as "a bitch who was bred to show and to work." The "working" part Mrs. Wood chose to do in obedience and in working trials, which she considered a new area since Shorthairs have been little used for either purpose in England. So far this year Ballarina has won the Weimaraner Club Tracking Stake and has done well at others.

At the St. Patrick's Day Show, on March 17th 1984, Ballarina won her fifth Green Star (she had gained the first four during the previous year). On each of these occasions she was Best of Breed as well, and at the St. Patrick's Day event she became the first German Shorthaired Pointer to win a Group there. In Ireland she also has won one beginners, two novices, and an A in obedience.

At the home shows, Ballarina has numerous Bests of Breed as well as Best in Show at South of England Gundog and Best Opposite Sex in Show at Windsor Gundog. Additionally, she has qualified to work A and B in obedience.

Mrs. Wood tries to divide time as equally as possible between showing, obedience competition and working trials. Not always an easy task!

As this is written, Ballarina is being mated to a son of Field Trial Champion Sky High Jonny. He is Wittekind Donner in the Autumn, the winner of two novice field trials.

Waldberg Cara of Bellandowa has a Junior Warrant, was born in 1978, bred by Mrs. C. Spoors, by Birkenwald Voss ex Birkenwald Mandel. Cara obtained a K.C. Junior Warrant, and went Best of Breed at her first open show at six months of age. Next she gained the Challenge Certificate at Bournemouth Championship Show from the Junior Class. Bred to Wittekind Zeppelin she had a litter of seven puppies in August 1981. Owing to complications caused by the litter, Mrs. Wood decided that she would not be bred again; thus she has been spayed and enjoys the life of a housedog, hunting, and generally being a dearly loved pet.

Bellandowa Ballarina, C.D.X., Junior Warrant winner, by Field Trial Ch. Sky High Jonny of Wittekind ex Ch. Bellandowa Cirio, one of the excellent Shorthairs bred and owned by Mrs. Barbara Wood, Shoreham, Sussex, England.

The English German Shorthaired Pointer Jagerheim Anatole, by Ch. and F.T. Ch. Swifthause Tufty ex Sh. Ch. Christingham Azalea Mist, achieved Junior Warrant at 15 months of age. At two years his awards include Res. C.C. at L.K.A. '83 and his first C.C. and Best of Breed at Manchester '84. Also has many Bests of Breed: the "Gold Medal" Award at Hammersmith Open Show as Best Gundog, earned firsts in two Working tests, and placed second in his only Novice test so far. Owned by Larry Wilks, London, England. Bred by Mrs. E.L. Boeree.

For the future, there is Bellandowa Exquisite, born in February 1983, bred and owned by Mrs. Wood. She is the baby, by Wittekind Zeppelin from Jangrath Irma of Bellandowa. Although only to a very few shows so far, she has always been placed. At the moment Mrs. Wood is deeply involved with her training for the field trials.

Wirehairs

It was in 1955 when Godfrey Gallia was in Germany in the National Service that he saw and acquired a German Wirehaired Pointer. Roland Buschung was her breeder, her parentage by Carin vom Larchenwald ex Adda Aus dem Potterhoek. This was Adda Aus dem Potterhoek, and when Mr. Gallia returned home to England, he arranged to have her do so, too, which in her case took a bit longer due to the quarantine. In due time she arrived, however. Although she was registered with the German Kennel Club, Mr. Gallia did not bother about

Bareve Bianca as a German Wirehair puppy. She has grown up to become the mother of Brombeere and is the sister to Baldur and Brunhilde. Not shown until three years old, she has won a 1st and a 2nd in the only two classes she has entered. Bred and owned by Barbara and Sharon Pinkerton.

registering her in England. Having a granddaughter to succeed his original bitch, in due time Mr. Gallia felt that he would like to breed his younger bitch, which led to two obstacles. First, she could not be registered under Kennel Club rules. Second, it proved impossible to find a German Wirehaired stud dog. Not to be overcome in his determination, Mr. Gallia finally bred her to a German *Shorthair*, a mixed litter resulting. He concentrated on the Wire coated puppies, but eventually most of the litter went to hunting homes anyway so had no influence on future generations so far as we have been able to ascertain.

A Wirehaired named Chang, by Hector of Raleigh from Asta, was finally admitted to Class II registration by the Kennel Club, but not until 1970. A gamekeeper, by the name of Mr. Meredith, owned this dog, and in 1975 Chang was mated to an important bitch who had come to England under the ownership of Mrs. Burnham. She was Hedda v.d. Reiberbeize, by Blucher von Buchborn ex Fietze v.d. Reiberbeize, and the ten liver and white puppies which she and Chang produced were the beginning of the Matravers line.

Vreda Vom Romersee was the next import to reach England from Germany in 1973. Mr. W. Warner imported this one, who was by

Hector vom Scheidelhof ex Resi vom Romersee. Again there was the problem of finding a suitable mate. So it was that Mr. Warner joined forces with Major George Wilkinson, who had been impressed with Wirehairs he had worked with in Germany, for the purpose of importing a pair of dogs.

As a result, Mr. Warner became the owner of Vasal v.d. Bocholter and Major Wilkinson owned Vicky v.D. Bocholter. They turned out to both be black and white, and they were brother and sister, by Ero vom Ortfeld ex Yirs v.d. Kibitzheide. Although a bit disconcerted at these developments, Mr. Warner went ahead with mating Vreda to Vasal, which produced a mixed color litter in July 1975.

Bareve Brombeere, January 1983, by Wittekind Ice King ex Bareve Bianca, bred and owned by Barbara and Sharon Pinkerton. This is the only Wirehaired Pointer to have won a Kennel Club Junior Warrant, which involves the dog needing to win 25 points before the age of 18 months. The scale of points for Wirehaireds, as this is still classed as a rare breed, is one point per breed class, and Brombeere gained this number of points just prior to reaching age 14 months. She has now won 30 classes at only 15 months old.

These two handsome German Wirehaired Pointers are representative of the breed in England. They are Stablaheim April Love, left, and Cody of Stablaheim, and they are owned by Mrs. Pam blay, Appledore, Kent.

Then another fancier began to take an interest in Wirehairs, Mr. A. Vaughan, sensibly sending Mrs. Mills de Hoog to Holland to make selections for him. The breed won her over so completely that when she returned she had one for herself as well.

Mrs. Mills de Hoog selected three Wirehairs which were unrelated to bring back with her. Rakker Ven de Mijzijde (by Kay v Almere ex Tjardine van de Mijzijde) and Matilda van Staringsland (International Champion Oscar ex Apasje) and Heloise (Datsun v.d. Beiesdel ex Annoeska v.d. Hertgang) were the three she chose, and following quarantine she took Matilda while Rakker and Heloise went to Mr. Vaughan.

Vicky was bred to Rakker, producing a litter of seven. One of these became the first Wirehaired in Ireland, going to Mr. O'Neill where she became Andersheim Alise v.d. Heide.

Sissi vom Reiler Hals Andersheim was next brought to England for Major Wilkinson, having been bred and her puppies whelped in quarantine. Only three of these survived, in late 1979.

A most valuable dog to the English breeding program and progress of the breed there has been Desert Mills Henry Tickencote (by American Champion Desert Mills Medow Rok Willy ex American Champion Desert Mills Tilly von Landhaus) which has brought to England the cream of our basic American breeding stock. Helen Shelley is the exporter of this fine dog.

Stablaheim April Love at 11 months. Mrs. Pam Blay, Draycott Kennels, Appledore, Kent, England.

Between 1955 and the early 1980's, there has been a very healthy rise in the quality and popularity of German Wirehaired Pointers in England. The culmination of many dedicated fanciers' dreams came about when, in 1980, the Kennel Club gave its official approval and recognition to the German Wirehaired Pointer Club, this following at least one disappointment on the matter in the past.

Now that it is "official," the club and the breed are forging full steam ahead.

As of 1983, the German Wirehaired Pointer Club in England has about 140 members, which include some from such distant points as Australia and New Zealand, the United States, Belgium, and even a member or two from Germany. A number of them have been involved since the very beginning (such as Major Wilkinson), Barbara Pinkerton and her daughter, Sharon (who is Secretary), these two ladies having bred the first Wirehair to have won a Group at a British Championship Show, and a number more of dedicated, accomplished people.

We are indebted to Mrs. Pam Blay, owner of the Draycott Kennels, for much of the above background information on what has been taking place among Wirehairs and their owners in Great Britain. Mrs. Blay is a lady of prominence in the breed there and has established an excellent line of her own as a Wirehaired breeder. Jolly Quirta of Stablaheim was the real foundation of Mrs. Blay's dogs. She was mated to the Swedish import Mr. Allround at Wittekind and produced a smashing good litter that included Stablaheim Aint Misbehavin and Stablaheim April Love, both of whom have succeeded admirably in the show ring.

Jolly Quirta and her litter brother and sisters, Merry Igor of Stablaheim and Abbey and Isara Drahtaar were bred in Ireland by Mr. O'Neill from the bitch he purchased from England. The puppies came to England when very young, and Mrs. Blay promptly took over Jolly and Igor. The litter from Ireland also included Abbey, who went to a pet home, and I.D. who became the foundation bitch for Mrs. Roberts. Although in a pet home, Abbey had a litter sired by an early Wittekind, from which Mrs. Blay kept a young dog, Cody of Stablaheim.

Attending a field trial during 1983, Pam Blay lost her heart to a nine-year-old dog, Lanka Bacchus vom Insul, who, it turned out, was a son of one of the original black and white imports. As luck would have it, there was a daughter of his available for sale (really luck, as he had been bred to only twice in his nine years) which Mrs. Blay promptly bought. She is Zoe of Stablaheim, of outstanding type, and Pam knew

Bareve Brunhilde, born February 1981, by Mr. Allround of Wittekind from Witte-kind Eva Braun at Bareve. Bred and owned by Barbara and Sharon Pinkerton. Brun-hilde is litter sister to Baldur, and has won very consistently during her show career with many firsts before retiring to have a litter.

at once that this was exactly what was needed in the show ring and in the field in England.

Pam Blay comments, "Our line is now quite unique, as we have mated April Love to Bacchus. The breeding produced eight puppies, four dogs and bitches, now three months old. Two of the bitches are also black and white, and these are the two we have kept. Their coats are fantastic and they are showing great promise."

We have already mentioned Barbara Pinkerton and her daughter, Sharon, who is Secretary of the German Wirehaired Pointer Club in England. The Pinkertons live at Market Harborough, Leics, where they operate the Bareve Kennels. This is the home of the famed Eva Braun, Top Wirehaired Bitch in England for 1980 and 1981 and leading Wirehair for 1982.

125

The German Wirehaired puppy, Stablaheim Aint Misbehavin at seven months. Photo courtesy of Mrs. Pam Blay, Draycott Kennels, Appledore, Kent, England.

Eva Braun is the dam of Bareve Baldur and Bareve Brunhilde, littermates sired by the Swedish import, Mr. Allround of Wittekind who was the first Wirehaired Pointer to appear in the Group at Crufts and the sire of the first Group winner at a British Championship Show, Bareve Baldur. Baldur still, as we write, holds his position as the *only* Wirehaired to win a Gundog Group at a Championship Show; this honor came to him at the Scottish Kennel Club in 1983. Baldur was the Best Dog at England's "first ever" Specialty Show for Wirehairs. Additionally he has been Best Wirehaired Pointer Dog three times and Reserve Best German Wirehaired Dog once. Brunhilde, Baldur's sister, has won very consistently during her show career, winning 41 Firsts before semi-retirement to have a litter.

Another littermate to Baldur and Brunhilde is Bareve Bianca, who is the mother of the beautiful Bareve Bromberg, sired by Wittekind Ice King, and also bred by Barbara and Sharon Pinkerton. Bianca was unshown until after she had turned three years of age, and has done well on both occasions when she has appeared in the ring.

The English winner, Bareve Baldur, born February 1981 by the Swedish import Mr. Allround of Wittekind from Wittekind eva Braun at Bareve. Bred and owned by Barbara and Sharon Pinkerton, Leics, England. Baldur is the *only* Wirehaired to have won a Gundog Group at a Championship Show, which he did at the Scottish Kennel Club in May 1983. He has been Best Wirehaired Pointer Dog three times and Reserve Best once. He was the Best Dog at their first ever German Wirehaired Pointer Club Specialty Show in 1983.

The Bianca-Ice King daughter, Bareve Brombeere, was born in January 1983. She is the only German Wirehaired Pointer to have won a Kennel Club Junior Warrant, an honor for which the dog needs to win 25 points before the age of 18 months. The requirements are particularly stringent for Wirehaireds, this being considered a "rare" breed, and only one point is awarded under these circumstances for each breed class. Nonetheless, Brombeere completed her needed points for the honor four months earlier than was actually necessary, when just 14 months of age.

Brombeere now has won 30 classes and she is still only 15 months old! She has been Best German Wirehaired bitch on one occasion and Reserve Best German Wirehaired bitch on two. At the time of this writing, Brombeere has yet to be beaten by another puppy during her puppy career.

Now the Pinkertons are eagerly anticipating the arrival, during early September 1984, of their long awaited "American Boy" who is now in quarantine. He is American Champion Geronimos Knickers von S.G., and he was born in 1982, bred by Joanne Burns-Steffes, to whom the Pinkertons feel deep gratitude for allowing them to have this beautiful dog. He should make a most wonderful part of the Bareve team for future shows and bring new blood to the breeding program.

Major Wilkinson is still active with his Andesheim Wirehaireds, and enjoys the respect and admiration of his fellow fanciers as the importer of the first Shorthairs from Germany.

Mrs. Mills De Moog owns the Wittekind Kennels, a familiar name to all Wirehaired fanciers. Among Wittekind dogs are American Champion Wittekind Hans owned by Mrs. M. Beeney, and Australian Champion Wittekind Cleo owned by Mrs. Oakes. Wittekind is strong in Dutch and Swedish bloodlines.

← **Overleaf:**

1. Ch. Gretchenhof Columbia River with Jo Shellenbarger winning Best in Show at Westminster in 1974.

2. Shannon's Wild Irish Rose, by Ch. Shannon's Irish Challenge ex Fieldfine's Megan of Sharon, was Best of Opposite Sex in the Sweepstakes at the German Shorthaired Pointer Club National Specialty in May 1984, St. Paul, Minnesota. Bred and owned by Patricia Crowley, Shannon Shorthairs, Old Saybrook, Connecticut.

3. Terry Strong of Maryland is the owner-trainer of this beautiful Shorthair, Happitee's Maybe This Time.

4. Mutual admiration! John Remondi with one of the Robin Crest puppies.

Overleaf:→

1. Ch. Gretchenhof Windjammer with Joyce Shellenbarger.

2. Ch. Froja's Gretel, by Ch. Rocky Run's Stoney ex Serakraut's Frojo, bred by F.J. Harshaw. Owned by Bob Arnold, Marcus Hook, Pennsylvania.

3. Ch. Fieldfine's Foxey Lady, by Am. and Can. Ch. Fieldfines Count Rambard ex Shaas River Risque, is a multiple Best of Breed winner and was Best of Opposite Sex at the 1980 National Specialty Show. Dot Vooris handling for Noel M. Nucks, South Salem, New York.

4. Ch. Serakraut's Hot Shot, by Ch. Strauss's Happy Go Lucky ex Strauss's Jodi, bred and owned by Ann Serak, Serakraut Shorthairs, Sturtevant, Wisconsin. Hot Shot was a Top Ten Shorthair in 1974, Best of Opposite at the National 1975, Multiple Group and Specialty winner, and Best in First Sweepstakes, National Specialty 1972.

5. Ch. Rocky Run's Katrin II, by Ch. Fieldfines Rocky Run ex Rocky Run's Windsong, bred, owned, and handled by Bob Arnold.

6. Ch. Fieldfines Rocky Run, by Ch. Rocky Run's Stoney ex Fieldfines Tasha, is a half brother to Rambard, a multiple Best of Breed winner, and the sire of the fantastic bitch Ch. Fieldfines Ribbons. Owned by Bob and Doris Arnold. Handled by Bob Arnold.

1 ▸
2 ▸
3 ▸
4 ▸
5 ◂
6 ▸
7 ▸
8 ▸

← **Overleaf:**

1. Can. Ch. Jaegershund's Firefox Quester, C.D. gained the latter title with three straight wins at Brantford, Ontario (two) and St. Catherine's, Ontario (one), scoring 189½, 192, and 194 points. Owned by Firefox Shorthairs, Jerry and Sharon Freeman, Alton, Ontario.

2. Ch. Wil-Lyn Sienna Gold, C.D. finished his C.D. title in four trials; finished championship with three majors; and Specialty Best in Sweepstakes at the German Shorthaired Pointer Club of Southern California, September 1981. Field-trained and will be campaigned for field championship and Dual title. Karen Detterich, owner, Paladen Shorthairs, Riverside, California.

3. A lovely portrait of a handsome German Shorthair in the field. This is Ch. Revil Raisin Mischief Maker, by Am. and Can. Ch. Fieldfines Count Rambard ex Ch. Scanpoint's Chocolate Raisin, a prominent show winner owned by Donna C. Bruce, Jacksonville, North Carolina.

4. Aust. Ch. Trolanda Arctic Tern, U.K. import, is also a C.D. title holder. Born in 1979, this bitch is the progeny of two English Dual Champions, both therefore being working dogs as well as show champions. Owned by W.W. Davies, Carlingford, New South Wales, Australia.

5. Ch. Arawak Blue Angel, by Ch. Conrad's Brio ex Ch. Traveler v Waldtaler, owned by J. and J. Tabor, Upper Montclair, New Jersey.

6. Hapitee Count Wilhelm, by Am. and Can. Ch. Fieldfines Count Rambard ex Shortt's Frau Jutta, C.D., born August 1977. This handsome Shorthair owned and trained by Terry L. Strong, Sykesville, Maryland.

7. Glenmajors Dunka's Top Boss "on point" to pheasant. Larry and Marlyn Kennedy, owners, Streetsville, Ontario, Canada.

8. Two handsome Shorthairs in the field: Ch. Legacy's Too Far Gone and Legacy's Easy From Now On. Both are by Am. and Can. Ch. Fieldfine's Count Rambard ex Monarch's Mein Grievous Angel and were bred by their owner, Donna Liberto.

Overleaf:→

1. Am. Ch. Abigail von Thurber, by Dual Ch. Biff Bangabird ex Sieglinda Thurber, completing her championship. Handled by Robert Schultz for breeder-owner Robert B. Leach, M.D., Birmingham, Michigan.

2. Ch. Berkshire's Dancing Star, multi-Best of Breed and Group placing bitch, bred by S. Fastiggi. Owned by Pat Crowley and S. Roy, Old Saybrook, Connecticut.

3. Ch. Kingswood's Miss Chiff, by Am. and Can. Ch. Kingswood's Windsong ex Am. and Can. Ch. Wentworth's Happy Wanderer, C.D., at the 1982 National Specialty took Best in Futurity, Best in Sweepstakes and Winners Bitch then the following year went Best of Breed at the National. Bred and owned by James M. and June D. Burns, Cuddebackville, New York.

4. The first time out as a Veteran at the Mason and Dixon Specialty in 1980, the great Am. and Can. Ch. Fieldfines Count Rambard goes straight through from there to Best of Breed under judge Anna K. Nicholas as the crowd roared their approval. An exciting moment in dog show history, as breeder-owner Dot Vooris proudly handles her magnificent dog.

5. Ch. St. Hubertus's Katie-Did, by Ch. Baron Pepper Von Pooh ex Ch. Johmar's Truly Scrumptious, owned by Patricia Crowley. Katie-Did is a multi-Best of Breed winner and a National Specialty winner.

6. Ch. Serakraut's Anxious, by Ch. Serakraut's Tailor Made ex Ch. Serakraut's Stardust, bred and owned by Ann Serak, was Best in Specialty over an entry of 182 Shorthairs, 50 of them specials, at the German Shorthaired Pointer Club of Wisconsin Specialty in May 1981.

135

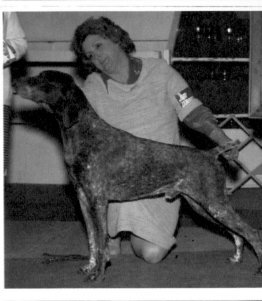

1 ▼
2 ▲

3 ▲
4 ▼

5 ▼
6 ▲

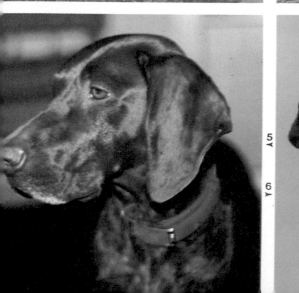

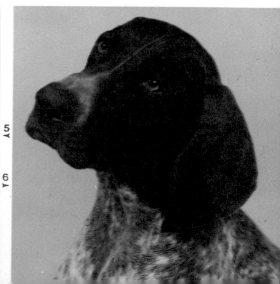

←Overleaf:

1. The outstanding German Shorthair Am. and Can. Ch. Fieldfines Count Rambard, by Ch. Whispering Pines Patos ex Fieldfines Tasha, owned by Dorothea and Robert Vooris, Ronkonkoma, New York. This great dog, the sire of 60 or more champions, has been a dominant competitor throughout his show career, with a record of consistent successes in keenest show competition.

2. Ch. Wil-Lyn's Wild Bear Cody, by Ch. Baron Erik Von Austin, C.D. ex Ch. Geezee Cinderella V. C'Sambra, bred by Jerry Ammel. Owned by Paul and Karen Detterich, Paladen German Shorthairs, Riverside, California.

3. Ch. Kaposia's Sun Dance, C.D.X., by Ch. Kaposia's Wildfire ex Ch. Ginger v Hockenschmidt, a distinguished Shorthair owned by Mrs. Nolan Noren, Lorene, Idaho.

4. The German Shorthaired Pointer, Ch. Tabor's Zephyr of Orion, owned by J. and J. Tabor, Upper Montclair, New Jersey.

5. Am. and Can. Ch. Katrina von Thurber, German Shorthair bitch, owned by Robert B. Leach, M.D., Birmingham, Michigan. Handled by James Berger.

6. Ch. Donavin's Magic Mischief, littermate to Ch. Donavin's Sir Ivanhoe, owned by Donavin Shorthairs, Christopher and Donna Saris, Stanton, California.

Overleaf:→

1. Ch. Serakraut's Tailor Made, by Ch. Strauss's Happy Go Lucky ex Ch. Misty Morn of Sigma Tau Gamma, bred and owned by Ann Serak. This Group winner is the sire of seven champions including Best in Show winner.

2. Shannon's War Paint (Tank), littermate to Challenge, has three majors and lacks just two points to finish despite limited showing. Breeder-owner, Patricia D. Crowley, Shannon's Shorthairs.

3. Ch. Serakraut's Exactly, by Ch. Serakraut's Rocky Mountain ex Ch. Serakraut's Stardust, was born March 1977. A multiple Specialty and Group winner and a Top Ten German Shorthair for 1979 and 1980, Exactly is the only Shorthair to date who has ever won a Group at the Chicago International.

4. Ch. Huntabirds Born Ready, a handsome and consistent Shorthair, owned by Robert P. Steward. Handled by Smokey Medeiros.

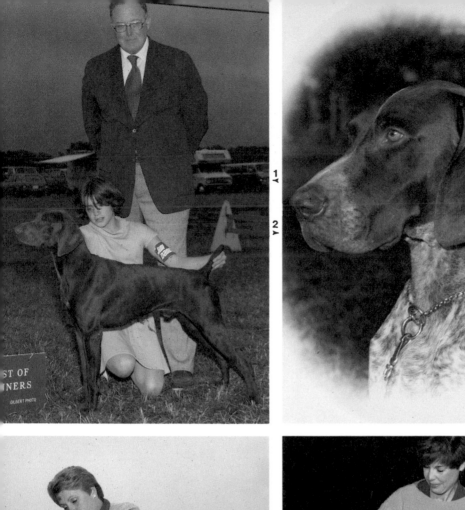

1 ▲

2 ▲

3 ▲

4 ▲

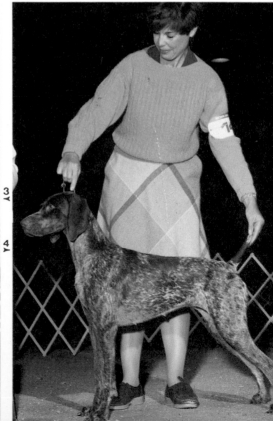

←Overleaf:

1. Wentworth's Benchmark, 11 months old, going Best of Winners for a 3-point major. Handled by Denine Vooris for owners Paul and Elena Fairfield.

2. The noted Ch. Geezee's Super Chief, the Nation's No. 2 German Shorthair in 1975 and 1976, West Coast's No. 1 (both years), is the sire of many champions and big record dogs including Ch. Donavin's Sir Ivanhoe. Owned by Donavin Shorthairs, Stanton, California.

3. Ch. Fieldfines Revil Raisin, by Am. and Can. Ch. Fieldfines Count Rambard ex Ch. Scanpoints Chocolate Raisin, C.D., was Best of Opposite Sex in 1983 Sweepstakes National. A Reserve Winners Dog at the age of six months, Mason and Dixon Specialty, he is now a Best of Breed and Group placing winner. Owned by Fieldfine Kennels and Stephanie Snyder. Handled by Dot Vooris.

4. Ch. Donavin's Chocolate Confetti, sired by Champion Donavin's Sir Ivanhoe, owned by Donavin Shorthairs, Christopher and Donna Saris, Stanton, California.

Overleaf:→

1. Ch. Fieldfines Rocky River, by Ch. Fieldfines Rocky Runt ex Am. and Can. Ch. Fieldfines River Shannon, is the litter sister to Ch. Fieldfines Ribbons and herself a multiple Best of Breed winner. She is also the Voorises' daughter's Junior Showmanship Dog with whom they qualified for Westminster Junior Handling. Here Rocky River is pictured with Dorothea May Vooris winning Best Junior Handler, Wallkill 1984.

2. Am. and Can. Ch. Hungerhausen's Dreimal Adam was the No. 1 German Shorthaired Pointer in 1975 and Parent Club Show Dog of the Year in 1974 and 1975. This fantastic show dog as well as devoted companion in the field is owned by Dennis G. and Ruth Ann Ricci, Vincentown, New Jersey.

3. Ch. Berkshire's Dancing Star, a multi-Best of Breed and Group placing bitch, bred by S. Fastiggi. Owned by Pat Crowley and S. Roy.

4. Ch. Rocky Run's Stoney, born May 12th 1968, by Ch. Adam v Fuehrerheim ex Ch. Rocky Run's Poldi, was a Best in Show winner and won five Specialty Bests of Breed. He had 105 Best of Breed wins to his credit, numerous Group placements, and is a member of the German Shorthaired Pointer Hall of Fame. Bred, handled, and owned by Robert Arnold, Marcus Hook, Pennsylvania.

5. Am. and Can. Ch. Fieldfines Ram of Ravenhurst, by Am. and Can. Ch. Fieldfine's Count Rambard ex Ch. Grouseflights Shadow Tara, is a multiple Best of Breed and Group placement winner in the States and in Canada. Owned by Keith and Donna Vooris. Handled by Keith Vooris.

6. Ch. Wilwyn's Acis, by Ch. Adam v Fuehrerheim ex Ch. Macho's Contessa of Kaposia, C.D., pictured here at Mispillion Kennel Club, August 1972, taking third in Group. This dog has ten Group placements and more than 45 Bests of Breed. Always handled by owner-breeder Clyde Wilkinson, his wife Jane, or their daughter.

143

1 ▸
2 ▸

3 ▸
4 ▸

5 ▸
6 ▸

← **Overleaf:**

1. Pelham West's Big Game Spotter at ten years old. Owned by Larry Berg, Wood-haven, New York.

2. Aust. and New Zealand Ch. Canawindra Winara, by Aust. Ch. Canawindra Audipi, C.D. ex Aust. Dual Ch. Deddick Tarshish, was bred by M.J. and F.L. Park and is owned by G. and R. Stewart, Australia.

3. A German Shorthaired Pointer owned by A.M. and J.M. Hayes at Chester Hill, New South Wales, Australia. This dog, Seltsam Errol Flynn, C.D. was born in January 1983, sired by Arlgarde Gemini (U.K. import) from Burnbrock Elena, and was bred by R. and M. Howarth, Seltsam Kennels. He has multiple show wins and placings although still a youngster, including winning the Minor Puppy Class at the 1983 Shorthair Championship and a placement at the Sydney Royal Easter Show in 1984. He was a member of the Easter Show open obedience demonstration team in 1984 and attained his Companion Dog title before a year old; also winner of the Novice Gundog Obedience Trial German Shorthair Parade, at 14 months and placed in his first Non-Slip Retriever Trial at 15 months.

4. Can. Dual Ch. Glenmajor's Dunks's Top Boss, by NFC Uodibar's Bossman ex Ch. Seigers Farina, C.D.X., 1979 No. 1 Shooting Dog in Canada, has seven points towards Open Field Championship and seven points towards Amateur Field Championship for the U.S.A. Field Trial Championship. He is Canada's First Dual Champion German Shorthaired Pointer. This sire of Dual Champions and Show Champions, is owned by Mrs. Maryln Kennedy, Streetsville, Ontario, Canada.

5. The noted British winner Bellandowa Ballarina, C.D.X. has some admirable wins to her credit in both England and Ireland. One of the outstanding Shorthairs owned by Mrs. Barbara Wood, Shoreham, Sussex, England.

6. English Ch. Bellandowa Cirio has won her seventh Challenge Certificate at the Southern Counties Championship Show. Owned by Mrs. Barbara Wood, Bellandowa Shorthairs, Shoreham, Sussex, England.

Overleaf:→

1. Ch. Kingswood's Chelsea Timer, by Ch. Conrad's Brio ex Ch. Kingswood's Encore, taking Best in Sweepstakes at the Nutmeg Specialty in 1983. This splendid youngster is owned by Regina Hairie, Wurtsboro, New York.

2. Am. and Can. Ch. Fieldfines River Shannon, by Am. and Can. Ch. Fieldfines Count Rambard ex Shaas River Risque, owned by Debby Vooris, Smithtown, New York. Handled by Dot Vooris.

3. Lieblinghaus Flagstaff, by Ch. Indian Country Columbia Moon ex Ch. Lieblinghaus April Snow, finished championship with four majors. A multiple breed winner and Group placing German Shorthair bred, owned, and handled by Dennis and Ruth Ann Ricci, Vincentown, New Jersey.

4. Am. and Can. Ch. James von Thurber, by Am. and Can. Ch. Galileo von Thurber ex Am. and Can. Ch. Katrina von Thurber, completed his championship in January 1984 under judge, Denis Grivas. Handler, James Berger. Owner-breeder, Robert B. Leach, M.D., Birmingham, Michigan.

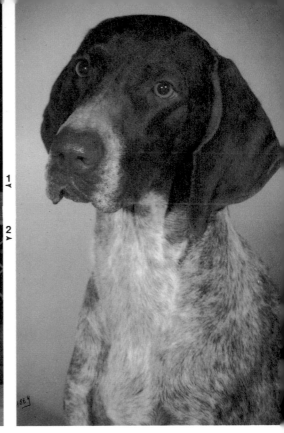

1. Am. and Can. Ch. Robin Crest Little John winning the breed for owner-handler John Remondi at Eastern Dog Club 1982.

2. Ch. Lieblinghaus Starshine, German Shorthaired Pointer from the Lieblinghaus Kennels, Dennis and Ruth Ann Ricci, Vincentown, New Jersey.

3. Ch. Donavin's Gusto, multiple Group winning and on Top Ten list prior to being killed on a plane at two and a half years of age. This littermate to Champion Donavin's Sir Ivanhoe was owned by Donavin's Shorthairs, Christopher and Donna Saris, Stanton, California.

4. The German Shorthaired Pointer, Ch. Rocky Run's Wildflower, by Ch. Fieldfine's Rocky Run ex Ch. Rocky Run's Shati, is the Group placing foundation bitch for Thomashenry Kennels. She was bred by Bob Arnold and is owned by Tom and Dorothy Alexander, Ste. Anne, Manitoba, Canada.

Overleaf:→

1. Am. and Can. Ch. Galileo von Thurber, by Ch. Ashbrook's Pagageno ex Lori von Thurber, handled by James Berger for breeder-owner Robert B. Leach, M.D., Von Thurber Shorthairs, Birmingham, Michigan.

2. Ch. Fieldfines Count Rambard winning Best of Breed under the author at Wallkill in 1977. Dot Vooris, as usual, owner-handling her great dog.

3. Am. and Can. Ch. Dee Tee's Fan Cede v Greif. C.D. is by Dual Ch. Oxton's Minado von Brunz ex Dual Champion Cede Mein Dolly der Orrian. Breeder, D.W. Tidrick. Owners, Sandra and John R. Trotter, Cedar Falls, Iowa.

4. Ch. Wilwin's Dionysus, Group winning German Shorthaired Pointer by Ch. Conrad's Brio ex Ch. Macho's Contessa of Kaposia, C.D., bred and owned by Clyde H. Wilkinson. Handled by daughter, Kym W. Kulis, winning the Sporting Group at Asheville, July 1982.

5. Ch. Fieldfines A Perfect Tasha, by Am. and Can. Ch. Fieldfines Count Rambard ex Monarch's Mein Grievous Angel, born May 1980, completed title at Southern Maryland in 1982, and winning since as a special. Owned by William Desmini, Nesconset, New York.

6. Ch. Baron Edward Von Pooh, bred by N. and C. Baldwin, owned by Patricia D. Crowley, winning the breed at Trenton Kennel Club in 1981, judged by the author. This lovely Shorthair, a multi-Best of Breed winner, is by Ch. Carol's Fancy Dan, C.D. ex Princess Gretchen Von Pooh.

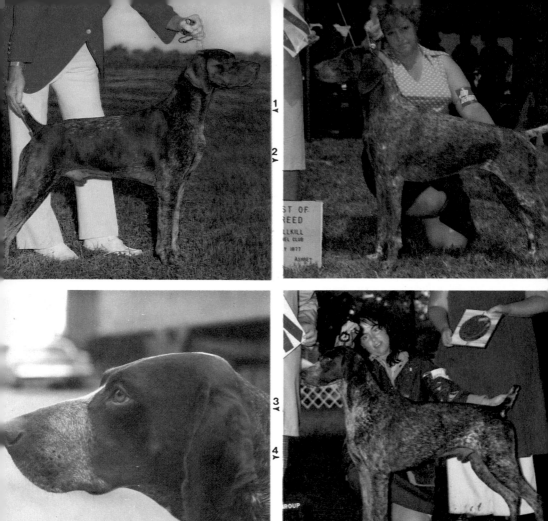

1 ►

2 ►

ST OF
REED
LLKILL
EL CLUB
Y 1977
ASHBEY

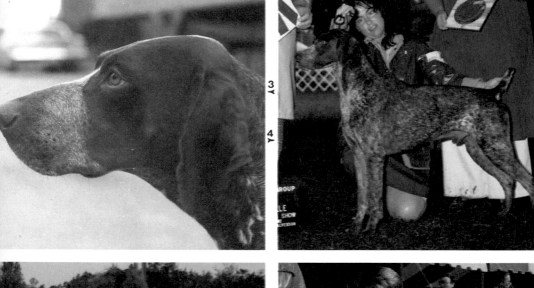

3 ►

4 ►

ROUP
LE
SHOW
FFERSON

5 ►

6 ►

1 ▶
2 ▶

3 ▶
4 ▶

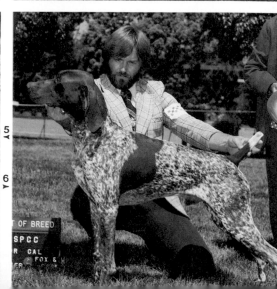

5 ▶
6 ▶

←**Overleaf:**

1. Ch. Lieblinghaus April Snow, by Ch. Gretchenhof Columbia River ex Ch. Lieblinghaus Snowstorm, winning Bred-by-Exhibitor Class at the Mason and Dixon Specialty in 1978. Owned by Debbie Pugsley Jackson in co-ownership with breeders-handlers Dennis and Ruth Ann Ricci, Vincentown, New Jersey.

2. Ch. Lieblinghaus Miss Liberty, by Ch. Gretchenhof Westminster ex Ch. Lieblinghaus Starshine, taking Best of Breed at Bucks County in 1983, judged by Tom Bradley. Bred, owned, and handled by Dennis and Ruth Ann Ricci, Vincentown, New Jersey.

3. Ch. Hawkeyes Dan Sir von Greif, by Ch. Schatzi's Greif der Ripper ex Am. and Can. Ch. Dee Tee's Fan Cede von Greif, C.D. Bred and owned by Sandra and John R. Trotter, Cedar Falls, Iowa.

4. Ch. Cede Mein Chat Nuga Chu Chu, by Am. and Can. Ch. Cede Brass Badge ex Am. and Can. Ch. Cede Mein Gadabout, C.D., bred by C.D. Lawrence. This handsome winner of the mid-1970's was owned for two years by P. Carl Tuttle, Gunhill Kennels, who showed him in the East and used him as a stud dog.

5. Ch. Serakraut's Lucky Buck, by Ch. Strauss's Happy Go Lucky ex Strauss's Jodi, bred and owned by Ann Serak. This Top Ten Shorthair in 1974, multiple Group and Specialty winner, and Veterans Class winner 1978 National Specialty, was also Winners Dog for 5-point major first time out as a puppy.

6. Ch. Wil-Lyn's Wild Bear Cody, whelped in 1980, by Ch. Baron Erik Von Austin, C.D. ex Ch. Geezee Cinderella V. C'Sambra, bred and handled by Jerry Ammel for owners Paul and Karen Detterich, Paladen German Shorthaired Pointers, Riverside, California. Pictured winning the German Shorthaired Club of California Specialty Best in Show in 1983. Judge was E.J. Kauffman.

Overleaf:→

1. Ch. Fieldfines Rocky Run, born 1977, by Ch. Rocky Run's Stoney ex Fieldfines Tascha, bred by Keith and Dorothea Vooris, owned by Robert Arnold, Marcus Hook, Pennsylvania. Rocky is the sire of the great winning bitch Ch. Fieldfines Ribbons, the Top German Shorthaired Pointer of 1982. Peggy Rousch handling here for owner.

2. Ch. Baron Pepper Von Pooh winning Best of Breed at Queensboro in 1978. Pat Horan handling for owners, Nancy C. Baldwin and D.G. Comstock.

3. Am. and Can. Ch. Juliet von Thurber, handled by James Berger for breeder-owner Robert B. Leach, M.D., Birmingham, Michigan.

4. Am. and Can. Ch. Tabor's Zephyr of Orion, by Ch. Tabor's Orion, C.D. ex Ch. Arawak Blue Angel, winning the Sporting Group under Donald Booxbaum en route to his third all-breed Best in Show. Handled by Raymond E. Scott for breeder-owners J. and J. Tabor, Upper Montclair, New Jersey.

← **Overleaf:**

1. Am. and Can. Ch. Fieldfines Lord Tanner, by Am. and Can. Ch. Fieldfines Count Rambard ex Ch. Cinnamon Duchess, is a multiple Best of Breed winner. Tanner is also a Best in Show dog and winner of the 1980 National Specialty. In Canada he is a Group and Best in Show winner. He is the sire of champions. Owned by Leonard and Mark Shulman. Handled by Keith and Dot Vooris.

2. Ch. Donavin's Sir Ivanhoe winning the National Specialty Show for Donavin's Shorthairs, Christopher and Donna Saris, Stanton, California. Handled by Ric Byrd.

3. Ch. Tabor's Twice As Spicey, by Ch. Tabor's Zephyr of Orion ex Ch. Tabor's Artemis of Buck Hollow, was bred by J. and J. Tabor. Owned by De Rafferty and J. Tabor, Upper Montclair, New Jersey.

4. Ch. Nock's Chocolate Morsel, by Ch. Nock's Chocolate Chip ex Ch. Kejan's Independence, pictured winning a Group, judged by Melbourne Downing. Bred by Jack Nock and Tom Greer, born January 1979. This noted Sporting Group, Specialty Show, and all-breed Best in Show winner is now owned by Sherri and Jack Nock, Jupiter, Florida.

1. Ch. Tabor's Banner of Hidden Acre, by Ch. Tabor's Orion, C.D. ex Ch. Conrad's Liberty Bell, bred by J. and J. Tabor. Owned by J. Tabor and De Rafferty, Upper Montclair, New Jersey.

2. Ch. Huntabird's Born Ready, well-known winning Shorthair owned by Robert P. Stewart, Noblesville, Indiana. By Ch. Huntabird's Mello Yellow Blues ex Ch. Huntabird's Born A Star, "Ready" finished his championship at a year old and had several Best of Breed and Group placements along the way. Now starting out as a special handled by Smokey and Chris Medeiros.

3. The very famous Shorthair Ch. Nock's Chocolate Chip, who was bred by K. Lytle, is owned by Sherri and Jack Nock, Jupiter, Florida. Here winning Best in Show at Central Florida in 1982. Handled by George Heitzman.

4. Am. and Can. Ch. Echo Run's Corteze's Choice, by Ch. Heidabrandt's Blitzdorf ex Grouseflight Holliday, C.D., winning the Group at Saginaw Valley K.C. A Top Ten German Shorthaired Pointer of 1982 and 1983, he has won first in six Sporting Groups to date with numerous other placements and close to 100 times Best of Breed. Also doing well as a sire, he already has three champions to his credit. An outstanding field dog and companion, "Corky" has been owner-handled to his show successes by Neil Ritter, Freedom, Pennsylvania.

5. Shannon's Fo Ha Finish, by Ch. P.W.'s Challenge Von Fieldfine ex Ch. St. Hubertus's Katie Did, owned by Kathleen Fo Ha. Breeder, Patricia Crowley, Shannon Shorthairs. Shown seven times by her novice owner, this lovely bitch has a 5-point, a 4-point, and a 3-point major.

6. Am. and Can. Ch. Katrina von Thurber taking a major at Lakeland-Winterhaven in 1982, judged by Mrs. Barbara Heller. One of the excellent Shorthairs owned by Robert B. Leach, M.D., Birmingham, Michigan. Handled by James Berger.

7. Ch. Macho's Contessa of Kaposia, C.D., by Kaposia's Comanche ex Champion Kaposia's Winona, tied in 1972 for Top Producing German Shorthaired Pointer Dam. Contessa finished championship at 14 months and C.D. at a year and a half in three shows. Produced six champions and numerous obedience title holders in her lifetime. Owner-handler, Clyde Wilkinson, Lynchburg, Virginia.

8. Ch. Nock's Chocolate Chip winning one of his many Group victories. Handled by George Heitzman for owners Jack and Sherri Nock, Jupiter, Florida.

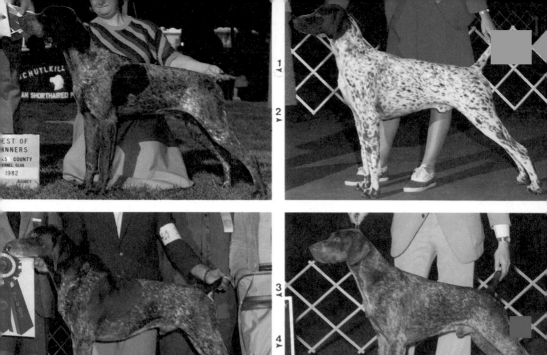

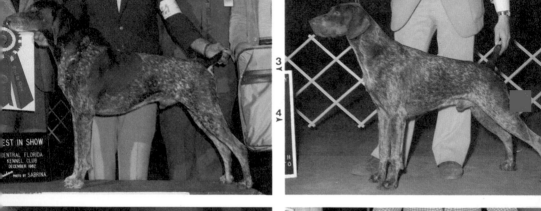

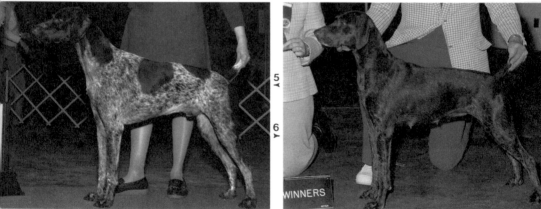

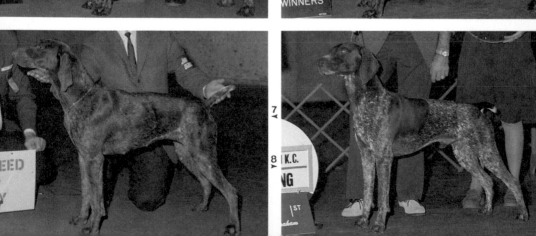

BEST OF
OPPOSITE
ERKS COUNTY
KENNEL CLUB
SEPTEMBER 1978
ASHBEY

← **Overleaf:**

1. Ch. Nock's Chocolate Morsel winning Best of Breed at Texas Kennel Club in March 1983. Handled by George Heitzman for breeder-owner Jack Nock, Jupiter, Florida.

2. Ch. Kingswood's Windsong, Group winner and multiple breed winner, the sire of Ch. Kingswood's Miss Chiff, owned by James M. and June D. Burns, Kingswood Shorthairs, Cuddebackville, New York.

3. Am. and Can. Ch. Robin Crest Rolls Royce taking Best of Opposite Sex at Chester Valley Kennel Club 1983. Owner-handled by John Remondi, Armonk, New York.

4. Ch. Kingswood's Night Rider was Winners Dog, Best of Winners, Best in Sweepstakes, and Best in Futurity at the 1979 National Specialty. Sired by Ch. Fieldfines Count Rambard ex Am. and Can. Ch. Wentworth's Happy Wanderer, C.D. Owned by James M. and June D. Burns, Cuddebackville, New York.

5. Ch. Donavin's Sir Ivanhoe winning one of his 62 Sporting Group Firsts, this time judged by Haworth Hoch. Ivanhoe, by Ch. Geezee Super Chief, has also eight all-breed Bests in Show to his credit, 16 Specialties, 171 Group placements, and has been Best of Breed a total of 261 times. Owned by Donavin Shorthairs, Christopher and Donna Saris, Stanton, California. Handled by Ric Byrd.

6. Ch. Shannon's Irish Challenge, by Ch. P.W.'s Challenger Von Fieldfine ex Ch. St. Hubertus's Katie Did, bred and owned by Patricia Crowley, Shannon Shorthairs, Old Saybrook, Connecticut.

7. Ch. Kingswood's Shady Lady taking Best of Winners en route to the title at Mohawk Valley in 1978. Owned by James M. and June D. Burns, Cuddebackville, New York.

8. Ch. Heidehof Hi-Spirit of Kaposia is the son of Ch. Kaposia's Wild Wind, grandson of Ch. Kaposia's Tucumcar, and great-grandson of Ch. Kaposia's Waupon II. This Top Ten German Shorthaired Pointer and sire of champions was bred and is owned by Mr. and Mrs. Robert Morrison, Minneapolis, Minnesota.

Overleaf:→

1. Am. and Can. Ch. Fieldfines River Shannon, by Am. and Can. Ch. Fieldfines Count Rambard ex Shaas River Risque, is the dam of the No. 6 Sporting Dog for 1982, Ch. Fieldfines Ribbons; of Ch. Fieldfines Rocky River; and of Fieldfines Shutter Bug, 1979 National Specialty Show Winners Bitch. Robert Vooris, handler, aged 16. Owners, Allen and Debra Vooris.

2. M. and J.'s Kit von Thurber, by Ch. Ashbrook's Papageno ex Am. and Can. Ch. Katrina von Thurber, bred by Robert B. Leach, M.D. Handled by Marie Henry, co-owner with Jeri Leach.

3. Am. and Can. Ch. Hungerhausen's Dreimal Adam "on point" at the Sporting Group sign. Owned by Dennis G. and Ruth Ann Ricci, Vincentown, New Jersey.

4. Shorthairs make neat Junior Showmanship Dogs, as Ch. Shannon's Irish Challenge is doing with breeder-owner Patricia Crowley's daughter at Putnam Kennel Club in 1983, judged by Jean Dills.

5. Ch. Broker's Best Offer, by Am. and Can. Ch. Fieldfine's Count Rambard ex Ch. Legacy's Mein Grievous Angel, owned by W.W. Bowman, Beltsville, Maryland. A Group winner and a Specialty Show winner, this dog, handled by Keith Vooris, is also already known as the sire of champions.

6. Ch. Serakraut's Bravo, by Ch. Serakraut's Tailor Made ex Ch. Serakraut's Stardust, bred and owned by Ann Serak. Bravo is an all-breed Best in Show dog, a multiple Specialty winner, and a multiple Group winner including a Group First from the classes.

1 ▶

2 ▶

3 ▶

4 ▶

5 ▶

6 ▶

1 ▶

2 ▼

3 ▶

4 ▼

5 ▶

6 ▼

← **Overleaf:**

1. Kingsacres Cordova, 1st Amateur Shooting Dog, owned by Mrs. Marlyn Kennedy, Streetsville, Ontario, Canada.

2. Ch. Fieldfines Ribbons, consistent and important winning bitch, taking Best of Breed at the German Shorthaired Pointer Club of California Specialty in May 1982. Handled by Dot Vooris for owners Joyce Oesch and Kathleen Plotts.

3. Ch. Eden Tasmin The Pilgrim, by Ch. Bleugras Bandy v Shadydell ex Ch. Eden Columbia Cameo, bred by Margaret Cass, belongs to Tom Crump, Greenwood, Indiana. A splendid working field dog as well as show winner, this lovely Shorthair has hunted pheasant in South Dakota, quail in south central Kansas, and has run in local field trials.

4. The German Shorthair, Ch. Lowenbrau's Ben von Greif, age three years, here taking first in the Sporting Group, Brazos Valley 1984, judged by Mr. Clinton M. Harris. Shirlee Murray handled for owners, Karen B. and David G. Beddow, Coat of Arms Kennel, Dallas, Texas.

5. The noted German Shorthair, Ch. Lowenbrau's Ben von Greif, at two years of age taking Best in Show at the Lone Star German Shorthaired Pointer Specialty Show, March 25th 1983. Judge, Miss Maxine Beam. Handler, Shirlee Murray. Owners, Karen B. and David G. Beddow, Dallas, Texas.

6. Ch. Lieblinghaus Storm Trooper is another of the many noted Shorthairs owned by Dennis G. and Ruth Ann Ricci. Vincentown, New Jersey.

1. The German Shorthaired Pointer Ch. Rocky Run's Robert, by Ch. Fieldfine's Rocky Run ex Rocky Run's Teal, is owned by Judith L. Sener, Hummelstown, Pennsylvania.

2. Three generations of show champions who are also retrieving trial winners. *Left to right*: Aust. Ch. Dunfriu Pluto, C.M., Aust. Ch. Burnbrook Atlas, C.D. (Group winner), and Aust. Ch. Burnbrook Othello (Group winner). Owned by Georgina and Michael Byrne, Burnbrook Kennels, Western Australia.

3. Three excellent Shorthair puppies, five weeks old here, who grew up to become Ch. Tabor's Orion, C.D., Ch. Arawak Blue Angel, and Am. and Can. Ch. Tabor's Zephyr of Orion. Bred by J. and J. Tabor, Upper Montclair, New Jersey.

4. Lord Shane of Pelham West at 12 years. Owned by Larry Berg, Woodhaven, New York.

5. Ch. Lieblinghaus Snowstorm, by Ch. Whispering Pines Ranger ex Ch. Mein Liebchen v Werner, C.D., was Top Ten in 1976 with over 50 Bests of Breed, Multiple Group wins and placements, and No. 1 Show Bitch in Country for 1976. This Dam of the Year 1982 and No. 5 All Time Top Producing Dam is dam of 14 Champions and eight pointed "get" from four litters. Dennis G. and Ruth Ann Ricci, owners, Lieblinghaus Shorthairs, Vincentown, New Jersey.

6. Am. and Can. Ch. Donavin's Auerback Ready Maid, daughter of Ch. Donavin's Sir Ivanhoe, owned by Donavin Shorthairs, Christopher and Donna Saris, Stanton, California.

7. Seltsam Errol Flynn, C.D., born January 1983, has done well in all types of competition for owners, A.M. and J.M. Hayes, Chester Hill, New South Wales, Australia.

8. Famed Australian German Shorthair, Ch. Canawindra Nandrena, was in 1982 Top Show Bitch among Shorthairs in Western Australia and in 1983 Top Show Shorthair in Victoria. Owned by M.J. and F.L. Park, Canawindra Kennels, Strathewen.

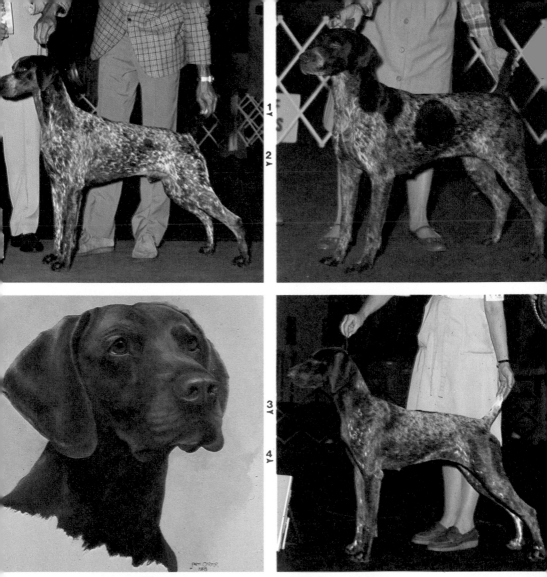
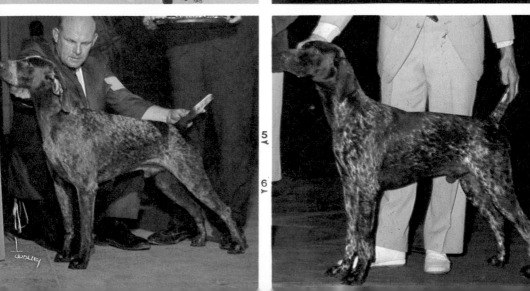

← Overleaf:

1. The German Shorthaired Pointer Ch. Bama Belle's Spectre, by Ch. Robin Crest Achilles ex Ch. Johmar Color Me Cocoa, C.D., is the winner of more than 50 Bests of Breed and 30 Group placements including multiple Group Firsts. Bred by Patricia A. Teer, D.V.M. and Donna H. Averill, D.V.M. and co-owned by Dr. Averill and Donna D. Averill. The Averills are from Marietta, Georgia.

2. Ch. Hawkeyes Yea Taylfuer V Greif, C.D., by Ch. Schatz's Greif der Ripper ex Am. and Can. Ch. Dee Tee's Fan Cede v. Greif, C.D., bred and owned by Sandra and John R. Trotter, Cedar Falls, Iowa. A litter sister to Ch. Lowenbraus Vahtzee vom Greif, C.D., she took second place to her in National Sweepstakes and National Futurity Classes in 1978.

3. Am. and Can. Ch. Wentworth's Benchmark, C.D. is by Am. and Can. Ch. Field-fines Count Rambard ex Am. and Can. Ch. Wentworth's Happy Wanderer, C.D. This No. 10 German Shorthair in the United States for 1979, earned his American Championship at 13 months of age, had A.K.C. Field Trial placements 1980-83, and took Prize III, Utility Test, October 1983 North American Versatile Hunting Dog Association. He is sire of two champions with more on the way and winner of Stud Dog Class at 1983 German Shorthair National. Paul A. Fairfield, owner, Wolfeboro, New Hampshire.

4. Ch. Revil Raisin Mischief Maker, by Am. and Can. Ch. Fieldfines Count Rambard ex Ch. Scanpoints Chocolate Raisin, is a multiple Best of Breed and Group placing Shorthair. Handled by Karen Ashe for owner Donna Bruce.

5. The German Shorthair Ch. Kaposia's Waupun II, winning Best in Show at Beaumont Kennel Club in 1971, judged by Dr. Frank Booth. Roy L. Murray handling for Helen B. Shelley. This dog during his lifetime, 1966-1978, won Best of Breed 151 times; three National Specialty Shows; Best of Breed at Westminster; first in 11 Sporting Groups; and 33 Group placements.

6. Ch. Hans Von Franzel taking Best of Breed at Savannah Kennel Club, November 1979. Owned by Walt and Betty Franzel, Land O'Lakes, Florida.

Overleaf:→

1. The German Shorthair Ch. Lieblinghaus Storm Hawk, C. D., by Ch. Gretchenhof Columbia River ex Ch. Lieblinghaus Snowstorm is the youngest of his breed ever to finish, having done so at three days before reaching nine months of age. Now a multiple Group placing breed winner. Owned by his breeders, Dennis G. and Ruth Ann Ricci, Vincentown, New Jersey.

2. Paladen's Brat Balou, whelped September 1982, by Ch. Wil-Lyn's Wild Bear Cody ex Sondra Von Brandenburg, is a homebred from Paladen Kennels, Karen Detterich, owner. At 18 months has both majors, having been Winners Bitch and Best of Winners for a four point major at six months of age, German Short-haired Pointer Club of Arizona Specialty among other good wins towards title.

3. This handsome dog is Ch. Kingswood's Leprechaun, owned by Harold Phillips, Jr., Sussex, New Jersey. Pictured here taking Winners Dog at the Eastern German Shorthaired Pointer Club Specialty Show in 1983. A son of Ch. Conrad's Brio ex Ch. Kingswood's Encore.

4. Ch. Tabor's Artemis of Buck Hollow, by Ch. Kooskia's Chief Joseph ex Buck Hollow's Valkyrie, bred by Julia Carroll, owned by J. and J. Tabor. Pictured with co-owner Joan Tabor taking Best of Opposite Sex at Lackawanna in 1980.

5. Am. and Can. Ch. Field Fines Count Rambard on the occasion of a Group victory. Owner-handled by Dot Vooris.

6. The German Shorthair Aust. Ch. Kazia Lord Nelson, by Klugerhund Von Igor (imported U.K.) ex Aust. Ch. Birdacre Kara, C. D. Bred by Mr. L. G. and Mrs. C. Butler, owned by Mr. R. and Mrs. P. Butler, Gladesville, New South Wales, Australia. Mr. R. Butler handling.

1

2

3

4

5

6

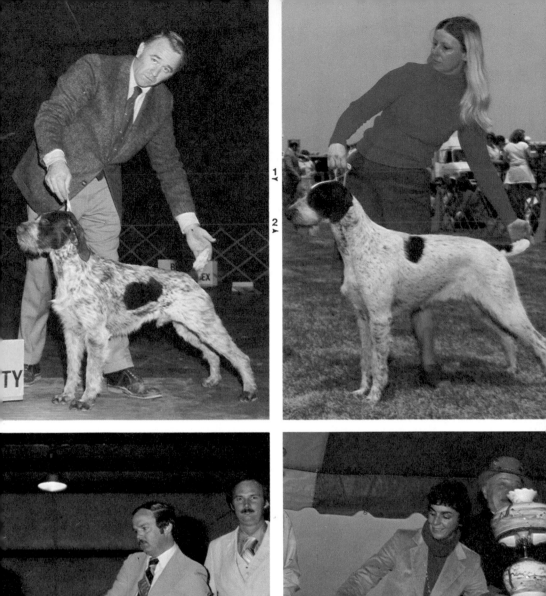

←**Overleaf:**

1. Ch. Jagersbo Friar Tuck, a son of Ch. Jagersbo Mills Stig ex Oldemill Flower, was second top winning German Wirehaired Pointer of his day. Erik Bergishagen, owner, Jagersbo Kennels, Birmingham, Michigan.

2. Ch. Laurwyn's Brie taking points at Trenton in 1979. Bred by Patricia Laurans. Owner-handled by Judy Cheshire.

3. Ch. Laurwyn's Cheeseburger winning the Sporting Group at Greater Kingsport in 1972. Owned by Spindrifter German Wirehaired Pointers, John H. and Ginger Writer and Patricia W. Laurans, Glen Ellyn, Illinois. This winner of two National Specialties is owner-handled.

4. Ch. Laurwyn's Banner winning the German Wirehaired Pointer Club of America National Specialty 1981. Bred and owned by Patricia W. Laurans. Handled here by Terry Lazzaro Hundt. Judge was Dr. Bernard M. McGivern. Robert McCarthy, Show Chairman, presented the trophy.

Overleaf:→

1. Field Champion and Amateur Field Champion Walker's Summer Wind, by Walker's Tanglefoot ex Field Ch. and Amateur Field Ch. Madchen, bred and owned by Phil Walker, Eagle, Wisconsin.

2. Ch. Briarpatch Ripsnorter Gal, by Ch. Windhaven's Stutzer Stumper ex Ch. Briarpatch Jaleska Wanda, finished undefeated in six shows. Owners, Jeffrey and Helen George, Ripsnorter German Wirehaired Pointers, Mt. Vernon, Ohio.

3. Laurwyn's American Cheese taking Best of Winners at Westminster in 1978. Terry Lazzaro Hundt handled for Gail Frazier.

4. Ch. Weidenhugel Moonraker, Deutscher Bundessieger 1983; 1983 Bundessieger Dortmund West Germany; Best of Breed Wirehaired; and third in Sporting Group, Arnheim, Holland. "Toto" was born August 1979, by Ch. Weidenhugel Aramis v Beau ex Heidi von Hohenzollern. Owned by Alaysia Hard, c/o M. Revell, Cotati, California.

5. Lutz and Cina at an "outing." These two Wirehairs are Dual and Amateur Field Ch. Lutz Zur Cadenburg, C.D., T.D. and Ch. Weidenhugel Capuccine, C.D., both owned by Silke Alberts, Cadenburg Wirehairs, Vallejo, California.

6. Ch. Weidenhugel Top Gunner, by Ch. Weidenhugel Aramis v Beau ex Herrlich Kelly Girl, goes back to Hilltop and Haar Baron bloodlines. Owned by M. Revell, R. Ehrlich and K. Hudson, Cotati, California.

175

1

2

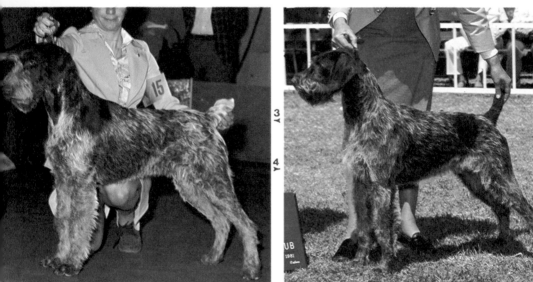

15

3

4

UB
1981

5

6

←**Overleaf:**

1. The German Wirehaired Pointer Ch. Laurwyn's Big Cheese owned by John H. Writer.

2. Ch. Hilltop's S.S. Cheese Cake going Group II at the Bucks County Kennel Club Show after winning the Delaware Valley German Wirehaired Pointer Club Specialty from the Veterans Class, age 11 years. In the Group, she defeated more than 350 dogs. Owner, Patricia W. Laurans, Laurwyn Kennel. Handler, Joy S. Brewster. Breeder, Hilltop Farm.

3. A seven- to eight-week-old Wirehaired puppy, just before the whiskers really start to appear. Laurwyn Kennels, owners, Newtown, Connecticut.

4. Zoe of Stablaheim, 8-month-old German Wirehaired puppy. Mrs. Pam Blay, Draycott Kennels, Appledore, Kent, England.

5. The noted Ch. Winterhawk Snow Owl, a multi-Best in Show dog who was No. 1 German Wirehaired Pointer over several years and the sire of many important winners, was owned by Berna Lee Akin and Peggy J. Clark, M.D. Snow Owl died in 1980.

6. Ch. Laurwyns Whynot Heidi, Best Junior Puppy, 1983 German Wirehaired Pointer Club of America Sweepstakes, was bred by Joanne Martin. Owner-handler, Barbara Halligan.

Overleaf:→

1. The German Wirehaired Ch. Brewster Von Lieben-waid, C.D., by Am. and Can. Ch. Windhaven's Stutzer Stumper ex Ch. Desert Mill's Ilda V Landhaus, bred by Diane L. Nordrum and Robert L. Calentine. Owners are Larry B. and Nancy Mason, Auburn, Washington. This dog was Best in Sweepstakes at the Wisconsin Specialty Show in 1982 and Reserve Winners Dog at the German Wirehaired Pointer Club National in 1982 at eight months of age. Finished conformation championship at age 16 months. Obtained C.D. in three shows.

2. The German Wirehair, Caden Berg Filou v. Lutz, T.D., by Dual and Amateur Field Ch. Lutz Zur Cadenburg, C.D., T.D., "on point." Bred and owned by Silke Alberts, Vallejo, California. This bitch, an A.K.C. Tracking Dog, is winner of NAUHDA NA Prize 1.

3. Winners Dog at the 1981 German Wirehaired Pointer Club of America National Specialty, Whynots Cointreau of Laurwyn, owned by Paul R. and Joanne K. Martin, co-breeders with Patricia Laurans.

4. Ch. Laurwyn's Big Cheese, by Ch. Hilltop's Bradshaw ex Ch. Hilltop's S.S. Cheese Cake, was bred by Patricia W. Laurans. Owned by John H. Writer, handled by Pamela De Hetre. Judge was the late A. Peter Knoop.

5. Patricia W. Laurans owner-handled her great bitch, Ch. Hillside's S.S. Cheese Cake, C.D., from the Veterans Class to Best of Opposite Sex, 11½ years *young*, at the 1981 Fall Specialty of the German Wirehaired Pointer Club of America.

6. Ch. Laurwyn's Bit of Cheese at age six months taking Best of Breed over specials, handled by Joy S. Brewster for breeder-owner Patricia W. Laurans, Laurwyn Kennels, Newtown, Connecticut.

7. Ch. Hilltop's Bradshaw, born June 1973, a Beau Brummel-Misty Lady winning son, owned and bred by Charles and Betty Stroh. He was No. 6 German Wirehaired Pointer 1976 and Top Producer 1977 and 1978.

8. The great Best in Show Wirehaired bitch, Ch. Hilltop's S.S. Cheese Cake, owned by Patricia W. Laurans, Newtown, Connecticut.

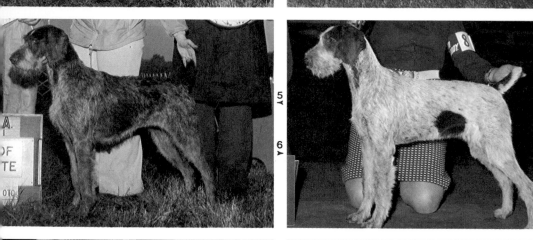

← **Overleaf:**

1. Am. and Can. Dual Ch. and Amateur Field Ch. Nordwest's Griff Von Der Feld in the field was one of the Top Ten German Wirehaired Pointer Gun Dogs in the U.S., 1978-1980. Entirely amateur trained and handled. Owners, Doug and Penny Ljungren, Kent, Washington.

2. Ch. Desert Mill's Medow Rok Willy, by Ch. Mueller Mill's Valentino II ex Ch. Desert Mill's Lily Marlene, winning a Sporting Group. One of the current winners from Desert Kennels as we go to press. Handled by Roy Murray for owner Helen B. Shelley.

3. Laurwyn's Macho Cheese, Best in Sweepstakes, German Wirehaired Pointer Club of America National Specialty, 1978. Owner, Patricia W. Laurans, handler, Joy S. Brewster.

4. Ch. Hilltop's S.S. Cheese Cake pictured on the occasion of her first Best in Show. This was at Champion Valley Kennel Club in July, 1972; the judge was the late Winnie Heckman. Handled by Joy S. Brewster and owned by Patricia W. Laurans.

5. Ch. Laurwyn's Shore Point Gis Tweed, Best in Sweepstakes, Winners Bitch and Best of Winners, German Wirehaired Pointer Club of America National Specialty 1981. Owner-handler Marcia Wolkerstorfer.

6. Ch. Laurwyn's Boursin, German Wirehaired Pointer, winning the Sporting Group at Newton Kennel Club in September 1977. Judged by Nial Koontz. Pat Horan handled for owners Bob and Mickey McCarthey.

7. Ch. Jagersbo Friar Tuck, by Ch. Jagersbo Mills Stig ex Oldemill Flower, one of the fine German Wirehairs owned by Erik Bergishagen, Jr., Jagersbo Kennels, Birmingham, Michigan.

8. A splendid German Wirehaired Pointer in the field. Ch. Jagersbo L.H. Harritt represents well the outstanding Wirehaireds from Jagersbo Kennels, Erik Bergishagen, Birmingham, Michigan.

Overleaf:→

1. Ch. Laurwyn's Shore Point Gis Tweed owned by Marcia Wolkerstorfer.

2. A handsome Wirehair Pointer headstudy from Ripsnorter Kennels, Jeff and Helen George, Mt. Vernon, Ohio.

3. These two handsome German Wirehairs are: *left*, Ch. Topwin's Macaroni, C.D.X. and *right*, Ch. Hilltop's Shula of Bogay, U.D.T. Both belong to Suzette M. Wood, Kissimmee, Florida, who tells us that Shula is the *only* German Wirehaired Pointer holding at that time a breed championship, Utility obedience degree and an *advanced* hunting skills title.

4. This handsome German Wirehaired Pointer is Am. and Can. Dual Ch. and Amateur Field Ch. Nordwest's Griff Von Dem Feld, by Am. and Can. Ch. Odell's Hansel, C.D.X. ex Odell's Anji, born January 6, 1976, owned by Doug and Penny Ljungren, Kent, Washington. This is the only German Wirehaired Pointer during his time to have completed Dual Championship in both the U.S. and in Canada.

1 ▶
2 ▶
◀ 3
◀ 4

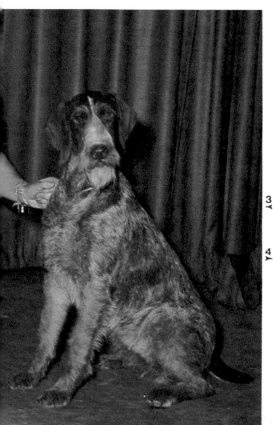

←**Overleaf:**

1. Titushill Alpine of Laurwyn winning four points on the way to the title. Handled by Mary Brooks at the Sun Maid Kennel Club, Fresno, California.

2. Laurwyn's Heywire Calliope taking points at Trenton K.C. by placing Best of Opposite Sex. Jack Writer, handler. Jim and Barbara Halligan, owners. Breeders, Judy Cheshire & Patricia W. Laurans.

3. Ch. S.S. Hilltop's Cheese Cake owned by Laurwyn Kennels, Patricia Laurans, Newtown, Connecticut. Joy S. Brewster handled this great Wirehaired bitch to so many thrilling victories.

4. Ch. Hilltop's S.S. Cheese Cake winning one of her many Sporting Group victories, this time judged by Mel Downing. Handled by Joy S. Brewster for owner Patricia W. Laurans, Newtown, Connecticut.

1. Dual Ch. Graf Bowser was top Field dog for many years. Entered the show ring at seven years of age to complete his Dual Championship. Owned by Norman Le Furge, Jersey City, New Jersey. Handled by Joy S. Brewster.

2. The German Wirehaired Pointer Ch. Laurwyn's Banner going Best in Show, all breeds, after winning the Delaware Valley German Wirehaired Pointer Club Specialty and the Sporting Group, judged by Ed Jenner. Joy S. Brewster handling for breeder-owner Patricia W. Laurans, Laurwyn Kennels, Newtown, Connecticut.

3. Ch. Weidenhugel Capuccine, C.D., T.D. owned by Silke Alberts, Cadenberg Wirehairs, Vallejo, California.

4. "Waiting for more ducks," photographed by R.L. Calentine. Ch. Desert Mill's Ilda V Landhaus, one year old, sitting in duck blind after making a couple of successful retrieves through ice and water. She is the foundation bitch at Diana L. Nordrum's Kennels, Maple Valley, Washington.

5. Am., Can., Bah. Ch. Windhaven's Stutzer Stumper, by Ch. Brewmeister of Brookside ex Ch. Fevus (Danish import), was bred by Robert J. Furlong and belongs to Jeffrey and Helen George, Mt. Vernon, Ohio.

6. Ch. Jagersbo Flying Turkey, German Wirehaired Pointer, is one of the current Wires owned by Erik Bergishagen, Jr., Jagersbo Kennels, Birmingham, Michigan.

1 ▸
2 ▸
3 ▸
4 ▸
5 ▸
6 ▸

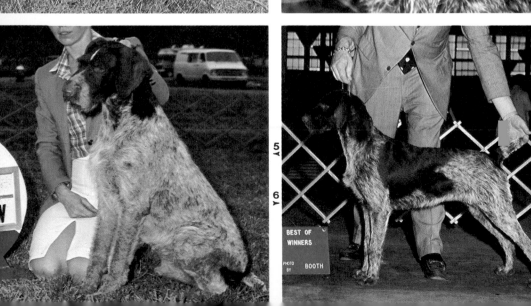

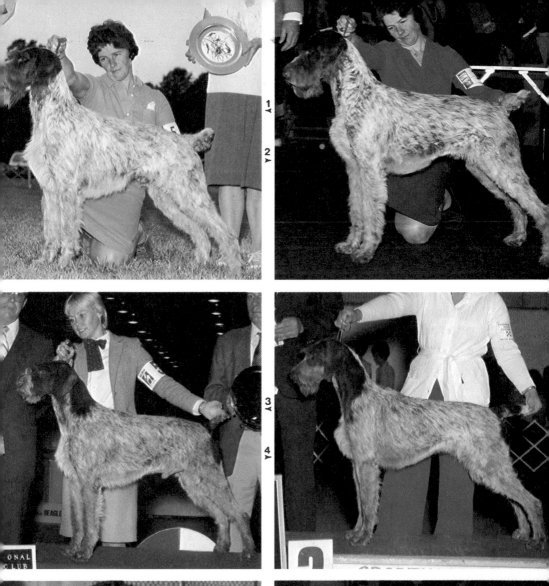

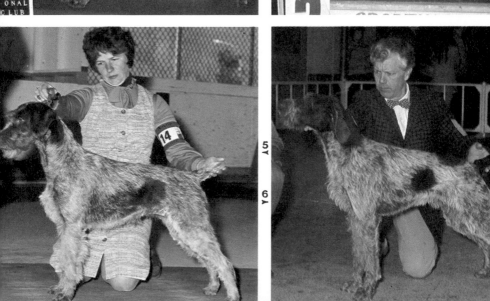

← Overleaf:

1. Ch. Laurwyn's Cheese Cobbler, handled by Joy Brewster, owned by Robert Hauslohner.

2. The German Wirehaired Ch. Laurwyn's Cheese Cobbler, winning the Best of Breed at Westminster in 1982. Joy S. Brewster, handler. Robert Hauslohner, owner.

3. Am., Can. and Bah. Ch. Windhaven's Stutzer Stumper winning the Sporting Group at Chicago International in October 1983, judged by D. Roy Holloway. Owned by Jeffrey and Helen George, Mt. Vernon, Ohio.

4. The No. 2 Wirehaired Producing Bitch Ch. Laurwyn's Barbed Wire owned by Jack Writer.

5. Ch. Laurwyn's Cheese Twist handled by Joy S. Brewster for owner Peter Loosen.

6. The noted Wirehaired sire and winner Ch. Weidenhugel Aramis v Beau is by Ch. Hilltop Honey's Beau Brummel ex Ch. Weidenhugel Anniversary. This famous and important Wirehair belongs to Norman D. and Mildred L. Revell, Cotati, California.

Overleaf:→

1. Ch. Winterhawk's Cholla in a thoughtful mood. Owned by Berna Lee Akin, Albuquerque, New Mexico. Photo courtesy of Pat Laurans.

2. "Good friends." Photo courtesy of Marcia Wolkerstorfer.

3. German Wirehaired Pointer Ch. Sandrifters Bang of Laurwyn, C.D., TT-2 GWP in the field retrieving a chukar, December 1982, six weeks after whelping a litter of nine. Owned by Robert J. Marks, Arkayem Kennels, Dundee, Illinois.

4. The great German Wirehaired Pointer bitch, top winning member of her breed, Champion Hilltop's S.S. Cheese Cake, C.D., owned by Patricia W. Laurans, Laurwyn Kennels. Handled throughout her show career by Joy S. Brewster. From a portrait in 1973 by Scott Griswold.

1 ▲
2 ▼

3 ▲
4 ▼

Chapter 6

Standards of the Breed

The standard of the breed, to which one sees and hears such frequent reference whenever and wherever purebred dogs are written of or discussed, is the word picture of what is considered to be the ideal specimen of the breed. It outlines, in minute detail, each and every feature of the breed, both in physical characteristics and in temperament, accurately describing the dog from whisker to tail, creating a clear impression of what is to be considered correct (or incorrect); the features comprising "breed type" (*i.e.*, those which set it apart from other breeds making it distinctive and unique); and the probable temperament and behavior pattern to expect in typical members of that breed.

The standard is the guide for breeders endeavoring to produce quality dogs, and for fanciers wishing to learn what is considered beautiful and typical within this individual breed. It is the tool with which judges evaluate and reach their decisions in the ring. The dog it describes as correct is the one in our mind's eye as we compare dogs and make our evaluations. It is the result of endless hours spent in consideration and study of the breed, its history, its reasons for being; and of its description and previous standards in our own country and the countries of the breed's origin and development from earliest days up until modern times. All such factors have been studied and examined most carefully by your breed's parent specialty club; usually by a special committee selected for the task; then by the board of directors, and later the general membership. When all are in agreement to that point, the results are turned in to the American Kennel Club for *their* further study and possible comments or suggestions, followed by pub-

Ch. Weidenbach Bridget moving right out. Owned by Weidenbach Kennels, Mildred Revell, Cotati, California. A Top Ten Shorthair of the 1970's.

lication, with the invitation to comment by interested parties, in the official American Kennel Club publication, *Pure-bred Dogs/American Kennel Gazette*. Following the satisfactory completion of all these steps, the Standard, or any changes in it which may have been under consideration, are approved and become official.

A similar routine is followed in other countries, too, for the drawing up of breed standards.

194

American Standard for the German Shorthaired Pointer

The Shorthair is a versatile hunter, an all purpose gun dog capable of high performance in field and water. The judgment of Shorthairs in the show ring should reflect this basic characteristic.

GENERAL APPEARANCE: The overall picture which is created in the observer's eye is that of an aristocratic, well-balanced, symmetrical animal with conformation indicating power, endurance and agility and a look of intelligence and animation. The dog is neither unduly small nor conspicuously large. It gives the impression of medium size, but is like the proper hunter, "with a short back but standing over plenty of ground." Tall, leggy dogs, or dogs which are ponderous or unbalanced because of excess substance should be definitely rejected. The first impression is that of a keenness which denotes full enthusiasm for work without indication of nervous or flighty character. Movements are alertly co-ordinated without waste motion. Grace of outline, clean-cut head, sloping shoulders, deep chest, powerful back, strong quarters, good bone composition, adequate muscle, well-carried tail and taut coat, all combine to produce a look of nobility and an indication of anatomical structure essential to correct gait which must indicate a heritage of purposefully conducted breeding. Doggy bitches and bitchy dogs are to be faulted. A judge must excuse a dog from the ring if it displays extreme shyness or viciousness toward its handler or the judge. Aggressiveness or belligerence toward another dog is not to be considered viciousness.

SYMMETRY: Symmetry and field quality are most essential. A dog in hard and lean field condition is not be be penalized; however, overly fat or poorly muscled dogs are to be penalized. A dog well-balanced in all points is preferable to one with outstanding good qualities and defects.

HEAD: Clean-cut, neither too light nor too heavy, in proper proportion to the body. Skull is reasonably broad, arched on side and slightly round on top. Scissura (median line between the eyes at the forehead) not too deep, occipital bone not as conspicuous as in the case of the Pointer. The foreface rises gradually from nose to forehead. The rise is more strongly pronounced in the dog than in the bitch as befitting his sex. The chops fall away from the somewhat projecting nose. Lips are full and deep, never flewy. The chops do not fall over too much, but from a proper fold in the angle. The jaw is powerful and the muscles well developed. The line to the forehead rises gradually and never has a definite stop as that of the Pointer, but rather a stop-effect when viewed from the side, due to the position of the eyebrows. The muzzle is sufficiently long to enable the dog to seize properly and to facilitate his carrying game a long time. A pointed muzzle is not desirable. The entire head never gives the impression of tapering to a point. The depth is in the right proportion to the length, both in the muzzle and in the skull proper. The length of the muzzle should equal the length of skull. A pointed muzzle is a fault. A dish-faced muzzle is a fault. A definite Pointer stop is a serious fault. Too many wrinkles in forehead is a fault.

Ears: Ears are broad and set fairly high, lie flat and never hang away from the head. Placement is just above eye level. The ears, when laid in front without being pulled, meet the lip angle. In the case of heavier dogs, the ears are correspondingly longer. Ears too long or fleshy are to be faulted.

Eyes: The eyes are of medium size, full of intelligence and expression, good humored and yet radiating energy, neither protruding nor sunken. The eye is almond shaped, not circular. The eyelids close well. The best color is dark brown. Light yellow (Bird of Prey) eyes are not desirable and are a fault. Closely set eyes are to be faulted. China or wall eyes are to be disqualified.

Nose: Brown, the larger the better, nostrils well-opened and broad. Spotted nose not desirable. Flesh colored nose disqualifies.

Teeth: The teeth are strong and healthy. The molars intermesh properly. The bite is a true scissors bite. A perfect level bite (without overlapping) is not desirable and must be penalized. Extreme overshot or undershot bite disqualifies.

NECK: Of proper length to permit the jaws reaching game to be retrieved, sloping downwards on beautifully curving lines. The nape is rather muscular, becoming gradually larger towards the shoulders. Moderate houndlike throatiness permitted.

CHEST: The chest in general gives the impression of depth rather than breadth; for all that, it should be in correct proportion to the other parts of the body with a fair depth. The chest reaches down to the elbows, the ribs forming the thorax show a rib spring and are not flat or slabsided; they are not perfectly round or barrel shaped. Ribs that are entirely round prevent the necessary expansion of the chest when taking breath. The back ribs reach well down. The circumference of the thorax immediately behind the elbows is smaller than that

196

of the thorax about a hands-breadth behind elbows, so that the upper arm has room for movement.

BACK, LOINS AND CROUP: Back is short, strong and straight with slight rise from root of tail to withers. Loin strong, of moderate length and slightly arched. Tuck-up is apparent. Excessively long, roached or swayed back must be penalized.

FOREQUARTERS: The shoulders are sloping, movable, well-covered with muscle. The shoulder blades lie flat and are well laid back nearing a 45° angle. The upper arm (the bones between the shoulder and elbow joints) is as long as possible, standing away somewhat from the trunk so that the straight and closely muscled legs, when viewed from the front appear to be parallel. Elbows which stand away from the body or are too close indicate toes turning inwards or outwards, which must be regarded as faults. Pasterns are strong, short and nearly vertical with a slight spring. Loose, short-bladed or straight shoulders must be faulted. Knuckling over is to be faulted. Down in the pasterns is to be faulted.

HINDQUARTERS: The hips are broad with hip sockets wide apart and fall slightly toward the tail in a graceful curve. Thighs are strong and well-muscled. Stifles well bent. Hock joints are well angulated and strong, straight bone structure from hock to pad. Angulation of both stifle and hock joint is such as to combine maximum combination of both drive and traction. Hocks turn neither in nor out. A steep croup is a fault. Cowhocked legs are a serious fault.

FEET: Are compact, close-knit and round to spoon-shaped. The toes sufficiently arched and heavily nailed. The pads are strong, hard and thick. Dewclaws on the forelegs may be removed. Feet pointing in or out is a fault.

COAT AND SKIN: The skin is close and tight. The hair is short and thick and feels tough to the hand; it is somewhat longer on the underside of the tail and the back edges of the haunches. It is softer, thinner and shorter on the ears and the head. Any dog with long hair in body coat is to be severely penalized.

TAIL: Is set high and firm, and must be docked, leaving 40% of length. The tail hangs down when the dog is quiet, is held horizontally when he is walking. The tail must never be curved over the back toward the head when the dog is moving. A tail curved or bent toward the head is to be severely penalized.

BONES: Thin and fine bones are by no means desirable in a dog which must possess strength and be able to work over any and every country. The main importance is not laid so much on the size of bones, but rather on their being in proper porportion to the body. Bone structure too heavy or too light is a fault. Dogs with coarse bones are handicapped in agility of movement and speed.

WEIGHT AND HEIGHT: Dogs, 55 to 70 pounds. Bitches, 45 to 60 pounds. Dogs, 23 to 25 inches. Bitches 21 to 23 inches at the withers. Deviations of one inch above or below the described heights are to be severely penalized.

COLOR: The color may be of solid liver or any combination of liver and white such as liver and white ticked, liver spotted and white ticked, or liver roan. A dog with any area of black, red, orange, lemon or tan, or a dog solid white will be disqualified.

GAIT: A smooth, lithe gait is essential. It is to be noted that as gait increases from the walk to a faster speed, the legs converge beneath the body. The tendency to single track is desirable. The forelegs reach well ahead as if to pull in the ground without giving the appearance of a hackney gait, and are followed by the back legs which give forceful propulsion. Dragging the rear feet is undesirable.

DISQUALIFICATIONS

China or wall eyes.

Flesh colored nose.

Extreme overshot or undershot.

A dog with any area of black, red, orange, lemon, or tan, or a dog solid white.

Approved October 14th 1975.

Kennel Club (English) Standard for the German Shorthaired Pointer

CHARACTERISTICS: The German Shorthaired Pointer is a dual-purpose Pointer-Retriever and this accounts for his excellence in the field, which requires a very keen nose, perseverance in searching, and enterprise. His style attracts attention; he is equally good on land and in water, is biddable, an extremely keen worker, and very loyal.

GENERAL APPEARANCE: A noble, steady dog showing power, endurance and speed, giving the immediate impression of an alert and energetic (not nervous) dog whose movements are well co-ordinated. Neither unduly small nor conspicuously large, but of medium size, and like the hunter, "With a short back stands over plenty of ground." Grace of outline, clean cut head, sloping long shoulders, deep chest, short back and powerful hindquarters, good bone composition, adequate muscle, well carried tail and taut coat giving a thoroughbred appearance.

HEAD AND SKULL: Clean-cut, neither too light nor too heavy, but well proportioned to the body. The skull sufficiently broad and slightly rounded. The furrow between the eyes not so deep, and the occiput not so pronounced as in the English Pointer. The nasal bone rises gradually from nose to forehead (this is more pronounced in the male) and should never possess a definite stop as in the English Pointer, but when viewed from the side there is a well defined stop effect due to the position of the eyebrows. The lips fall away almost vertically from a somewhat protruding nose and continue in a slight curve to the corner of the mouth. Lips well developed but not over hung. Jaws powerful and sufficiently long to enable the dog to pick up and carry game. Dish-faced and spiny muzzle are not desirable. Nose solid brown, wide nostrils well opened and soft.

EYES: Medium size, soft and intelligent, not protruding nor too deep set. Varying in shades of brown to tone with coat. Light eye not desirable. Eyelids should close properly.

EARS: Broad and set high; neither too fleshy nor too thin with a short soft coat; hung close to the head, no pronounced fold, rounded at the tip and should reach almost to the corner of the mouth when brought forward.

MOUTH: Teeth sound and strong. Molar teeth meeting exactly and the eyeteeth should fit close in a true scissor bite. Neither overshot nor undershot.

NECK: Moderately long, muscular and slightly arched, becoming larger towards the shoulders. Skin should not fit too closely.

FOREQUARTERS: Shoulder sloping and very muscular with top of shoulder blades close; upper arm bones between shoulder and elbow long. Elbows well laid back, neither pointing outwards nor inwards. Forelegs straight and lean, sufficiently muscular and strong but not coarse-boned. Pasterns slightly sloping, almost straight but not quite.

BODY: Chest must appear deep rather than wide but not out of proportion to the rest of the body; ribs deep and well sprung, never barrel-shaped nor flat as in the hound; back ribs reaching well down to tucked up loins. Chest measurement immediately behind the elbows smaller than about a handsbreadth behind the elbows, so that the upper arm has freedom of movement. Firm, short back, not arched. The loin wide and slightly arched; the croup wide and sufficiently long, neither too heavy nor too sloping starting on a level with the back and sloping gradually towards the tail. Bones solid and strong not clumsy and porous.

HINDQUARTERS: The hips broad and wide falling slightly towards the tail. Thighs strong and well muscled. Stifles well bent. Hocks square with the body and slightly bent, turning neither in nor out. Pasterns nearly upright.

FEET: Compact, close-knit, round to spoon shaped, well padded, should turn neither in nor out. Toes well arched and heavily nailed.

TAIL: Starts high and thick growing gradually thinner. Docked to medium length by two-fifths to half its length. When quiet tail should be carried down and when moving horizontally, never held high over the back or bent.

COAT: Skin should not fit loosely or fold. Coat short, flat and coarse to the touch, slightly longer under the tail.

COLOUR: Solid liver, liver and white spotted, liver and white spotted and ticked, liver and white ticked, black and white.

WEIGHT AND SIZE: Dogs 25-31.8Kg (55-70 lbs.), bitches 20.4-27.2Kg (45-60 lbs.). Size—dogs 58-64cm (23-25″) and bitches 53-59cm (21-23″) at the shoulder. Symmetry is most essential.

FAULTS: Bone structure too clumsy, sway-back, head too large, deep wrinkles in forehead, cone-shaped skull or occiput too prominent. Ears too long or too closely set together, eye-lids not closing properly. Wrinkles in neck. Feet or elbows turned inwards or outwards. Soft, sunken or splayed toes; cowhocks, straight hindlegs, or down on pasterns. Tail starting too low, undocked, too thick, curled up or too furry. Tri-coloured.

NOTE: Male animals should have two apparently normal testicles fully descended into the scrotum.

American Standard for the German Wirehaired Pointer

The German Wirehaired Pointer is a dog that is essentially Pointer in type, of sturdy build, lively manner and an intelligent, determined expression. In disposition the dog has been described as energetic, rather aloof but not unfriendly.

HEAD: The *head* is moderately long, the *skull* broad, the occipital bone not too prominent. The *stop* is medium, the *muzzle* fairly long with nasal bone straight and broad, the *lips* a trifle pendulous but close and bearded. The *nose* is dark brown with nostrils wide open, the *teeth* are strong with scissors bite. The *ears*, rounded but not too broad, hang close to the sides of the head. *Eyes* are brown, medium in size, oval in contour, bright and clear and overhung with bushy eyebrows. Yellow eyes are not desirable. The *neck* is of medium length, slightly arched and devoid of dewlap; in fact the skin throughout is notably tight to the body.

BODY AND TAIL: The body is a little longer than it is high, as ten is to nine, with the back short, straight and strong, the entire back line showing a perceptible slope down from withers to croup. The chest is deep and capacious, the ribs well sprung, loins taut and slender, the tuck-up apparent. Hips are broad with croup nicely rounded and the tail docked, approximately two-fifths of original length.

LEGS AND FEET: Forelegs are straight, with shoulders obliquely set and elbows close. The thighs are strong and muscular. The hind legs are moderately angulated at stifle and hock and, as viewed from behind, parallel to each other. Round in outline, the feet are webbed, high arched with toes close, their pads thick and hard, and their nails strong and quite heavy. Leg bones are flat rather than round, and strong, but not so heavy or coarse as to militate against the dog's natural ability.

COAT: The coat is weather-resisting and to some extent water-repellent. The undercoat is dense enough in winter to insulate against the cold but so thin in summer as to be almost invisible. The distinctive outer coat is straight, harsh, wiry and rather flat-lying, from one and one half to two inches in length; it is long enough to protect against the punishment of rough cover but not so long as to hide the outline. On the lower legs it is shorter and between the toes of softer texture. On the skull it is naturally short and close fitting, while over the shoulders and around the tail it is very dense and heavy. The tail is nicely coated, particularly on the underside, but devoid of feather. These dogs have bushy eyebrows of strong, straight hair and beards and whiskers of medium length. A short smooth coat, a soft woolly coat, or an excessively long coat is to be severely penalized.

COLOR: The coat is liver and white, usually either liver and white spotted, liver roan, liver and white spotted with ticking and roaning or sometimes solid liver. The nose is dark brown. The head is brown, sometimes with a white blaze, the ears brown. Any black in the coat is to be severely penalized. Spotted and flesh colored noses are undesirable and are to be penalized.

SIZE: Height of males should be from 24 to 26 inches at the withers, bitches smaller but not under 22 inches.

Approved February 7th 1959

Kennel Club (English) Interim Standard for the German Wirehaired Pointer

CHARACTERISTICS: Wire haired dual-purpose Pointer-Retriever excellent in the field, with a very keen nose. Perseverance in searching, and initiative are required. His style attracts attention; he is equally good on land and in water, is biddable, and extremely keen worker, and very loyal.

GENERAL APPEARANCE: A medium sized hunting dog of noble bearing, colour unimportant; very harsh hair completely covering the skin; active temperament, intelligent expression; devoted and energetic.

HEAD AND SKULL: The head should be of medium length with a long strong muzzle.

EYES: Dark hazel. Bright and intelligent with eyelids closing properly.

EARS: Medium sized.

MOUTH: Teeth strong. The jaws should be strong, with a perfect regular and complete scissor bite, i.e. the upper teeth closely overlapping the lower teeth and set square to the jaws.

NECK: Strong and of medium length.

FOREQUARTERS: Shoulders sloping and very muscular with top of shoulder blades close; upper arm bones between shoulder and elbow long. Elbows close to the body, neither pointing outwards nor inwards. Forelegs straight and lean, sufficiently muscular and strong but not coarse-boned. Pasterns slightly sloping, almost straight but not quite.

BODY: Chest must appear deep rather than wide but not out of proportion to the rest of the body; ribs deep and well sprung, never barrel-shaped nor flat as in the hound; back ribs reaching well down to tucked up loins. Chest measurement immediately behind the elbows smaller than that about a handsbreadth behind the elbows, so that the upper arm has freedom of movement. Firm, short back, not arched. The loin wide and slightly arched; the croup wide and sufficiently long, neither too heavy nor too sloping starting on a level with the back and sloping gradually towards the tail. Bone solid and strong.

HINDQUARTERS: The hips broad and wide falling slightly towards the tail. Thighs strong and well muscled. Stifles well bent. Hocks square with the body and slightly bent, turning neither in nor out. Pasterns nearly upright.

FEET: Compact, close-knit, round to spoon-shaped, well padded, should turn neither in nor out. Toes well arched and heavily nailed.

GAIT: Smooth, covering plenty of ground with each stride, driving hind action, elbows neither turning in nor out. Definitely not a hackney action.

TAIL: Starts high and thick growing gradually thinner. Docked by half its length. When quiet, tail should be carried down; when moving horizontally, never held high over the back or bent.

COAT: Hair very harsh, medium length, abundant with a close fitting undercoat. It should not hide the body shape but it should be long enough to give good protection. The coat should lie close to the body. The hair on the lower parts of the legs should be shorter. Very thick on the ears. Bushy eyebrows, full but not over-long beard. Skin fairly fine and close fitting.

COLOUR: Solid liver, liver and white spotted, liver and white spotted and ticked, liver and white ticked, black and white.

WEIGHT AND SIZE: Ideal height at shoulder: 60-65cm (23½"-25½"). Bitches not smaller than 56cm (22"). Weight: Dogs 25-32Kg (55-70½ lbs). Bitches 20½-27Kg (45-59½ lbs).

FAULTS: Any departure from the foregoing points should be considered a fault and the seriousness with which the fault is regarded should be in exact proportion to its degree.

NOTE: Male animals should have two apparently normal testicles fully descended into the scrotum.

An informal pose of the great Ch. Gretchenhof Columbia River with Joyce Shellen-barger and a puppy. Gretchenhof German Shorthairs, Huntington Beach, California.

Chapter 7

You and Your German Pointer

If you have selected either a German Shorthair or a German Wirehair Pointer to become your "family dog," you have indeed made an excellent choice. The versatility of these two breeds seems almost endless. The intelligence is very well known, as is their loyalty to home and family, their devotion to children, and the fact that they are not a difficult dog to train, if one is firmly patient.

They are very much "people dogs," enjoying family life and human companionship and prospering best in a home environment. They are wonderful "outdoor companions" if hunting interests you; attractive, successful show dogs if that is your thing; and they are proving themselves right out front in obedience, too.

The day your puppy comes home, his education should start. Since you have selected a sporting breed, we assume that some sort of outdoor activity is in his future. It is important that he be *correctly* taught if he is to compete in field trials; and this is somewhat different than the way you will teach him if he is to be your hunting companion. There are many fine books on field training, which is quite a specialized subject. Ask the breeder of your puppy for suggestions. And have fun, as this dog should be a source of great pleasure to you and to your family.

Obviously, being good sized and bred for the outdoors, these two breeds fare better in a suburban or country setting than in a city apartment. It is not quite fair to them to limit them to apartment living, although I do know of some who have prospered even under these conditions. What it comes right down to, I guess, is that if your German Pointer is with *you* he will be *happy*.

The German Wirehaired Pointer Ch. Trollebros Paw, a Danish import who finished here in July 1967. Photo courtesy of Erik Bergishagen, Birmingham, Michigan.

Chapter 8

The German Wirehaired Pointer

by Patricia W. Laurans

"Ask the man (or woman, or child) who owns one to get the truest picture of a breed" has always been my policy, and so, when it came to the Wirehairs, I thought immediately of Patricia Laurans, who lives quite nearby in my home area, and whom I therefore know to be an owner who truly lives with, enjoys the company of and gets to *know* her dogs and their breed. Who better to comment on their personality and character, tell us a bit about their background, and generally reminisce on what she has found most lovable about them? We are proud to present the following, which she has written for use in this book.   A.K.N.

The German Wirehaired Pointer as we know the breed today is the result of careful, selective breeding programs done by a number of extremely dedicated people. It traces all the way back to ancient times when early German fanciers wished to develop what they could consider to be an ideal all-purpose working-sporting dog—a dog that could not just *either* point or retrieve; but that could be used successfully for *both*, which at the time was a new school of thought which would take at least several generations of careful experimentation and planning.

Those who were interested formed the Verein Deutsch Drahthaar in 1902, and worked selectively towards the perfection of a rough-coated (for protection in all weather and tough cover), true all-purpose dog who could function with equal efficiency as a pointer and as a land and water retriever. This necessitated experimentation, breeding with German Shorthaired Pointers, Griffons, Pudel-pointers and Stichelhaars (the latter two the then-existent rough-coated German working breeds). The hopefully anticipated results developed, and by 1928 when the Verein Deutsch Drahthaar was accepted for membership by the German Kartel, the Drahthaar was already faring well as the perfect rough-haired dog for all types of sporting. One notes that in modern Germany more Drahthaars are registered annually than any of the breeds which figured in its creation.

In the 1920's Drahthaars, or German Wirehaired Pointers as they were to become known over here, arrived in the United States. In 1959 the breed became the 114th to be recognized by the American Kennel Club. There has been a steady growth rate since then, with the number of dogs competing in both field and show competition, and general recognition and appreciation of the merits of the breed in all phases of dog ownership, increasing at a quite fast pace. For example, over the first ten years of recognition here, 1959-1969, there were 69 German Wirehaired Pointers completing their show championships. During the next four years the number increased sharply with 72 championships completed during that much shorter length of time. And it is significant that in the two years between 1973-1975 more than one hundred Wirehaired championships were completed.

Now the German Wirehaired is a well established breed with a loyal following of devoted admirers. As show dogs, they are making their presence felt in Group and Best in Show competition most satisfactorily. Quite different from the beginning when 1961 saw the first two Group placements made by the breed; the number growing to six in 1968; in 1971 nine; and in 1975 an impressive total of fifteen of the breed were awarded placements.

By mid-1984, ten individual Wirehaireds have achieved the distinction of taking Best in Show All Breeds. The first of these was Champion Oldmill's Casanova, owned by Anamary E. Compere, in October 1960, followed nine years later by his son, Champion Mueller Mills Valentino owned by Helen B. Shelley. Third was Champion Rusty von Schnellberg, owned by David and Patsy Hillstead; fourth Wirehair, and the first bitch, to take an all breed Best in Show was

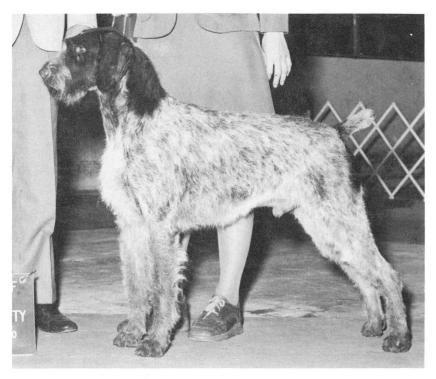

The German Wirehaired Pointer, Am., Can. and Bah. Ch. Windhaven's Stutzer Stumper, owned by Ripsnorter Kennels, Jeff and Helen George, Mt. Vernon, Ohio.

Champion Hilltop's S.S. Cheese Cake owned by Patricia Laurans.

Fifth was Champion Desert Mills Lon Chaney, Berna Lee Akin, owner; sixth, Champion Winterhawk Snow Owl co-owned by Berna Lee Akin and Peggy J. Clark, M.D.; seventh, Champion Laurwyn's Banner, owned by Patricia W. Laurans; eighth, Champion Brewmeister of Brookside, owner Robert Furlong; ninth, Champion Windhaven's Stutzer Stumper, Jeffrey and Helen George, and tenth, Champion Trysle Helix Arrose, C.D., owners Mark G. and Cynthia Tilly and Margarette Voorhes.

The German Wirehaired Pointer as a companion is intelligent, energetic and determined—a friendly yet not overbearing sort who might even be considered aloof to all except his own people. He is a very possessive protector, a hunter, companion, and clown whose fierce loyalty to those he knows and loves is unbounded. Being a clown, he

has a sense of humor which makes him fun to live with. His many good qualities, talents and versatility make him a dog to be enjoyed in many ways.

Yet with all these attributes, the Wirehair is by no means the ideal dog for every person and every situation. Individual love and attention are important to these dogs, and they do not fare well living strictly as "kennel dogs." Wirehairs need a consistent, firm and fair upbringing by someone capable of keeping a step or two ahead of them. Work and patience are required to bring out the best in a Wirehaired and to enjoy him to the utmost. His versatility and devotion which result make the work all well worthwhile.

Ch. Oldemill Casanova, handsome German Wirehaired Pointer from Newton Compere's famous kennels. Photo courtesy of Erik Bergishagen, Birmingham, Michigan.

German Wirehaired Pointer breeders can, and do, take pride as well as pleasure in the strides they have achieved in producing such sound and successful show dogs; the fact that they still retain their dual qualities which make them excel in field competition and as hunting companions for their owners; and success, as it has been coming too, in the obedience ring.

Shorthair puppies at play. Sired by Count Rambard, owned by Dot Vooris.

Chapter 9

The Purchase of Your German Pointer

Careful consideration should be given to what breed of dog you wish to own prior to your purchase of one. If several breeds are attractive to you, and you are undecided which you prefer, learn all you can about the characteristics of each before making your decision. As you do so, you are thus preparing yourself to make an intelligent choice; and this is very important when buying a dog who will be, with reasonable luck, a member of your household for at least a dozen years or more. Obviously since you are reading this book, you have decided on the breed—so now all that remains is to make a good choice.

It is never wise to just rush out and buy the first cute puppy who catches your eye. Whether you wish a dog to show, one with whom to compete in obedience, or one as a family dog purely for his (or her) companionship, the more time and thought you invest as you plan the purchase, the more likely you are to meet with complete satisfaction. The background and early care behind your pet will reflect in the dog's future health and temperament. Even if you are planning the purchase purely as a pet, with no thoughts of showing or breeding in the dog's or puppy's future, it is essential that if the dog is to enjoy a trouble-free future you assure yourself of a healthy, properly raised puppy or adult from sturdy, well-bred stock.

Throughout the pages of this book you will find the names and locations of many well-known and well-established kennels in various areas. Another source of information is the American Kennel Club (51 Madison Avenue, New York, NY 10010) from whom you can obtain a list of recognized breeders in the vicinity of your home. If you plan to have your dog campaigned by a professional handler, by all means let the handler help you locate and select a good dog. Through their numerous clients, handlers have access to a variety of interesting show prospects; and the usual arrangement is that the handler re-sells the dog to you for what his cost has been, with the agreement that the dog be campaigned for you by him throughout the dog's career. It is most strongly recommended that a prospective purchaser follow these suggestions, as you thus will be better able to locate and select a satisfactory puppy or dog.

Your first step in searching for your puppy is to make appointments at kennels specializing in the chosen breed, where you can visit and inspect the dogs, both those available for sale and the kennel's basic breeding stock. You are looking for an active, sturdy puppy with bright eyes and intelligent expression and who is friendly and alert; avoid puppies who are hyperactive, dull, or listless. The coat should be clean and thick, with no sign of parasites. The premises on which he was raised should look (and smell) clean and be tidy, making it obvious that the puppies and their surroundings are in capable hands. Should the kennels featuring the breed you intend owning be sparse in your area or not have what you consider attractive, do not hesitate to contact others at a distance and purchase from them if they seem better able to supply a puppy or dog who will please you *so long as it is a recognized breeding kennel of that breed*. Shipping dogs is a regular practice nowadays, with comparatively few problems when one considers the number of dogs shipped each year. A reputable, well-known breeder wants the customer to be satisfied; thus he will represent the puppy fairly. Should you not be pleased with the puppy upon arrival, a breeder such as one described above will almost certainly permit its return. A conscientious breeder takes real interest and concern in the welfare of the dogs he or she causes to be brought into the world. Such a breeder also is proud of a reputation for integrity. Thus on two counts, for the sake of the dog's future and the breeder's reputation, to such a person a *satisfied* customer takes precedence over a sale at any cost.

If your puppy is to be a pet or "family dog," the earlier the age at which it joins your household the better. Puppies are weaned and ready to start out on their own, under the care of a sensible new owner, at about six weeks old; and if you take a young one, it is often easier to train it to the routine of your household and your requirements of it than is the case with an older dog which, even though still a puppy

Moonwalk (on the left) and Traveler (future Ch. Gretchenhof Columbia River) at three months of age in Jo Shellenbarger's arms.

Starting your show prospect puppy correctly. Future Champion Rocky Run's Robert at three months of age poses like a veteran for owner Judy Sener. Bred by Bob Arnold.

technically, may have already started habits you will find difficult to change. The younger puppy is usually less costly, too, as it stands to reason the breeder will not have as much expense invested in it. Obviously, a puppy that has been raised to five or six months old represents more in care and cash expenditure on the breeder's part than one sold earlier and therefore should be and generally is priced accordingly.

There is an enormous amount of truth in the statement that "bargain" puppies seldom turn out to be that. A "cheap" puppy, cheaply raised purely for sale and profit, can and often does lead to great heartbreak including problems and veterinarian's bills which can add up to many times the initial cost of a properly reared dog. On the other hand, just because a puppy is expensive does not assure one that is healthy and well reared. Numerous cases are known where unscrupulous dealers have sold for several hundred dollars puppies that were sickly, in poor condition, and such poor specimens that the breed of which they were supposedly members was barely recognizable. So one cannot always judge a puppy by price alone. Common sense must guide a prospective purchaser, plus the selection of a *reliable,* well-recommended dealer whom you know to have well-satisfied customers or, best of all, a specialized breeder. You will probably find the fairest pricing at the kennel of a breeder. Such a person, experienced with the breed in general and with his or her own stock in particular, through extensive association with these dogs has watched enough of them mature to have obviously learned to assess quite accurately each puppy's potential—something impossible where such background is non-existent.

Ch. P.W.'s Challenger von Fieldfine taken shortly after winning Best of Breed for the second time from the Veterans Class at the Eastern German Shorthaired Pointer Specialty on his way to a Group First. Owner-handler, Larry Berg, Woodhaven, NY.

Laura Myles owns these beautiful German Wirehaired puppies, six and a half weeks old when photographed in September 1980.

One more word on the subject of pets. Bitches make a fine choice for this purpose as they are usually quieter and more gentle than the males, easier to house train, more affectionate, and less inclined to roam. If you do select a bitch and have no intention of breeding or showing her, by all means have her spayed, for your sake and for hers. The advantages to the owner of a spayed bitch include avoiding the nuisance of "in season" periods which normally occur twice yearly, with the accompanying eager canine swains haunting your premises in an effort to get close to your female, plus the unavoidable messiness and spotting of furniture and rugs at this time, which can be annoying if she is a household companion in the habit of sharing your sofa or bed. As for the spayed bitch, she benefits as she grows older because this simple operation almost entirely eliminates the possibility of breast cancer ever occurring. The consensus is that all bitches should eventually be spayed—even those used for show or breeding when their careers are ended—in order that they may enjoy a happier, healthier old age. Please take note, however, that a bitch who has been spayed (or an altered dog) *cannot be shown at American Kennel Club Dog shows once this operation has been performed.* Be certain that you are *not* interested in showing her before taking this step.

Also in selecting a pet, never underestimate the advantages of an older dog, perhaps a retired show dog or a bitch no longer needed for breeding, who may be available quite reasonably priced by a breeder anxious to place such a dog in a loving home. These dogs are settled and can be a delight to own, as they make wonderful companions, especially in a household of adults where raising a puppy can sometimes be a trial.

Everything we have said about careful selection of your pet puppy and its place of purchase applies, but with many further considerations, when you plan to buy a show dog or foundation stock for a future breeding program. Now is the time for an in-depth study of the breed, starting with every word and every illustration in this book and all others you can find written on the subject. The standard of the breed now has become your guide, and you must learn not only the words but also how to interpret them and how they are applicable in actual dogs before you are ready to make an intelligent selection of a show dog.

If you are thinking in terms of a dog to show, obviously you must have learned about dog shows and must be in the habit of attending them. This is fine, but now your activity in this direction should be increased, with your attending every single dog show within a reasonable distance from your home. Much can be learned about a breed at ringside at these events. Talk with the breeders who are exhibiting. Study the dogs they are showing. Watch the judging with concentration, noting each decision made and attempt to follow the reasoning by which the judge has reached it. Note carefully the attributes of the dogs who win and, for your later use, the manner in which each is presented. Close your ears to the ringside know-it-alls, usually novice owners of only a dog or two and very new to the fancy, who have only derogatory remarks to make about all that is taking place unless they happen to win. This is the type of exhibitor who "comes and goes" through the fancy and whose interest is usually of very short duration owing to lack of knowledge and dissatisfaction caused by the failure to recognize the need to learn. You, as a fancier who we hope will last and enjoy our sport over many future years, should develop independent thinking at this stage; you should learn to draw your own conclusions about the merits, or lack of them, seen before you in the ring and

SECOND IN GROUP

KENOSHA K.C.

SEPT. 11, 1983

PHOTO BY TERI

SPORTING GROUP

Ch. Serakraut's Bit O'Luck, by Ch. Serakraut's Gamesman ex Bleugras Lil Dipper, bred by Ann Serak, owned by John and Marilyn Murray, Wisconsin. Best of Breed three times at Chicago International. Winner of 24 other Bests of Breed, four Specialty "Bests" and seven Group placements.

thus, sharpen your own judgment in preparation for choosing wisely and well.

Note carefully which breeders campaign winning dogs, not just an occasional isolated good one but consistent, homebred winners. It is from one of these people that you should select your own future "star."

If you are located in an area where dog shows take place only occasionally or where there are long travel distances involved, you will need to find another testing ground for your ability to select a worthy show dog. Possibly, there are some representative kennels raising this breed within a reasonable distance. If so, by all means ask permission of the owners to visit the kennels and do so when permission is granted. You may not necessarily buy then and there, as they may not have available what you are seeking that very day, but you will be able to see the type of dog being raised there and to discuss the dogs with the breeder. Every time you do this, you add to your knowledge. Should one of these kennels have dogs which especially appeal to you, perhaps you could reserve a show-prospect puppy from a coming litter. This is frequently done, and it is often worth waiting for a puppy, unless you have seen a dog with which you are truly greatly impressed and which is immediately available.

We have already discussed the purchase of a pet puppy. Obviously this same approach applies in a far greater degree when the purchase involved is a future show dog. The only place at which to purchase a show prospect is from a breeder who raises show-type stock; otherwise, you are almost certainly doomed to disappointment as the puppy matures. Show and breeding kennels obviously cannot keep all of their fine young stock. An active breeder-exhibitor is, therefore, happy to place promising youngsters in the hands of people also interested in showing and winning with them, doing so at a fair price according to the quality and prospects of the dog involved. Here again, if no kennel in your immediate area has what you are seeking, do not hesitate to contact top breeders in other areas and to buy at long distance. Ask for pictures, pedigrees, and a complete description. Heed the breeder's advice and recommendations, after truthfully telling exactly what your expectations are for the dog you purchase. Do you want something with which to win just a few ribbons now and then? Do you want a dog who can complete his championship? Are you thinking of the real "big time" (*i.e.,* seriously campaigning with Best of Breed, Group wins, and possibly even Best in Show as your eventual goal)? Consider it all carefully in advance; then honestly discuss your plans with the breeder. You will be better satisfied with the results if you do this, as the breeder is then in the best position to help you choose the dog who is most likely to come through for you. A breeder selling a show dog is just as anxious as the buyer for the dog to succeed, and the breeder will represent the dog to you with truth and honesty. Also, this type of breeder does not lose interest the moment the sale has been made but when necessary will be right there ready to assist you with beneficial advice and suggestions based on years of experience.

As you make inquiries of at least several kennels, keep in mind that show-prospect puppies are less expensive than mature show dogs, the latter often costing close to four figures, and sometimes more. The reason for this is that, with a puppy, there is always an element of chance, the possibility of its developing unexpected faults as it matures or failing to develop the excellence and quality that earlier had seemed probable. There definitely is a risk factor in buying a show-prospect puppy. Sometimes all goes well, but occasionally the swan becomes an ugly duckling. Reflect on this as you consider available puppies and young adults. It just might be a good idea to go with a more mature, though more costly, dog if one you like is available.

When you buy a mature show dog, "what you see is what you get"; and it is not likely to change beyond coat and condition which are dependent on your care. Also advantageous for a novice owner is the fact that a mature dog of show quality almost certainly will have received show ring training and probably match show experience, which will make your earliest handling ventures far easier.

Frequently it is possible to purchase a beautiful dog who has completed championship but who, owing to similarity in bloodlines, is not needed for the breeder's future program. Here you have the opportunity of owning a champion, usually in the two- to five-year-old range, which you can enjoy campaigning as a "special" (for Best of Breed competition) and which will be a settled, handsome dog for you and your family to enjoy with pride.

If you are planning foundation for a future kennel, concentrate on acquiring one or two really superior bitches. These need not necessarily be top show-quality, but they should represent your breed's finest producing bloodlines from a strain noted for producing quality, generation after generation. A proven matron who is already the dam of show-type puppies is, of course, the ideal selection; but these are usually difficult to obtain, no one being anxious to part with so valuable an asset. You just might strike it lucky, though, in which case you are off to a flying start. If you cannot find such a matron available, select a young bitch of finest background from top producing lines who is herself of decent type, free of obvious faults, and of good quality.

Great attention should be paid to the pedigree of the bitch from whom you intend to breed. If not already known to you, try to see the sire and dam. It is generally agreed that someone starting with a breed should concentrate on a fine collection of top-flight bitches and raise a few litters from these before considering keeping one's own stud dog. The practice of buying a stud and then breeding everything you own or acquire to that dog does not always work out well. It is better to take advantage of the many noted sires who are available to be used at stud, who represent all of the leading strains, and in each case carefully to select the one who in type and pedigree seems most compatible to each of your bitches, at least for your first several litters.

To summarize, if you want a "family dog" as a companion, it is best to buy it young and raise it to the habits of your household. If you are buying a show dog, the more mature it is, the more certain you can be of its future beauty. If you are buying foundation stock for a kennel, then bitches are better, but they must be from the finest *producing* bloodlines.

When you buy a pure-bred dog that you are told is eligible for registration with the American Kennel Club, you are entitled to receive from the seller an application form which will enable you to register your dog. If the seller cannot give you the application form you should demand and receive an identification of your dog consisting of the name of the breed, the registered names and numbers of the sire and dam, the name of the breeder, and your dog's date of birth. If the litter of which your dog is a part is already recorded with the American Kennel Club, then the litter number is sufficient identification.

Do not be misled by promises of papers at some later date. Demand a registration application form or proper identification as described above. If neither is supplied, do not buy the dog. So warns the American Kennel Club, and this is especially important in the purchase of show or breeding stock.

Ch. Robin Crest Little John taking Best of Breed at the 1984 Greater Pittsburgh Specialty. This handsome young Shorthair is the latest "star" at Robin Crest Kennels owned by Rita and Jon Remondi, Armonk, NY.

Chapter 10

The Care of Your German Pointer Puppy

Preparing for Your Puppy's Arrival

The moment you decide to be the new owner of a puppy is not one second too soon to start planning for the puppy's arrival in your home. Both the new family member and you will find the transition period easier if your home is geared in advance for the arrival.

The first things to be prepared are a bed for the puppy and a place where you can pen him up for rest periods. Every dog should have a crate of its own from the very beginning, so that he will come to know and love it as his special place where he is safe and happy. It is an ideal arrangement, for when you want him to be free, the crate stays open. At other times you can securely latch it and know that the pup is safely out of mischief. If you travel with him, his crate comes along in the car; and, of course, in traveling by plane there is no alternative but to have a carrier for the dog. If you show your dog, you will want him upon occasion to be in a crate a good deal of the day. So from every consideration, a crate is a very sensible and sound investment in your puppy's future safety and happiness and for your own peace of mind.

Wooden crates with removable side panels are ideal for cold weather (with the panels in place to keep out drafts) and in hot weather (with the panels removed to allow better air circulation). Wire crates are all right in the summer, but they give no protection from cold or drafts. Aluminum crates are undesirable due to the manner in which aluminum reflects surrounding temperatures. If it is cold, so is the metal of the crate; if it is hot, the crate becomes burning hot. For this reason aluminum crates are neither comfortable nor safe.

This adorable eight-week-old Wirehaired puppy belongs to Laura Myles.

When you choose the puppy's crate, be certain that it is roomy enough not to become outgrown. The crate should have sufficient height so the dog can stand up in it as a mature dog and sufficient area so that he can stretch out full length when relaxed. When the puppy is young, first give him shredded newspaper as a bed; the papers can be replaced with a mat or turkish towels when the dog is older. Carpet remnants are great for the bottom of the crate, as they are inexpensive and in case of accidents can be quite easily replaced. As the dog matures and is past the chewing age, a pillow or blanket in the crate is an appreciated comfort.

Sharing importance with the crate is a safe area in which the puppy can exercise and play. If you are an apartment dweller, a baby's play-pen or a portable exercise pen works out well; the portable exercise pen you can then use later when traveling with your dog or for dog shows. If you have a yard, an area where he can be outside in safety should be fenced in prior to the dog's arrival at your home. This area does not need to be huge, but it does need to be made safe and secure. If you are in a suburban area where there are close neighbors, stockade

226

Fieldcrest Remington Steele, promising young Shorthair sired by Ch. Eden Tasmin The Pilgrim ex Ch. Secrets To Share, belongs to Tom Crump, Greenwood, Indiana.

fencing works out best as then the neighbors are less aware of the dog and the dog cannot see and bark at everything passing by. If you are out in the country where no problems with neighbors are likely to occur, then regular chain-link fencing is fine. For added precaution in both cases, use a row of concrete blocks or railroad ties inside against the entire bottom of the fence; this precludes or at least considerably lessens the chances of your dog digging his way out.

Be advised that if yours is a single dog, it is very unlikely that it will get sufficient exercise just sitting in the fenced area, which is what most of them do when they are there alone. Two or more dogs will play and move themselves around, but from my own experience, one by itself does little more than make a leisurely tour once around the area to check things over and then lie down. You must include a daily walk or two in your plans if your puppy is to be rugged and well. Exercise is extremely important to a puppy's muscular development and to keep a mature dog fit and trim. So make sure that those exercise periods, or walks, a game of ball, and other such activities, are part of your daily program as a dog owner.

If your fenced area has an outside gate, provide a padlock and key and a strong fastening for it, and use them, so that the gate can not be opened by others and the dog taken or turned free. The ultimate convenience in this regard is, of course, a door (unused for other purposes) from the house around which the fenced area can be enclosed, so that all you have to do is open the door and out into his area he goes. This arrangement is safest of all, as then you need not be using a gate, and it is easier in bad weather since then you can send the dog out without taking him and becoming soaked yourself at the same time. This is not always possible to manage, but if your house is arranged so that you could do it this way, you would never regret it due to the convenience and added safety thus provided. Fencing in the entire yard, with gates to be opened and closed whenever a caller, deliveryman, postman, or some other person comes on your property, really is not safe at all because people not used to gates and their importance are frequently careless about closing and latching gates *securely.* Many heartbreaking incidents brought about by someone carelessly only half closing a gate which the owner had thought to be firmly latched and the dog wandering out are frequently reported. For greatest security a fenced *area* definitely takes precedence over a fenced *yard.*

The puppy will need a collar (one that fits now, not one to be grown into) and lead from the moment you bring him home. Both should be an appropriate weight and type for his size. Also needed are a feeding dish and a water dish, both made preferably of unbreakable material. Your pet supply shop should have an interesting assortment of these and other accessories from which you can choose. Then you will need grooming tools of the type the breeder recommends and some toys. One of the best toys is a beef bone, either rib, leg, or knuckle (the latter the type you can purchase to make soup), cut to an appropriate size for your puppy dog. These are absolutely safe and are great exercise for the teething period, helping to get the baby teeth quickly out of the way with no problems. Equally satisfactory is Nylabone® , a nylon bone that does not chip or splinter and that "frizzles" as the puppy chews, providing healthful gum massage. Rawhide chews are safe, too, *IF made in the United States.* There was a problem a few years back owing to the chemicals with which some foreign rawhide toys had been treated, since which time we have carefully avoided giving them to our own dogs. Also avoid plastics and any sort of rubber toys, *particularly* those with squeakers which the puppy may remove and swallow. If you want a ball for the puppy to use when playing with him, select one of very hard construction (such as Nylaball) made for this purpose; do not leave a rubber ball alone with him, because he may chew off and swallow bits of it. Take the ball with you when the game is over. This also applies to some of those "tug of war" type rub-

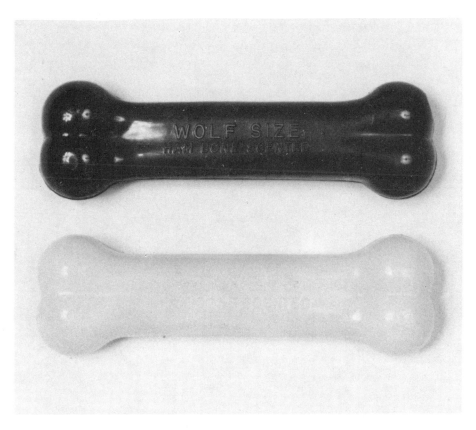

For variety, offer your German Pointer both the meat-flavored and the chocolate-flavored Nylabone. In addition to the traditional bone-shaped type shown, Nylabone is available in other shapes as well; in the form of a ball, knot, or ring. Manufactured in a range of sizes, select the one suited to your dog's age and size.

ber toys which are fun when used with the two of you for that purpose but again should *not* be left behind for the dog to work on with his teeth. Bits of swallowed rubber, squeakers, and other such foreign articles can wreak great havoc in the intestinal tract—do all you can to guard against them.

Too many changes all at once can be difficult for a puppy. For at least the first few days he is with you, keep him on the food and feeding schedule to which he is accustomed. Find out ahead of time from the breeder what he feeds his puppies, how frequently, and at what times of the day. Also find out what, if any, food supplements the breeder has been using and recommends. Then be prepared by getting in a supply of the same food so that you will have it there when you

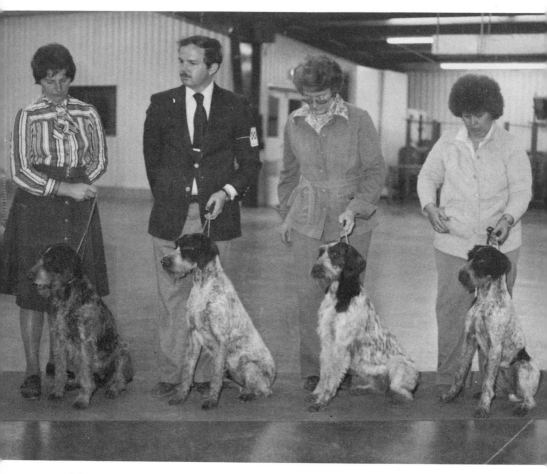

A beautiful "family portrait" courtesy of John H. Writer, Glen Ellyn, Illinois. *Left to right*: Ch. Hilltop's S.S. Cheese Cake, C.D.; Ch. Laurwyn's Cheeseburger; Ch. Laurwyn's Barbed Wire; and Ch. Spindrifter's Bang of Laurwyn, C.D. April 1980.

bring the puppy home. Once the puppy is accustomed to his new surroundings, then you can switch the type of food and schedule to fit your convenience, but for the first several days do it as the puppy expects.

Your selection of a veterinarian also should be attended to before the puppy comes home, because you should stop at the vet's office for the puppy to be checked over as soon as you leave the breeder's premises. If the breeder is from your area, ask him for recommendations. Ask your dog-owning friends for their opinions of the local veterinarians, and see what their experiences with those available have been. Choose someone whom several of your friends recommend highly, then contact him about your puppy, perhaps making an appointment to stop in at his office. If the premises are clean, modern, and well equipped, and if you like the veterinarian, make an appointment to bring the puppy in on the day of purchase. Be sure to obtain the puppy's health record from the breeder, including information on such things as shots and worming that the puppy has had.

Joining the Family

Remember that, exciting and happy an occasion as it is for you, the puppy's move from his place of birth to your home can be, for him, a traumatic experience. His mother and littermates will be missed. He quite likely will be awed or frightened by the change of surroundings. The person on whom he depended will be gone. Everything should be planned to make his arrival at your home pleasant—to give him confidence and to help him realize that yours is a pretty nice place to be after all.

Never bring a puppy home on a holiday. There just is too much going on with people and gifts and excitement. If he is in honor of an "occasion," work it out so that his arrival will be a few days earlier or, perhaps even better, a few days later than the "occasion." Then your home will be back to its normal routine and the puppy can enjoy your undivided attention. Try not to bring the puppy home in the evening. Early morning is the ideal time, as then he has the opportunity of getting acquainted and the initial strangeness should wear off before bedtime. You will find it a more peaceful night that way, surely. Allow the puppy to investigate as he likes, under your watchful eye. If you already have a pet in the household, keep a careful watch that the relationship between the two gets off to a friendly start or you may quickly find yourself with a lasting problem. Much of the future attitude of each toward the other will depend on what takes place that first day, so keep your mind on what they are doing and let your other activities slide for the moment. Be careful not to let your older pet become jealous by paying more attention to the puppy than to him, as that will start a bad situation immediately.

If you have a child, here again it is important that the relationship start out well. Before the puppy is brought home, you should have a talk with the youngster about puppies, so that it will be clearly understood that puppies are fragile and can easily be injured; therefore, they should not be teased, hurt, mauled, or overly rough-housed. A puppy is not an inanimate toy; it is a living thing with a right to be loved and handled respectfully, treatment which will reflect in the dog's attitude toward your child as both mature together. Never permit your children's playmates to mishandle the puppy, tormenting the puppy until it turns on the children in self-defense. Children often do not realize how rough is too rough. You, as a responsible adult, are obligated to assure that your puppy's relationship with children is a pleasant one.

Do not start out by spoiling your puppy. A puppy is usually pretty smart and can be quite demanding. What you had considered to be "just for tonight" may be accepted by the puppy as "for keeps." Be firm with him, strike a routine, and stick to it. The puppy will learn more quickly this way, and everyone will be happier at the result. A radio playing softly or a dim night light are often comforting to a puppy as it gets accustomed to new surroundings and should be provided in preference to bringing the puppy to bed with you—unless, of course, you intend him to share the bed as a permanent arrangement.

Socializing and Training Your New Puppy

Socialization and training of your puppy should start the very day of his arrival in your home. Never address him without calling him by name. A short, simple name is the easiest to teach as it catches the dog's attention quickly, so avoid elaborate call names. Always address the dog by the same name, not a whole series of pet names; the latter will only confuse the puppy.

Using his name clearly, call the puppy over to you when you see him awake and wandering about. When he comes, make a big fuss over him for being such a good dog. He thus will quickly associate the sound of his name with coming to you and a pleasant happening.

Several hours after the puppy's arrival is not too soon to start accustoming him to the feel of a light collar. He may hardly notice it; or he may struggle, roll over, and try to rub it off his neck with his paws. Divert his attention when this occurs by offering a tasty snack or a toy (starting a game with him) or by petting him. Before long he will have accepted the strange feeling around his neck and no longer appear aware of it. Next comes the lead. Attach it and then immediately take the puppy outside or otherwise try to divert his attention with things to see and sniff. He may struggle against the lead at first, biting at it and trying to free himself. Do not pull him with it at this point; just hold the end loosely and try to follow him if he starts off in any direction. Normally his attention will soon turn to investigating his surroundings if he is outside or you have taken him into an unfamiliar room in your house; curiosity will take over and he will become interested in sniffing around the surroundings. Just follow him with the lead slackly held until he seems to have completely forgotten about it; then try with gentle urging to get him to follow you. Don't be rough or jerk at him; just tug gently on the lead in short quick motions (steady pulling can become a battle of wills), repeating his name or trying to get him to follow your hand which is holding a bit of food or an interesting toy. If you have an older lead-trained dog, then it should be a cinch to get the puppy to follow along after *him*. In any event, the average puppy learns quite quickly and will soon be trotting along nicely on the lead. Once that point has been reached, the next step is to teach him to follow on your left side, or heel. Of course this will not likely be accomplished all in one day but should be done with short training periods over the course of several days until you are satisfied with the result.

During the course of house training your puppy, you will need to take him out frequently and at regular intervals: first thing in the morning directly from the crate, immediately after meals, after the puppy has been napping, or when you notice that the puppy is looking for a spot. Choose more or less the same place to take the puppy each time so that a pattern will be established. If he does not go immediately, do not return him to the house as he will probably relieve himself the moment he is inside. Stay out with him until he has finished; then be lavish with your praise for his good behavior. If you catch the puppy having an accident indoors, grab him firmly and rush him outside, sharply saying "No!" as you pick him up. If you do not see the accident occur, there is little point in doing anything except cleaning it up, as once it has happened and been forgotten, the puppy will most likely not even realize why you are scolding him.

Especially if you live in a big city or are away many hours at a time, having a dog that is trained to go on paper has some very definite advantages. To do this, one proceeds pretty much the same way as taking the puppy outdoors, except now you place the puppy on the newspaper at the proper time. The paper should always be kept in the same spot. An easy way to paper train a puppy if you have a playpen for it or an exercise pen is to line the area with newspapers; then gradually, every day or so, remove a section of newspaper until you are

Paladen's Pine Hill Lone Star at four months of age, by Ch. Wil-Lyn's Wild Bear Cody ex Am. and Mex. Ch. Pine Hill Royal Star Brandy, homebred owned by Karen Detterich, Paladen German Shorthairs, Riverside, California.

down to just one or two. The puppy acquires the habit of using the paper; and as the prepared area grows smaller, in the majority of cases the dog will continue to use whatever paper is still available. Experience with dogs has proved that this works out well. It is pleasant, if the dog is alone for an excessive length of time, to be able to feel that if he needs it the paper is there and will be used.

The puppy should form the habit of spending a certain amount of time in his crate, even when you are home. Sometimes the puppy will do this voluntarily, but if not it should be taught to do so, which is accomplished by leading the puppy over by his collar, gently pushing him inside, and saying firmly "Down" or "Stay." Whatever expression you use to give a command, stick to the very same one each time for each act. Repetition is the big thing in training—and so is association with what the dog is expected to do. When you mean "Sit" always say exactly that. "Stay" should mean *only* that the dog should remain where he receives the command. "Down" means something else again. Do not confuse the dog by shuffling the commands, as this will create training problems for you.

As soon as he has had his immunization shots, take your puppy with you whenever and wherever possible. There is nothing that will build a self-confident, stable dog like socialization, and it is extremely important that you plan and give the time and energy necessary for this whether your dog is to be a show dog or a pleasant, well-adjusted family member. Take your puppy in the car so that he will learn to enjoy riding and not become carsick as dogs may do if they are infrequent travelers. Take him anywhere you are going where you are certain he will be welcome: visiting friends and relatives (if they do not have housepets who may resent the visit), busy shopping centers (keeping him always on lead), or just walking around the streets of your town. If someone admires him (as always seems to happen when we are out with puppies), encourage the stranger to pet and talk with him. Socialization of this type brings out the best in your puppy and helps him to grow up with a friendly outlook, liking the world and its inhabitants. The worst thing that can be done to a puppy's personality is to overly shelter him. By keeping him always at home away from things and people unfamiliar to him you may be creating a personality problem for the mature dog that will be a cross for you to bear later on.

Feeding Your Dog

Time was when providing nourishing food for our dogs involved a far more complicated procedure than people now feel is necessary. The old school of thought was that the daily ration must consist of fresh beef, vegetables, cereal, egg yolks, and cottage cheese as basics with such additions as brewer's yeast and vitamin tablets on a daily basis.

During recent years, however, many minds have changed regarding this procedure. We still give eggs, cottage cheese, and supplements to the diet, but the basic method of feeding dogs has changed; and the change has been, in the opinion of many authorities, definitely for the better. The school of thought now is that you are doing your dogs a favor when you feed them some of the fine commercially prepared dog foods in preference to your own home-cooked concoctions.

The reason behind this new outlook is easily understandable. The dog food industry has grown to be a major one, participated in by some of the best known and most respected names in the American way of life. These trusted firms, it is agreed, turn out excellent products, so people are feeding their dog food preparations with confidence and the dogs are thriving, living longer, happier, and healthier lives than ever before. What more could we want?

The Shorthaired Pointer Ch. P.W.'s Challenger von Fieldfine being prepared for judging by owner-handler Larry Berg.

There are at least half a dozen absolutely top-grade dry foods to be mixed with broth or water and served to your dog according to directions. There are all sorts of canned meats, and there are several kinds of "convenience foods," those in a packet which you open and dump out into the dog's dish. It is just that simple. The "convenience" foods are neat and easy to use when you are away from home, but generally speaking we prefer a dry food mixed with hot water or soup and meat. We also feel that the canned meat, with its added fortifiers, is more beneficial to the dogs than the fresh meat. However, the two can be alternated or, if you prefer and your dog does well on it, by all means use fresh ground beef. A dog enjoys changes in the meat part of his diet, which is easy with the canned food since all sorts of beef are available (chunk, ground, stewed, and so on), plus lamb, chicken, and even such concoctions as liver and egg, just plain liver flavor, and a blend of five meats.

There also is prepared food geared to every age bracket of your dog's life, from puppyhood on through old age, with special additions or modifications to make it particularly nourishing and beneficial. Our grandparents, and even our parents, never had it so good where the canine dinner is concerned, because these commercially prepared foods are tasty and geared to meeting the dog's gastronomic approval.

Additionally, contents and nutrients are clearly listed on the labels, as are careful instructions for feeding just the right amount for the size, weight, and age of each dog.

With these foods we do not feel the addition of extra vitamins is necessary, but if you do there are several kinds of those, too, that serve as taste treats as well as being beneficial. Your pet supplier has a full array of them.

Of course there is no reason not to cook up something for your dog if you would feel happier doing so. But it seems to us unnecessary when such truly satisfactory rations are available with so much less trouble and expense.

How often you feed your dog is a matter of how it works out best for you. Many owners prefer to do it once a day. Others think that two meals, each of smaller quantity, are better for the digestion and more satisfying to the dog, particularly if yours is a household member who stands around and watches preparations for the family meals. Do not overfeed. That is the shortest route to all sorts of problems. Follow directions and note carefully how your dog is looking. If your dog is overweight, cut back the quantity of food a bit. If the dog looks thin, then increase the amount. Each dog is an individual and the food intake should be adjusted to his requirements to keep him feeling and looking trim and in top condition.

From the time puppies are fully weaned until they are about twelve weeks old, they should be fed four times daily. From three months to six months of age, three meals should suffice. At six months of age the puppies can be fed two meals, and the twice daily feedings can be continued until the puppies are close to one year old, at which time feeding can be changed to once daily if desired.

If you do feed just once a day, do so by early afternoon at the latest and give the dog a snack, or biscuit or two, at bedtime.

Remember that plenty of fresh water should always be available to your puppy or dog for drinking. This is of utmost importance to his health.

A historic and beautiful Wirehaired photo. Ch. Mueller-Mill's Valentino, Helen Shelley's famous dog; and Ch. Oldemill Flower, the dam of Ch. Jagersbo Frier Tuck. Photo courtesy of Erik Bergishagen, Jagersbro Wirehairs.

Chapter 11

Care of Your Wirehaired's Coat

by Joy S. Brewster

How happy we are that so famous and successful a professional handler as Joy S. Brewster, known for her expertise in making a German Wirehaired Pointer look his or her best, has taken the time to make some suggestions for our readers regarding care of the Wirehaired coat. Joy has perfected the art of making a Wirehaired look *right*. Her years of success and experience with this, and many other breeds, qualify her well and you will find that following her suggestions will keep your Wirehaired's coat at its very best.   A.K.N.

Stripping a dog totally by hand generally produces the best texture. However, those individuals lucky enough to have an exceptionally proper coated dog may sometimes, when time is limited, choose to use other than their fingers or a stripping knife.

For show grooming, round the feet by trimming hair around outside edges even with the pads. With #10 blade, use clipper around anus, then clip hair with grain up underside of tail to tip. Round end with scissors. Using #10 blade, clip with grain along area under tail to cowlick, then cut long hair from vulva or penis. Trim down back side of thigh from point of rump to about halfway to hock with single edge thinning shear.

Trim area under neck (as with a Setter), either by hand stripper or with #10 blade; trim with the grain to cowlick and down to prow (or breastbone).

Either hand strip or with #10 blade trim under chin from whiskers back to Adam's apple and with grain up to back edge (corner) of mouth; with grain from outer edge of eye to corner of mouth. Do not trim under the eye.

Continue from indentation over eye back to occiput and half down ears (as when trimming a Setter, always with grain). Clip inside of ears and bell with grain.

Trim edge of ears half up to head by hand or with straight scissors to even off. Brush whiskers and eyebrows forward. Use stripping knife or thinning shears to get a straight edge from outer edge of eyes down to back edge (corner) of mouth.

Comb eyebrows to outside of head. Clean out stop by pulling or with thinning shears against grain down the middle to a point almost on line with the inner corner of eye.

Neaten hair at inner corner of eye by stripping or trimming slightly at base of eyebrows (or bridge of nose). Do not trim eyebrows except at outer edge to blend into cheek line.

Even out neck (front) cowlicks by hand or with thinning shears by trimming up. Do not trim on top of neck; only trim on front from prow upward towards ear.

Use ear powder in ears. Pull hair inside of ear by hand or forceps.

Strip or use #10 blade with grain to clip hair from back hocks to pad. Using thinning shears to trim tufts of hair at elbows.

Brush front leg furnishings upward as length of hair increases. Pull hair at knuckles (with thumb and forefinger) to keep them even with rest of leg.

Only *pull* hair on leg furnishings. Do not cut hair except at back of elbows.

Keep main coat brushed with grain with slicker brush. Pull any stray hairs that are sticking up. If bathed the dog should be towelled as with a Setter.

When working main coat use slicker with grain. If pulling hair use thumb and forefinger or use wide-toothed terrier stripping knife. Make sure to pull, not cut or break off hair. This will pull out long hairs and some undercoat. Especially useful over hip area. Other places to keep short are down sides of shoulder and side of neck into shoulder.

Use fine-toothed terrier knife on knuckles if necessary.

Ch. Mueller Mills Valentino, the magnificent "Rudy," 1962-1976, winning Best in Show at Waco, Texas, in 1970 under judge Hollis Wilson. Handler Roy Murray for owner Helen B. Shelley. A seven times all-breed Best in Show winner, twice Best in National Specialties, 88 times first in the Sporting Group, plus many other honors to his credit. One of the truly important German Wirehaired Pointer dogs.

GENERAL GROOMING:

Use slicker brush every few days. Keep area around *anus trimmed*. Keep hair in ears pulled.

Keep teeth cleaned.

Keep nails back.

Beware! They like to dry their whiskers and eyebrows on rugs and furniture, and can rub them off!

Ch. Fieldfines Rumbunctious, by Am. and Can. Ch. Fieldfines Count Rambard ex Ch. Lieblinghaus's Lucky Lady is a multiple Best of Breed winner with Group placements from the classes. Owned by Jinny and Jack Nealon, Jinny Nealon handling.

Chapter 12

The Making of a Show Dog

If you have decided to become a show dog exhibitor, you have accepted a very real and very exciting challenge. The groundwork has been accomplished with the selection of your future show prospect. If you have purchased a puppy, we assume that you have gone through all the proper preliminaries concerning good care, which should be the same if the puppy is a pet or future show dog with a few added precautions for the latter.

General Considerations

Remember the importance of keeping your future winner in trim, top condition. Since you want him neither too fat nor too thin, his appetite for his proper diet should be guarded, and children and guests should not be permitted to constantly be feeding him "goodies." The best treat of all is a small wad of raw ground beef or a packaged dog treat. To be avoided are ice cream, cake, cookies, potato chips, and other fattening items which will cause the dog to put on weight and may additionally spoil his appetite for the proper, nourishing, well-balanced diet so essential to good health and condition.

The importance of temperament and showmanship cannot possibly be overestimated. They have put many a mediocre dog across while lack of them can ruin the career of an otherwise outstanding specimen. From the day your dog joins your family, socialize him. Keep him accustomed to being with people and to being handled by people. Encourage your friends and relatives to "go over" him as the judges will in the ring so this will not seem a strange and upsetting experience. Practice showing his "bite" (the manner in which his teeth meet)

"Moving on out" nicely. Ch. Broker's Best Offer owned by W.W. Bowman, Beltsville, MD. This Count Rambard son has Specialty Shows and Group wins: Best of Breed, Nutmeg Specialty 1981; and Best of Opposite Sex at Mason-Dixon in 1982 and National in 1983. As a sire already with some half dozen champions representing him in Sweepstakes and Specialty competition.

quickly and deftly. It is quite simple to slip the lips apart with your fingers, and the puppy should be willing to accept this from you or the judge without struggle. This is also true of further mouth examination when necessary. Where the standard demands examination of the roof of the mouth and the tongue, accustom the dog to having his jaws opened wide in order for the judge to make this required examination. When missing teeth must be noted, again, teach the dog to permit his jaws to be opened wide and his side lips separated as judges will need to check them one or both of these ways.

Ch. Swift's Light and Lively, by Ch. Fire Hawk of Kaposia ex Kaposia's Shashone Maiden, C.D.X., bred and owned by Leslie Swift from Virginia.

Some judges prefer that the exhibitors display the dog's bite and other mouth features themselves. These are the considerate ones, who do not wish to chance the spreading of possible infection from dog to dog with their hands on each one's mouth—a courtesy particularly appreciated in these days of virus epidemics. But the old-fashioned judges still persist in doing it themselves, so the dog should be ready for either possibility.

Take your future show dog with you in the car, thus accustoming him to riding so that he will not become carsick on the day of a dog

245

Aust. Ch. Moruada Wish Me Well, one of the winning German Shorthairs owned by Mrs. S.H. Wright, Liverpool, New South Wales.

show. He should associate pleasure and attention with going in the car, or van or motor home. Take him where it is crowded: downtown, to the shops, everywhere you go that dogs are permitted. Make the expeditions fun for him by frequent petting and words of praise; do not just ignore him as you go about your errands.

Do not overly shelter your future show dog. Instinctively you may want to keep him at home where he is safe from germs or danger. This can be foolish on two counts. The first reason is that a puppy kept away from other dogs builds up no natural immunity against all the things with which he will come in contact at dog shows, so it is wiser actually to keep him well up to date on all protective shots and then let him become accustomed to being among dogs and dog owners. Also, a dog who never is among strange people, in strange places, or among strange dogs, may grow up with a shyness or timidity of spirit that will cause you real problems as his show career draws near.

Keep your show prospect's coat in immaculate condition with frequent grooming and daily brushing. When bathing is necessary, use a mild baby shampoo or whatever the breeder of your puppy may suggest. Several of the brand-name products do an excellent job. Be sure to rinse thoroughly so as not to risk skin irritation by traces of soap left behind and protect against soap entering the eyes by a drop of castor oil in each before you lather up. Use warm water (be sure it is not uncomfortably hot or chillingly cold) and a good spray. A hair dryer is a real convenience and can be used for thorough drying after first blotting off the excess moisture with a turkish towel. A wad of cotton in each ear will prevent water entering the ear cavity.

Toenails also should be watched and trimmed every few weeks. It is important not to permit nails to grow excessively long, as they will ruin the appearance of both the feet and pasterns.

Assuming that you will be handling the dog yourself, or even if he will be professionally handled, a few moments each day of dog show routine is important. Practice setting him up as you have seen the exhibitors do at the shows you've attended, and teach him to hold this position once you have him stacked to your satisfaction. Make the learning period pleasant by being firm but lavish in your praise when he responds correctly. Teach him to gait at your side at a moderate rate on a loose lead. When you have mastered the basic essentials at home, then hunt out and join a training class for future work. Training classes are sponsored by show-giving clubs in many areas, and their popularity is steadily increasing. If you have no other way of locating one, perhaps your veterinarian would know of one through some of his other clients; but if you are sufficiently aware of the dog show world to want a show dog, you will probably be personally acquainted with other people who will share information of this type with you.

Accustom your show dog to being in a crate (which you should be doing with a pet dog as well). He should relax in his crate at the shows "between times" for his own well being and safety.

A show dog's teeth must be kept clean and free of tartar. Hard dog-biscuits can help toward this, but if tartar accumulates, see that it is removed promptly by your veterinarian. Real bones are not suitable for show dogs as they tend to damage and wear down the tooth enamel.

The famous German Wirehaired, Ch. Gretchenhof White Frost, owned by Margo Bryant, Casanova, Virginia, winning a Sporting Group during 1967. Handled by Jerry Rigden.

Ideal hindquarters of
Ch. Gretchenhof
White Frost, set up
nicely by Erik
Thomee.

Match Shows

Your show dog's initial experience in the ring should be in match show competition for several reasons. First, this type of event is intended as a learning experience for both the dog and the exhibitor. You will not feel embarrassed or out of place no matter how poorly your puppy may behave or how inept your attempts at handling may be, as you will find others there with the same type of problems. The important thing is that you get the puppy out and into a show ring where the two of you can practice together and learn the ropes.

Only on rare occasions is it necessary to make match show entries in advance, and even those with a pre-entry policy will usually accept entries at the door as well. Thus you need not plan several weeks ahead, as is the case with point shows, but can go when the mood strikes you. Also there is a vast difference in the cost, as match show entries only cost a few dollars while entry fees for the point shows may be over ten dollars, an amount none of us needs to waste until we have some idea of how the puppy will behave or how much more pre-show training is needed.

Match shows very frequently are judged by professional handlers who, in addition to making the awards, are happy to help new exhibitors with comments and advice on their puppies and their presentation of them. Avail yourself of all these opportunities before heading out to the sophisticated world of the point shows.

Point Shows

As previously mentioned, entries for American Kennel Club point shows must be made in advance. This must be done on an official entry blank of the show-giving club. The entry must then be filed either personally or by mail with the show superintendent or the show secretary (if the event is being run by the club members alone and a superintendent has not been hired, this information will appear on the premium list) in time to reach its destination prior to the published closing date or filling of the quota. These entries must be made carefully, must be signed by the owner of the dog or the owner's agent (your professional handler), and must be accompanied by the entry fee; otherwise they will not be accepted. Remember that it is not when the entry leaves your hands that counts but the date of arrival at its destination. If you are relying on the mails, which are not always dependable, get the entry off well before the deadline to avoid disappointment.

A dog must be entered at a dog show in the name of the actual owner at the time of the entry closing date of that specific show. If a registered dog has been acquired by a new owner, it must be entered in the name of the new owner in any show for which entries close after the date of acquirement, regardless of whether the new owner has or has not actually received the registration certificate indicating that the dog is recorded in his name. State on the entry form whether or not transfer application has been mailed to the American Kennel Club, and it goes without saying that the latter should be attended to promptly when you purchase a registered dog.

In filling out your entry blank, type, print, or write clearly, paying particular attention to the spelling of names, correct registration numbers, and so on. Also, if there is more than one variety in your breed, be sure to indicate into which category your dog is being entered.

The Puppy Class is for dogs or bitches who are six months of age and under twelve months, were whelped in the United States, and are not champions. The age of a dog shall be calculated up to and inclusive of the first day of a show. For example, the first day a dog whelped on January 1st is eligible to compete in a Puppy Class at a show is July 1st of the same year; and he may continue to compete in Puppy Classes up to and including a show on December 31st of the same year, but he is *not* eligible to compete in a Puppy Class at a show held on or after January 1st of the following year.

The Puppy Class is the first one in which you should enter your puppy. In it a certain allowance will be made for the fact that they *are* puppies, thus an immature dog or one displaying less than perfect showmanship will be less severely penalized than, for instance, would be the case in Open. It is also quite likely that others in the class will be suffering from these problems, too. When you enter a puppy, be sure to check the classification with care, as some shows divide their Puppy Class into a 6-9 months old section and a 9-12 months old section.

The Novice Class is for dogs six months of age and over, whelped in the United States or Canada, who *prior to the official closing date for entries* have *not* won three first prizes in the Novice Class, any first prize at all in the Bred-by-Exhibitor, American-bred, or Open Classes, or one or more points toward championship. The provisions for this class are confusing to many people, which is probably the reason exhibitors do not enter in it more frequently. A dog may win any number of first prizes in the Puppy Class and still retain his eligibility for Novice. He may place second, third or fourth not only in Novice on an unlimited number of occasions but also in Bred-by-Exhibitor, American-bred and Open and still remain eligible for Novice. But he may no longer be shown in Novice when he has won three blue ribbons in that class, when he has won even one blue ribbon in either Bred-by-Exhibitor, American-bred, or Open, or when he has won a single championship point.

In determining whether or not a dog is eligible for the Novice Class, keep in mind the fact that previous wins are calculated according to the official published date for closing of entries, not by the date on which you may actually have made the entry. So if in the interim, between the time you made the entry and the official closing date, your dog makes a win causing him to become ineligible for Novice, change your class *immediately* to another for which he will be eligible, prefer-

Moruada Bold Venture, two points short of Australian championship, is a son of Australian Ch. Gillbrae Nice'n Easy ex Aust. Ch. Moruada Liebe Ziggy. Best Dog in Parade and Best Open in Parade, German Shorthaired Pointer Society, 1984. Note: Parades are for non-champion dogs only. Junior Dog, Sydney Royal 1983. Junior in Parade, German Shorthaired Pointer Society 1983. Multiple "Age in Group" and "In Show" winner. Multiple Sweepstakes winner, all breeds. The sire of top winning puppies now being campaigned. Owned by Alex and Olga Gillies, Wallacia, New South Wales, Australia.

Opposite page: *(Top)* The German Shorthaired Pointer Ch. Gretchenhof New Moon, Joyce Shellenbarger, owner, Huntington Beach, California. *(Bottom)* Ch. Gretchenhof Moonshine, winner of 15 all-breed Bests in Show, owned by Joyce Shellenbarger, Gretchenhof Kennels, Huntington Beach, California.

ably such as either Bred-by-Exhibitor or American-bred. To do this, you must contact the show's superintendent or secretary, at first by telephone to save time and at the same time confirm it in writing. The Novice Class always seems to have the fewest entries of any class, and therefore it is a splendid "practice ground" for you and your young dog while you are getting the "feel" of being in the ring.

Bred-by-Exhibitor Class is for dogs whelped in the United States or, if individually registered in the American Kennel Club Stud Book, for dogs whelped in Canada who are six months of age or older, are not champions, and are owned wholly or in part by the person or by the spouse of the person who was the breeder or one of the breeders of record. Dogs entered in this class must be handled in the class by an owner or by a member of the immediate family of the owner. Members of an immediate family for this purpose are husband, wife, father, mother, son, daughter, brother or sister. This is the class which is really the "breeders' showcase," and the one which breeders should enter with particular pride to show off their achievements.

The American-bred Class is for all dogs excepting champions, six months of age or older, who were whelped in the United States by reason of a mating which took place in the United States.

The Open Class is for any dog six months of age or older (this is the only restriction for this class). Dogs with championship points compete in it, dogs who are already champions are eligible to do so, dogs who are imported can be entered, and, of course, American-bred dogs compete in it. This class is, for some strange reason, the favorite of exhibitors who are "out to win." They rush to enter their pointed dogs in it, under the false impression that by doing so they assure themselves of greater attention from the judges. This really is not so, and in my opinion to enter in one of the less competitive classes, with a better chance of winning it and thus earning a second opportunity of gaining the judge's approval by returning to the ring in the Winners Class, can often be a more effective strategy.

One does not enter for the Winners Class. One earns the right to compete in it by winning first prize in Puppy, Novice, Bred-by-Exhibitor, American-bred, or Open. No dog who has been defeated on the same day in one of these classes is eligible to compete for Winners, and every dog who has been a blue-ribbon winner in one of them and not defeated in another, should he have been entered in more than one class, (as occasionally happens) *must* do so. Following the selection of the Winners Dog or the Winners Bitch, the dog or bitch receiving that

Looking at this photo of Ch. Gunhill's Mesa Maverick makes it easy to understand why this dog was reputed to have been one of the best moving German Short-haired Pointers of his day. The National Parent club shows moving pictures of this splendid dog at its Annual Specialty Shows. P. Carl Tuttle was Maverick's breeder-owner-handler.

award leaves the ring. Then the dog or bitch who placed second in that class, unless previously beaten by another dog or bitch in another class at the same show, re-enters the ring to compete against the remaining first-prize winners for Reserve. The latter award indicates that the dog or bitch selected for it is standing "in reserve" should the one who received Winners be disqualified or declared ineligible through any technicality when the awards are checked at the American Kennel Club. In that case, the one who placed Reserve is moved up to Winners, at the same time receiving the appropriate championship points.

Winners Dog and Winners Bitch are the awards which carry points toward championship with them. The points are based on the number of dogs or bitches actually in competition, and the points are scaled one through five, the latter being the greatest number available to any

The Aust. Ch. Shorthair, Gillbrae Mi-Masquerade, by Aust. Ch. Wildheart Mennen, C.D. ex Klugerhund Seigi (U.K. import). Owned by Klugerhund Shorthairs, J.R. Maxwell, Werombi, New South Wales, Australia.

one dog or bitch at any one show. Three-, four-, or five-point wins are considered majors. In order to become a champion, a dog or bitch must have won two majors under two different judges, plus at least one point from a third judge, and the additional points necessary to bring the total to fifteen. When your dog has gained fifteen points as described above, a championship certificate will be issued to you, and your dog's name will be published in the champions of record list in the *Pure-Bred Dogs/American Kennel Gazette,* the official publication of the American Kennel Club.

The scale of championship points for each breed is worked out by the American Kennel Club and reviewed annually, at which time the number required in competition may be either changed (raised or

The German Shorthaired Pointer Ch. P.W.'s Challenger von Fieldfine, top winning son of Ch. Fieldfine's Count Rambard, was produced in the first litter sired by Rambard, and owner-handled by Larry Berg of Woodhaven, New York. His wins are Best of Breed at the German Shorthaired Pointer National Specialty in 1981, all-breed Best in Show, German Shorthaired Pointer Club of America Show Dog of the Year 1980, and Best of Breed at Westminster and Chicago International. Most notable among Challenger's winning get is Cruz's Princess De Shannon, C.D.X., T.D., the youngest dog, *all breeds*, to receive a C.D. in American Kennel Club history, at six months of age!

lowered) or remain the same. The scale of championship points for all breeds is published annually in the May issue of the *Gazette,* and the current ratings for each breed within that area are published in every show catalog.

When a dog or bitch is adjudged Best of Winners, its championship points are, for that show, compiled on the basis of which sex had the greater number of points. If there are two points in dogs and four in bitches and the dog goes Best of Winners, then *both* the dog and the bitch are awarded an equal number of points, in this case four. Should the Winners Dog or the Winners Bitch go on to win Best of Breed or Best of Variety, additional points are accorded for the additional dogs and bitches defeated by so doing, provided, of course, that there were entries specifically for Best of Breed Competition or Specials, as these specific entries are generally called.

If your dog or bitch takes Best of Opposite Sex after going Winners, points are credited according to the number of the same sex defeated in both the regular classes and Specials competition. If Best of Winners is also won, then whatever additional points for each of these awards are available will be credited. Many a one- or two-point win has grown into a major in this manner.

Best of Breed, Ch. Berkshire's Dancing Star. Best of Opposite Sex, Ch. Baron Edward Von Pooh. Both of these good Shorthairs are owned by Patricia Crowley. Handlers, Patty Crowley and daughter Erin at the Pioneer Valley Kennel Club in 1981 judged by Dr. McGivern.

Moving further along, should your dog win its Variety Group from the classes (in other words, if it has taken either Winners Dog or Winners Bitch), you then receive points based on the greatest number of points awarded to any member of any breed included within that Group during that show's competition. Should the day's winning also include Best in Show, the same rule of thumb applies, and your dog or bitch receives the highest number of points awarded to any other dog of any breed at that event.

Best of Breed competition consists of the Winners Dog and the Winners Bitch, who automatically compete on the strength of those awards, in addition to whatever dogs and bitches have been entered specifically for this class for which champions of record are eligible. Since July 1980, dogs who, according to their owner's records, have completed the requirements for a championship after the closing of entries for the show, but whose championships are unconfirmed, may be transferred from one of the regular classes to the Best of Breed competition, provided this transfer is made by the show superintendent or show secretary *prior to the start of any judging at the show.*

This has proved an extremely popular new rule, as under it a dog can finish on Saturday and then be transferred and compete as a Special on Sunday. It must be emphasized that the change *must* be made *prior* to the start of *any* part of the day's judging, not for just your individual breed.

In the United States, Best of Breed winners are entitled to compete in the Variety Group which includes them. This is not mandatory, it is a privilege which exhibitors value. (In Canada, Best of Breed winners *must* compete in the Variety Group, or they lose any points already won.) The dogs winning *first* in each of the seven Variety Groups *must* compete for Best in Show. Missing the opportunity of taking your dog in for competition in its Group is foolish as it is there where the general public is most likely to notice your breed and become interested in learning about it.

Non-regular classes are sometimes included at the all-breed shows, and they are almost invariably included at Specialty Shows. These include Stud Dog Class and Brood Bitch Class, which are judged on the basis of the quality of the two offspring accompanying the sire or dam. The quality of the latter two is beside the point and should not be considered by the judge; it is the youngsters who count, and the quality of *both* are to be averaged to decide which sire or dam is the best and most consistent producer. Then there is the Brace Class (which, at all-breed shows, moves up to Best Brace in each Variety Group and then Best Brace in Show), which is judged on the similarity and evenness of appearance of the two members of the brace. In other words, the two dogs should look like identical twins in size, color, and conformation and should move together almost as a single dog, one person handling with precision and ease. The same applies to the Team Class competition, except that four dogs are involved and, if necessary, two handlers.

The Veterans Class is for the older dogs, the minimum age of whom is seven years. This class is judged on the quality of the dogs, as the winner competes in Best of Breed competition and has, on a respectable number of occasions, been known to take that top award. So the point is *not* to pick out the oldest dog, as some judges seem to believe, but the best specimen of the breed, exactly as in the regular classes.

Then there are Sweepstakes and Futurity Stakes sponsored by many Specialty clubs, sometimes as part of their regular Specialty Shows and sometimes as separate events on an entirely different occasion. The difference between the two stakes is that Sweepstakes entries usually include dogs from six to eighteen months of age with entries made at the same time as the others for the show while for a Futurity the entries are bitches nominated when bred and the individual puppies entered at or shortly following their birth.

If you already show your dog, if you plan on being an exhibitor in the future, or if you simply enjoy attending dog shows, there is a book, written by me, which you will find to be an invaluable source of detailed information about all aspects of show dog competition. This book is *Successful Dog Show Exhibiting* (T.F.H. Publications, Inc.) and is available wherever the one you are reading was purchased.

Junior Showmanship Competition

If there is a youngster in your family between the ages of ten and sixteen, I can suggest no better or more rewarding hobby than becoming an active participant in Junior Showmanship. This is a marvelous activity for young people. It teaches responsibility, good sportsmanship, the fun of competition where one's own skills are the deciding factor of success, proper care of a pet, and how to socialize with other young folks. Any youngster may experience the thrill of emerging from the ring a winner and the satisfaction of a good job well done.

Entry in Junior Showmanship Classes is open to any boy or girl who is at least ten years old and under seventeen years old on the day of the show. The Novice Junior Showmanship Class is open to youngsters who have not already won, at the time the entries close, three firsts in this class. Youngsters who have won three firsts in Novice may compete in the Open Junior Showmanship Class. Any junior handler who wins his third first-place award in Novice may participate in the Open Class at the same show, provided that the Open Class has at least one other junior handler entered and competing in it that day. The Novice and Open Classes may be divided into Junior and Senior Classes. Youngsters between the ages of ten and twelve, inclusively, are eligible

Miss Valerie Nunes winning Best in Junior Showmanship at Westminster in 1981 with the German Shorthair Ch. Donavin's Sir Ivanhoe owned by Christopher Saris, Donavin Shorthairs, Stanton, California.

Ch. Serakraut's Stardust, by Ch. Serakraut's Lucky Buck ex Ch. Serakraut's Lucky Star, bred and owned by Ann Serak, is the dam of ten champions including Best in Show, Specialty and multiple Group winning "Bravo"; multiple Specialty and Group winner "Exactly"; multiple Specialty and Group winner, Sir Valiant Laurel. Dam of the Year (Show Type) 1981 and Top Producer 1981, German Shorthaired Pointer Club of America Annual Awards.

for the Junior division; and youngsters between thirteen and seventeen, inclusively, are eligible for the Senior division.

Any of the foregoing classes may be separated into individual classes for boys and for girls. If such a division is made, it must be so indicated on the premium list. The premium list also indicates the prize for Best Junior Handler, if such a prize is being offered at the show. Any youngster who wins a first in any of the regular classes may enter the competition for this prize, provided the youngster has been undefeated in any other Junior Showmanship Class at that show.

Junior Showmanship Classes, unlike regular conformation classes in which the quality of the dog is judged, are judged solely on the skill and ability of the junior handling the dog. Which dog is best is not the point—it is which youngster does the best job with the dog that is under consideration. Eligibility requirements for the dog being shown in Junior Showmanship, and other detailed information, can be found in *Regulations for Junior Showmanship,* available from the American Kennel Club.

Ch. Rocky Run's Stoney handled here by Jim Rathburn for breeder-owner Bob Arnold, winning Best of Breed at the Eastern German Shorthaired Pointer Club Specialty and on to Best in Show at Sand and Sea Kennel Club, 1972.

A junior who has a dog that he or she can enter in both Junior Showmanship and conformation classes has twice the opportunity for success and twice the opportunity to get into the ring and work with the dog, a combination which can lead to not only awards for expert handling but also, if the dog is of sufficient quality, for making a conformation champion.

Pre-Show Preparations for Your Dog and You

Preparation of the items you will need as a dog show exhibitor should not be left until the last moment. They should be planned and arranged for at least several days in advance of the show in order for you to remain calm and relaxed as the countdown starts.

The German Shorthaired Pointer Ch. Wynward's Bifrost, C.D., by Ch. Ashbrook Papageno ex Ch. Macho's Contessa of Kaposia, C.D., Best in Sweepstakes, Mason-Dixon German Shorthaired Pointer Club Sweepstakes April 1983, finished her championship from the Puppy and Bred-by-Exhibitor classes, and her C.D. in three straight shows.

The importance of the crate has already been mentioned, and we hope it is already part of your equipment. Of equal importance is the grooming table, which very likely you have also already acquired for use at home. You should take it along with you to the shows, as your dog will need last minute touches before entering the ring. Should you have not yet made this purchase, folding tables with rubber tops are made specifically for this purpose and can be purchased at most dog shows, where concession booths with marvelous assortments of "doggy" necessities are to be found, or at your pet supplier. You will also need a sturdy tack box (also available at the dog show concessions) in which to carry your grooming tools and equipment. The latter should include brushes, comb, scissors, nail clippers, whatever you use for last minute clean-up jobs, cotton swabs, first-aid equipment, and anything you are in the habit of using on the dog, including a leash or two of the type you prefer, some well-cooked and dried-out liver or any of the small packaged "dog treats" for use as bait in the ring, an atomizer in case you wish to dampen your dog's coat when you are preparing him for the ring, and so on. A large turkish towel to spread under the dog on the grooming table is also useful.

Take a large thermos or cooler of ice, the biggest one you can accommodate in your vehicle, for use by "man and beast." Take a jug of water (there are lightweight, inexpensive ones available at all sporting goods shops) and a water dish. If you plan to feed the dog at the show, or if you and the dog will be away from home more than one day, bring food for him from home so that he will have the type to which he is accustomed.

You may or may not have an exercise pen. It is a *must*, even if you only have one dog. While the shows do provide areas for the exercise of the dogs, these are among the most likely places to have your dog come in contact with any illnesses which may be going around, and having a pen of your own for your dog's use is excellent protection. Such a pen can be used in other ways, too, such as a place other than the crate in which to put the dog to relax (that is roomier than the crate) and a place in which the dog can exercise at motels and rest areas. These, too, are available at the show concession stands and come in a variety of heights and sizes. A set of "pooper scoopers" should also be part of your equipment, along with a package of plastic bags for cleaning up after your dog.

Bring along folding chairs for the members of your party, unless all of you are fond of standing, as these are almost never provided anymore by the clubs. Have your name stamped on the chairs so that there will be no doubt as to whom the chairs belong. Bring whatever you and your family enjoy for drinks or snacks in a picnic basket or cooler, as show food, in general, is expensive and usually not great. You should always have a pair of boots, a raincoat, and a rain hat with you (they should remain permanently in your vehicle if you plan to attend shows regularly), as well as a sweater, a warm coat, and a change of shoes. A smock or big cover-up apron will assure that you remain tidy as you prepare the dog for the ring. Your overnight case should include a small sewing kit for emergency repairs, bandaids, headache

Ch. Spindrifter's Bang of Laurwyn, C.D., TT-2, is owned by Bob and Kathy Marks, Arkayem Kennels, Dundee, Illinois. A German Wirehaired distinguished in the field, obedience and the show ring.

Opposite page: *(Top)* Ch. Gretchenhof Cimarron with Joyce Shellenbarger. *(Bottom)* Aust. Ch. Birdacre Maximilian, C.D., by Aust. Ch. Ianbarr Krishna ex Southcreek Gold Dust. Owned by Klugerhund Shorthairs, J.R. Maxwell, Werombi, New South Wales, Australia.

267

Mrs. Ann Stevenson chooses her Shorthair winners at a 1977 event. Am. and Can. Ch. Fieldfines Count Rambard, at the head of the line with breeder-owner-handler Dot Vooris takes Best of Breed; Fieldfines River Shannon Winners Bitch; Ch. Fieldfines Dawn von Stillwater, Best of Opposite Sex; Fieldfines Yankee Clipper, Winners Dog.

and indigestion remedies, and any personal products or medications you normally use.

In your car you should always carry maps of the area where you are headed and an assortment of motel directories. Generally speaking, we have found Holiday Inns to be the nicest about taking dogs. Ramadas and Howard Johnsons generally do as cheerfully (with a few exceptions). Best Western generally frowns on pets (not always, but often enough to make it necessary to find out which do). Some of the smaller chains welcome pets. The majority of privately owned motels do not.

Have everything prepared the night before the show to expedite your departure. Be sure that the dog's identification and your judging program and other show information are in your purse or briefcase. If you are taking sandwiches, have them ready. Anything that goes into the car the night before the show will be one thing less to remember in the morning. Decide upon what you will wear and have it out and ready. If there is any question in your mind about what to wear, try on the possibilities before the day of the show; don't risk feeling you may want to change when you see yourself dressed a few moments prior to departure time!

In planning your outfit, make it something simple that will not detract from your dog. Remember that a dark dog silhouettes attractively against a light background and vice-versa. Sport clothes always seem to look best at dog shows, preferably conservative in type and not overly "loud" as you do not want to detract from your dog, who should be the focus of interest at this point. What you wear on your feet is important. Many types of flooring can be hazardously slippery, as can wet grass. Make it a habit to wear rubber soles and low or flat heels in the ring for your own safety, especially if you are showing a dog that likes to move out smartly.

Your final step in pre-show preparation is to leave yourself plenty of time to reach the show that morning. Traffic can get amazingly heavy as one nears the immediate area of the show, finding a parking place can be difficult, and other delays may occur. You'll be in better humor to enjoy the day if your trip to the show is not fraught with panic over fear of not arriving in time!

Enjoying the Dog Show

From the moment of your arrival at the show until after your dog has been judged, keep foremost in your mind the fact the he is your reason for being there and that he should therefore be the center of your attention. Arrive early enough to have time for those last-minute touches that can make such a great difference when he enters the ring. Be sure that he has ample time to exercise and that he attends to personal matters. A dog arriving in the ring and immediately using it as an exercise pen hardly makes a favorable impression on the judge.

When you reach ringside, ask the steward for your arm-card and anchor it firmly into place on your arm. Make sure that you are where you should be when your class is called. The fact that you have picked up your arm-card does not guarantee, as some seem to think, that the judge will wait for you. The judge has a full schedule which he wishes to complete on time. Even though you may be nervous, assume an air of calm self-confidence. Remember that this is a hobby to be enjoyed, so approach it in that state of mind. The dog will do better, too, as he will be quick to reflect your attitude.

Always show your dog with an air of pride. If you make mistakes in presenting him, don't worry about it. Next time you will do better. Do not permit the presence of more experienced exhibitors to intimidate you. After all, they, too, once were newcomers.

The judging routine usually starts when the judge asks that the dogs be gaited in a circle around the ring. During this period the judge is watching each dog as it moves, noting style, topline, reach and drive, head and tail carriage, and general balance. Keep your mind and your eye on your dog, moving him at his most becoming gait and keeping your place in line without coming too close to the exhibitor ahead of you. Always keep your dog on the inside of the circle, between yourself and the judge, so that the judge's view of the dog is unobstructed.

Calmly pose the dog when requested to set up for examination. If you are at the head of the line and many dogs are in the class, go all the way to the end of the ring before starting to stack the dog, leaving sufficient space for those behind you to line theirs up as well as requested by the judge. If you are not at the head of the line but between other exhibitors, leave sufficient space ahead of your dog for the judge to examine him. The dogs should be spaced so that the judge is able to move among them to see them from all angles. In practicing to "set up" or "stack" your dog for the judge's examination, bear in mind the importance of doing so quickly and with dexterity. The judge has a schedule to meet and only a few moments in which to evaluate each dog. You will immeasurably help yours to make a favorable impression if you are able to "get it all together" in a minimum amount of time. Practice at home before a mirror can be a great help toward bringing this about, facing the dog so that you see him from the same side that the judge will and working to make him look right in the shortest length of time.

Listen carefully as the judge describes the manner in which the dog is to be gaited, whether it is straight down and straight back; down the ring, across, and back; or in a triangle. The latter has become the most popular pattern with the majority of judges. "In a triangle" means the dog should move down the outer side of the ring to the first corner, across that end of the ring to the second corner, and then back to the judge from the second corner, using the center of the ring in a diagonal line. Please learn to do this pattern without breaking at each corner to twirl the dog around you, a senseless maneuver we sometimes have noted. Judges like to see the dog in an uninterrupted triangle, as they are thus able to get a better idea of the dog's gait.

It is impossible to overemphasize that the gait at which you move your dog is tremendously important, and considerable study and thought should be given to the matter. At home, have someone move the dog for you at different speeds so that you can tell which shows him off to best advantage. The most becoming action almost invariably is seen at a moderate gait, head up and topline holding. Do not

Ch. Gretchenhof Moonwalk with Joyce Shellenbarger.

gallop your dog around the ring or hurry him into a speed atypical of his breed. Nothing being rushed appears at its best; give your dog a chance to move along at his (and the breed's) natural gait. For a dog's action to be judged accurately, that dog should move with strength and power but not excessive speed, holding a straight line as he goes to and from the judge.

As you bring the dog back to the judge, stop him a few feet away and be sure that he is standing in a becoming position. Bait him to show the judge an alert expression, using whatever tasty morsel he has been trained to expect for this purpose or, if that works better for you, use a small squeak-toy in your hand. A reminder, please, to those using liver or treats. Take them with you when you leave the ring. Do not just drop them on the ground where they will be found by another dog.

When the awards have been made, accept yours graciously, no matter how you actually may feel about it. What's done is done, and arguing with a judge or stomping out of the ring is useless and a reflection on your sportsmanship. Be courteous, congratulate the winner if your dog was defeated, and try not to show your disappointment. By the same token, please be a gracious winner; this, surprisingly, sometimes seems to be still more difficult.

271

Ch. Sigurd's Hexa, U.D., Can. C.D.X. is owned, trained and handled by Doug and Chris Jones, Berkley, Michigan.

Ch. Sigurd's Hexa, U.D., Can. C.D.X. at work in obedience. Doug and Chris Jones, owners, Berkley, Michigan.

Chapter 13

Your Dog and Obedience

For its own protection and safety, every dog should be taught, at the very least, to recognize and obey the commands "Come," "Heel," "Down," "Sit," and "Stay." Doing so at some time might save the dog's life and in less extreme circumstances will certainly make him a better behaved, more pleasant member of society. If you are patient and enjoy working with your dog, study some of the excellent books available on the subject of obedience and then teach your canine friend these basic manners. If you need the stimulus of working with a group, find out where obedience training classes are held (usually your veterinarian, your dog's breeder, or a dog-owning friend can tell you) and you and your dog can join up. Alternatively, you could let someone else do the training by sending the dog to class, but this is not very rewarding because you lose the opportunity of working with your dog and the pleasure of the rapport thus established.

If you are going to do it yourself, there are some basic rules which you should follow. You must remain calm and confident in attitude. Never lose your temper and frighten or punish your dog unjustly. Be quick and lavish with praise each time a command is correctly followed. Make it fun for the dog and he will be eager to please you by responding correctly. Repetition is the keynote, but it should not be continued without recess to the point of tedium. Limit the training sessions to ten- or fifteen-minute periods at a time.

Obedience Trials

Formal obedience training can be followed, and very frequently is, by entering the dog in obedience competition to work toward an obedience degree, or several of them, depending on the dog's aptitude and

Cruz's Princess De Shannon, C.D.X., T.D. by Ch. P.W.'s Challenger von Fieldfine ex Ch. St. Hubert's Katy Did, is the *youngest dog of any breed* to have achieved a C.D. in the *history* of A.K.C. which degree he attained at age six months. Owner, Walter Cruz.

your own enjoyment. Obedience trials are held in conjunction with the majority of all-breed conformation dog shows, with Specialty shows, and frequently as separate Specialty events. If you are working alone with your dog, a list of trial dates might be obtained from your dog's veterinarian, your dog breeder, or a dog-owning friend; the A.K.C. *Gazette* lists shows and trials to be scheduled in the coming months; and if you are a member of a training class, you will find the information readily available.

The goals for which one works in the formal A.K.C. Member or Licensed Trials are the following titles: Companion Dog (C.D.), Companion Dog Excellent (C.D.X.), and Utility Dog (U.D.). These degrees are earned by receiving three "legs," or qualifying scores, at each level of competition. The degrees must be earned in order, with one completed prior to starting work on the next. For example, a dog must have earned C.D. prior to starting work on C.D.X.; then C.D.X. must be completed before U.D. work begins. The ultimate title attainable in obedience work is Obedience Trial Champion (O.T.Ch.).

When you see the letters "C.D." following a dog's name, you will know that this dog has satisfactorily completed the following exercises: heel on leash, heel free, stand for examination, recall, long sit and long stay. "C.D.X." means that tests have been passed on all of those just mentioned plus heel free, drop on recall, retrieve over high jump, broad jump, long sit, and long down. "U.D." indicates that the

Ch. Sigurd's Hexa, owned by Doug and Chris Jones, here is flyball racing, one of her favorite activities.

dog has additionally passed tests in scent discrimination (leather article), scent discrimination (metal article), signal exercises, directed retrieve, directed jumping, and group stand for examination. The letters "O.T.Ch." are the abbreviation for the only obedience title which precedes rather than follows a dog's name. To gain an obedience trial championship, a dog who already holds a Utility Dog degree must win a total of one hundred points and must win three firsts, under three different judges, in Utility and Open B Classes.

There is also a Tracking Dog title (T.D.) which can be earned at tracking trials. In order to pass the tracking tests the dog must follow the trail of a stranger along a path on which the trail was laid between thirty minutes and two hours previously. Along this track there must be more than two right-angle turns, at least two of which are well out in the open where no fences or other boundaries exist for the guidance of the dog or the handler. The dog wears a harness and is connected to the handler by a lead twenty to forty feet in length. Inconspicuously dropped at the end of the track is an article to be retrieved, usually a glove or wallet, which the dog is expected to locate and the handler to pick up. The letters "T.D.X." are the abbreviation for Tracking Dog Excellent, a more difficult version of the Tracking Dog test with a longer track and more turns to be worked through.

The German Wirehaired Pointer Ch. Spindrift's Bang of Laurwyn, C.D. achieved her first leg on her C.D.X. at Kalamazoo, Michigan, in 1983. A daughter of Ch. Laurwyn's Cheeseburger from Am. and Can. Ch. Laurwyn's Barbed Wire. Robert J. Marks, owner, Arkayem Kennels, Dundee, Illinois.

Wirehair Obedience Stars

Generally speaking, German Wirehaired Pointers are not known for tremendous success in the obedience ring. Chris Jones, co-owner with Doug Jones of the very widely admired and successful obedience titlist Champion Sigurd's Hexa, U.D., Canadian C.D.X. says she, for one, believes this situation to be the fault of the handler, not of the dog. To quote, "They (Wirehairs) are clowns, love to jump, only do willingly what they want to do. But what they do is great. They need good trainers who will give a variety in their training and not exercise too much drilling all at once. Handlers from day one must move at a brisk pace with them and insist (with proper method) that the dog stay with them. You cannot brow-beat a Wirehaired, but neither can you let yourself be outsmarted by them."

In her entire career, Hexa never scored less than 190. Almost always she was 195 or better, bringing her average, Mrs. Jones believes, around 197. She was two years old before she went to obedience school, and was the Jones' first obedience titled dog.

Hexa did many other things besides obedience work in the ring. She is her owner's favorite to take to the elementary school as she loves children and always shows off especially well for them. She was on the Sportsmen's Dog Training Club of Detroit's original Flyball and Drill Team, plus being one of the original eight dogs who performed square dancing. She briefly appeared on the television show "Those Amazing Animals," and one of her very favorite activities is scent hurdle relay racing.

Hexa is an excellent hunting companion. What does she hate more than anything in the world??? Snakes, which she goes after and kills on sight.

Doug and Chris Jones live at Berkley, Michigan. Need we add that Hexa is a well-known citizen of that town?

Suzette M. Wood of Kissimmee, Florida, has the distinction of owning two very talented and famous Wirehairs, Champion Topwin's Macaroni, C.D.X., and Champion Hilltop's Shula of Bogay, U.D.T., NAVHDA Utility.

Shula, her owner tells us, is the only German Wirehaired Pointer to hold a breed championship title, tracking title, Utility obedience degree, and *advanced* hunting skills title, certainly an exciting combination of talents! Shula has received several Highest Score in Trial awards in open utility. For her C.D. degree she received the DOG WORLD Award. And she was the first German Wirehaired Pointer in Florida to obtain a prize qualification for the NAVHDA Utility test.

A daughter of Champion Hilltop's Coffee of Laurwyn ex Hilltop's Show Squall, Shula was bred by B. Stroh and R.S. Barge. She is the dam of Champion Topwin's Macaroni, C.D.X., who is sired by Champion Laurwyn's Banner.

Two Wirehairs at work. On the bank, Ch. Hilltop's Shula of Bogay, U.D.T. In the water, Ch. Topwin's Macaroni, C.D.X. Both owned by Suzette Wood, Kissimmee, Florida.

Am. Field Ch., Amateur Field Ch., Can. Field Ch. Halb's Miss Chief, by F.C., A.F.C. Halb Von Grofenberg II, born April 13th 1979. Owned by Doug and Penny Ljungren, Kent, Washington.

278

Chapter 14

German Pointers in the Field

Under rules of the American Kennel Club, German Shorthaired Pointers and German Wirehaired Pointers are eligible to compete in field trials held for the Pointing breeds.

Field Trial Rules

To become a field champion, a dog of a Pointing breed must win ten points under the point ratings listed below in regular stakes in at least three licensed or member field trials, provided that three points have been awarded in one 3-point win or better Open All-Age, Open Gun Dog, Open Limited All Age, or Open Limited Gun Dog Stake, that no more than two points each have been won in Open Puppy and Open Derby Stakes, and that no more than four of the ten points have been won by placing first in Amateur Stakes.

A German Shorthaired Pointer, German Wirehaired Pointer, Vizsla, or Weimaraner shall *not* be recorded a Field Champion unless it has won at least four points in Retriever Stakes at Field Trials held by Specialty Clubs of one of these four breeds.

A German Shorthaired Pointer, German Wirehaired Pointer, or Weimaraner shall *not* be recorded a Field Champion unless it has been certified by two of the approved judges to have passed a Water Test at a licensed or member Field Trial held by a Specialty Club for one of these three breeds.

Championship points shall be credited only to dogs placed first in regular stakes. The number of points shall be based on the actual number of eligible starters in each stake according to the following schedule:

Four to Seven Starters	1 point
Eight to Twelve Starters	2 points
Thirteen to Seventeen Starters	3 points
Eighteen to Twenty-Four Starters	4 points
Twenty-five or More Starters	5 points

An Amateur Field Championship will be recorded in one of the Pointing breeds after all of the same above requirements have been fulfilled *but* at *Amateur Trials*. Amateur Championship Points are awarded as below.

	Placement		
	1st	2nd	3rd
4 to 7 starters	1 point		
8 to 12 starters	2 points		
13 to 17 starters	3 points	1 point	
18 to 24 starters	4 points	2 points	
25 or more starters	5 points	3 points	1 point

Championship points from first placements in Amateur Stakes that are credited towards a Field Championship will also be credited towards an Amateur Field Championship.

The complete rules and regulations governing A.K.C. licensed or approved field trials can be obtained, free of charge, from The American Kennel Club, 51 Madison Avenue, New York, N.Y. 10010. Anyone interested in entering Field Trials should obtain a copy immediately, as rules do change and it is important that exhibitors keep right up to the moment on them.

Wirehaired Pointers in the Field

Having read with considerable interest of the Field accomplishments of German Wirehaired Pointers owned by Doug and Penny Ljungren of Kent, Washington, we have asked for photos of these dogs to show our readers, and also for some comments on Wirehairs in the field from their owners.

The Ljungren Wirehairs are very famous. American and Canadian Dual Champion, Amateur Field Champion Griff Von Dem Feld is the first and only German Wirehaired Pointer who has accomplished this feat. He was one of the Top Ten Wirehair Gun Dogs in the United States, 1978-1980. Entirely amateur owner-trained and handled, he is

Ch. Brewster Von Lieben-wald, C.D. entering the water in his usual manner. Owned by Larry B. and Nancy Mason, Auburn, Washington.

a truly versatile hunting dog with an easy going personality, equally at home in the duck blind or hunting upland game.

Sired by American and Canadian Champion Odell's Hansel, C.D.X. (who has produced titled offspring from eight different bitches) from Odell's Anji, Griff was born January 6th 1976.

Then there are the two sisters, Halb's Miss Chief and Halb's Sure Shot, same breeding but different litters. "Missy" is an American Field Champion, Amateur Field Champion, and Canadian Field Champion sired by Field Champion and Amateur Field Champion Holb Von Pommoregon from Gisela Von Grafenberg II, born April 13th 1979.

The Ljungrens are basing their major breeding program on the above two bitches, who represent a budding line having its roots in Field Champion and American Field Champion Wirehairs through Halb Von Pommoregon (Field Champion/Amateur Field Champion) and Imp Von Pommoregon (Dual Champion/Amateur Field Champion) who are full brothers from different litters. Both have produced excellent field caliber dogs.

We understand that the Haar Baron Wirehairs were one Field Trial line that was producing. This line has been largely stopped now with its own identity, and it is dispersed through the backgrounds of very different groups. Mr. Ljungren is proud of having this line represented in his dog, Griff, along with some German import crosses.

In 1982 the German Wirehaired Pointer Club of America upgraded the status of the National Field Trial by making it tougher and giving the winner the title of "National Champion." Halb's Miss Chief has won the National Amateur Championship in both 1982 and 1983, making her the only Wirehair thus far to hold this title.

The following list of German Wirehaired Pointer Field Champions since the breed was recognized by the American Kennel Club in 1959 has been submitted to us by Mr. Ljungren to be included in this chapter.

Doug Ljungren calls to our attention the fact that in the nearly 25 years since German Wirehaired Pointers first were recognized by the American Kennel Club, only 41 of the breed have earned the title of Field Champion or Amateur Field Champion. To help put this number into proper perspective, he further comments that in 1983 alone, 66 members of the breed completed show championships. Obviously the testing and refining of field trial lines in the United States is proceeding very slowly!

As reasons for the latter, Mr. Ljungren further points out that fewer people are working at this facet of the breed than are working to produce show champions. An additional reason is that time is often long in training these dogs for the field, with a dog owned by a field trial competitor normally not being fully trained until it is two years old. The average field champion probably finishes between four and five years age. A great deal of skill and knowledge goes into the proper development of a fully trained competitive field trial dog. Most "field trial" litters are sold to hunters who have neither the knowledge nor the desire to take their dog further than becoming a good companion for their own hunting activities.

We are told that it is due to these reasons that field trial lines in the United States are not better defined. This is evidenced by the fact that there is not a German Wirehaired Pointer alive in the United States today that is a three-generation Field Champion (that is, that it is itself a Field Champion, one of its parents is a Field Champion, and one of its grandparents a Field Champion). Obviously there are many show champions that can boast a six-generation show champion pedigree.

Wirehair Field Champions

FC Haar Baron's Mike (D)	12/59	Faestal	Wisconsin
DC Haar Baron's Gremlin (B)	5/60	Faestal	Wisconsin
DC Quandu v.d. Elbmarsch (B)	12/60	Hoffman	Illinois
DC Strauss's Melodie (B)	5/61	Glodowski	Wisconsin
FC Mitchen of Lowenberg (B)	6/62	Faestal	Wisconsin
DC Haar Baron's Tina, CD (B)	6/63	Faestal	Wisconsin
DC Haar Baron's Hans (D)	6/64	Capstaff	Illinois
FC Haar Baron's Jo (D)	5/65	Rieckhoff	Wisconsin
DC Haar Baron's Gretchen (B)	6/67	Faestal	Wisconsin
DC Herr Schmidt's Boy Yancy (D)	6/69	Gallagher	Illinois
DC Queen Vom Stoppelsberg CDX (B)	7/69	Floege-Boehm	Tennessee
DC Haar Baron's Shean (D)	11/70	Arkema	Illinois
DC Wotan Zur Wolfschlucht CD (D)	12/70	Floege-Boehm	Tennessee
DC/AFC Loki Zur Wolfschlucht (D)	2/71	Byrne	Virginia
DC/AFC Graf Bowser (D)	1/72	LeFurge	New Jersey
FC/AFC Rebel's Madchen (B)	6/73	Walker	Wisconsin
FC Haar Baron's Miss Keli (B)	7/73	Wyderka	Wisconsin
FC/AFC/CFC Halb Von Pommoregon (D)	11/74	Marquart	Washington
DC/AFC Imp Von Pommoregon (D)	8/75	Ruess	Iowa
FC/AFC Bur-Oaks Trixie (B)	11/75	Burke	Illinois
FC/AFC Miss Keli's Tonya (B)	11/76	Wyderka	Wisconsin
FC Aras von Grafenberg (D)	12/76	Strakeljohn	Washington
DC/AFC Lutz zur Cadenberg CD, TD (D)	8/77	Alberts/Berry	N. California
DC/AFC Bit of Sigurd (D)	5/78	Uhl	S. California
DC/AFC Miss Keli's Annabelle (B)	7/78	Schoonover	Indiana
FC/AFC Ahlin's Dyke Ann (B)	12/79	Ahlin	Wisconsin
FC Whitewing's Baby von Arni (B)	3/80	Haviland	Arizona
AFC Draufganger's Sinta (B)	6/80	Wagner	Michigan
Am/Can DC/AFC Nordwest's Griff Von Feld (D)	7/80	Ljungren	Washington
DC/AFC Walker's Blue Movie (B)	9/80	Haag	Iowa
FC Chancellor's Sierra Drifter (D)	11/80	Calkins	Oregon
FC/AFC Walker's Summer Wind (B)	2/81	Walker	Wisconsin
FC Fredrich's Wolfgang (D)	3/81	Fredrich	Washington
DC Flintlock's Not Too Shabby (B)	4/81	Fernandez/Berry	N. California
FC/AFC Fredrich's Figure It Out (D)	7/81	Fredrich	Washington
FC/AFC/CFC Halb's Sure Shot (B)	12/81	Ljungren	Washington
FC/AFC Baron Vom Schyrental (D)	12/81	Weatheron	N. California
FC/AFC/CFC Halb's Miss Chief (B)	1/83	Ljungren	Washington
FC Walker's Gye Wire (D)	2/83	Ciolkowski	Illinois
FC Schroeder's Maine Heir (D)	1/84	Wilkins	Maine
FC Dallimore's Gretta (B)	2/84	T. Dallimore	Oregon

(Listed through April, 1984 Gazette)

Ch. Columbia River Jill, the foundation bitch at Gretchenhof Kennels, Joyce Shellenbarger, Huntington Beach, California

Chapter 15

Breeding Your German Pointer

The German Pointer Brood Bitch

We have in an earlier chapter discussed selection of a bitch you plan to use for breeding. In making this important purchase, you will be choosing a bitch who you hope will become the foundation of your kennel. Thus she must be of the finest producing bloodlines, excellent in temperament, of good type, and free of major faults or unsoundness. If you are offered a "bargain" brood bitch, be wary, as for this purchase you should not settle for less than the best and the price will be in accordance with the quality.

Conscientious breeders feel quite strongly that the only possible reason for producing puppies is the ambition to improve and uphold quality and temperament within the breed—definitely *not* because one hopes to make a quick cash profit on a mediocre litter, which never seems to work out that way in the long run and which accomplishes little beyond perhaps adding to the nation's heartbreaking number of unwanted canines. The only reason ever for breeding a litter is, with conscientious people, a desire to improve the quality of dogs in their own kennel or, as pet owners, because they wish to add to the number of dogs they themselves own with a puppy or two from their present favorites. In either case breeding should not take place unless one has definitely prospective owners for as many puppies as the litter may contain, lest you find yourself with several fast-growing young dogs and no homes in which to place them.

Bitches should not be mated earlier than their second season, by which time they should be from fifteen to eighteen months old. Many breeders prefer to wait and first finish the championships of their show bitches before breeding them, as pregnancy can be a disaster to a show coat and getting the bitch back in shape again takes time. When you have decided what will be the proper time, start watching at least several months ahead for what you feel would be the perfect mate to best complement your bitch's quality and bloodlines. Subscribe to the magazines which feature your breed exclusively and to some which cover all breeds in order to familiarize yourself with outstanding stud dogs in areas other than your own for there is no necessity nowadays to limit your choice to a nearby dog unless you truly like him and feel that he is the most suitable. It is quite usual to ship a bitch to a stud dog a distance away, and this generally works out with no ill effects. The important thing is that you need a stud dog strong in those features where your bitch is weak or lacking and of bloodlines compatible to hers. Compare the background of both your bitch and the stud dog under consideration, paying particular attention to the quality of the puppies from bitches with backgrounds similar to your bitch's. If the puppies have been of the type and quality you admire, then this dog would seem a sensible choice for yours, too.

Stud fees may be a few hundred dollars, sometimes even more under special situations for a particularly successful sire. It is money well spent, however. Do *not* ever breed to a dog because he is less expensive than the others unless you honestly believe that he can sire the kind of puppies who will be a credit to your kennel and your breed.

Contacting the owners of the stud dogs you find interesting will bring you pedigrees and pictures which you can then study in relation to your bitch's pedigree and conformation. Discuss your plans with other breeders who are knowledgeable (including the one who bred your own bitch). You may not always receive an entirely unbiased opinion (particularly if the person giving it also has an available stud dog), but one learns by discussion so listen to what they say, consider their opinions, and then you may be better qualified to form your own opinion.

As soon as you have made a choice, phone the owner of the stud dog you wish to use to find out if this will be agreeable. You will be asked about the bitch's health, soundness, temperament, and freedom from serious faults. A copy of her pedigree may be requested, as might a picture of her. A discussion of her background over the telephone may be sufficient to assure the stud's owner that she is suitable for the stud dog and of type, breeding, and quality herself to produce puppies of the quality for which the dog is noted. The owner of a top-quality stud is often extremely selective in the bitches permitted to be bred to his dog, in an effort to keep the standard of his puppies high. The owner of a stud dog may require that the bitch be tested for brucellosis, which should be attended to not more than a month previous to the breeding.

Check out which airport will be most convenient for the person meeting and returning the bitch if she is to be shipped and also what airlines use that airport. You will find that the airlines are also apt to have special requirements concerning acceptance of animals for shipping. These include weather limitations and types of crates which are acceptable. The weather limits have to do with extreme heat and extreme cold at the point of destination, as some airlines will not fly dogs into temperatures above or below certain levels, fearing for their safety. The crate problem is a simple one, since if your own crate is not suitable, most of the airlines have specially designed crates available for purchase at a fair and moderate price. It is a good plan to purchase one of these if you intend to be shipping dogs with any sort of frequency. They are made of fiberglass and are the safest type to use for shipping.

Normally you must notify the airline several days in advance to make a reservation, as they are able to accommodate only a certain number of dogs on each flight. Plan on shipping the bitch on about her eighth or ninth day of season, but be careful to avoid shipping her on a weekend, when schedules often vary and freight offices are apt to be closed. Whenever you can, ship your bitch on a direct flight. Changing planes always carries a certain amount of risk of a dog being overlooked or wrongly routed at the middle stop, so avoid this danger if at all possible. The bitch must be accompanied by a health certificate which you must obtain from your veterinarian before taking her to the airport. Usually it will be necessary to have the bitch at the airport about two hours prior to flight time. Before finalizing arrangements, find out from the stud's owner at what time of day it will be most convenient to have the bitch picked up promptly upon arrival.

It is simpler if you can plan to bring the bitch to the stud dog. Some people feel that the trauma of the flight may cause the bitch to not conceive; and, of course, undeniably there is a slight risk in shipping which can be avoided if you are able to drive the bitch to her destination. Be sure to leave yourself sufficient time to assure your arrival at the right time for her for breeding (normally the tenth to fourteenth day following the first signs of color); and remember that if you want the bitch bred twice, you should allow a day to elapse between the two matings. Do not expect the stud's owner to house you while you are there. Locate a nearby motel that takes dogs and make that your headquarters.

Just prior to the time your bitch is due in season, you should take her to visit your veterinarian. She should be checked for worms and should receive all the booster shots for which she is due plus one for parvo virus, unless she has had the latter shot fairly recently. The brucellosis test can also be done then, and the health certificate can be obtained for shipping if she is to travel by air. Should the bitch be at all overweight, now is the time to get the surplus off. She should be in good condition, neither underweight nor overweight, at the time of breeding.

The moment you notice the swelling of the vulva, for which you should be checking daily as the time for her season approaches, and the appearance of color, immediately contact the stud's owner and settle on the day for shipping or make the appointment for your arrival with the bitch for breeding. If you are shipping the bitch, the stud fee check should be mailed immediately, leaving ample time for it to have been received when the bitch arrives and the mating takes place. Be sure to call the airline making her reservation at that time, too.

Do not feed the bitch within a few hours before shipping her. Be certain that she has had a drink of water and been well exercised before closing her in the crate. Several layers of newspapers, topped with some shredded newspaper, make a good bed and can be discarded when she arrives at her destination; these can be replaced with fresh newspapers for her return home. Remember that the bitch should be brought to the airport about two hours before flight time as sometimes the airlines refuse to accept late arrivals.

If you are taking your bitch by car, be certain that you will arrive at a reasonable time of day. Do not appear late in the evening. If your arrival in town is not until late, get a good night's sleep at your motel and contact the stud's owner first thing in the morning. If possible, leave children and relatives at home, as they will only be in the way and perhaps unwelcome by the stud's owner. Most stud dog owners prefer not to have any unnecessary people on hand during the actual mating.

After the breeding has taken place, if you wish to sit and visit for awhile and the stud's owner has the time, return the bitch to her crate in your car (first ascertaining, of course, that the temperature is comfortable for her and that there is proper ventilation). She should not be permitted to urinate for at least one hour following the breeding. This is the time when you get the business part of the transaction attended to. Pay the stud fee, upon which you should receive your breeding certificate and, if you do not already have it, a copy of the stud dog's pedigree. The owner of the stud dog does not sign or furnish a litter

Ch. Rocky Run's Rascal, by Crissy's Treth Fuehrerheim ex Arnold's Lady Hedi, bred and owned by Bob Arnold, Marcus Hook, Pennsylvania. Finished with Best of Winners at Mason-Dixon German Shorthaired Pointer Specialty under judge Alfred Sausse. Rascal was the first Rocky Run champion and the sire of Champion Rocky Run's Poldi, the Arnolds' Top Producing bitch.

registration application until the puppies have been born.

Upon your return home, you can settle down and plan in happy anticipation a wonderful litter of puppies. A word of caution! Remember that although she has been bred, your bitch is still an interesting target for all male dogs, so guard her carefully for the next week or until you are absolutely certain that her season has entirely ended. This would be no time to have any unfortunate incident with another dog.

Ch. Columbia River Thundercloud, the foundation dog at Gretchenhof Kennels, Joyce Shellenbarger, Huntington Beach, California.

The German Pointer Stud Dog

Choosing the best stud dog to complement your bitch is often very difficult. The two principal factors to be considered should be the stud's conformation and his pedigree. Conformation is fairly obvious; you want a dog that is typical of the breed in the words of the standard of perfection. Understanding pedigrees is a bit more subtle since the pedigree lists the ancestry of the dog and involves individuals and bloodlines with which you may not be entirely familiar.

To a novice in the breed, then, the correct interpretation of a pedigree may at first be difficult to grasp. Study the pictures and text of this book and you will find many names of important bloodlines and members of the breed. Also make an effort to discuss the various dogs behind the proposed stud with some of the more experienced breeders, starting with the breeder of your own bitch. Frequently these folks will be personally familiar with many of the dogs in question, can offer opinions of them, and may have access to additional pictures which you would benefit by seeing.

290

It is very important that the stud's pedigree should be harmonious with that of the bitch you plan on breeding to him. Do not rush out and breed to the latest winner with no thought of whether or not he can produce true quality. By no means are all great show dogs great producers. It is the producing record of the dog in question and the dogs and bitches from which he has come which should be the basis on which you make your choice.

Breeding dogs is never a money-making operation. By the time you pay a stud fee, care for the bitch during pregnancy, whelp the litter, and rear the puppies through their early shots, worming, and so on, you will be fortunate to break even financially once the puppies have been sold. Your chances of doing this are greater if you are breeding for a show-quality litter which will bring you higher prices as the pups are sold as show prospects. Therefore, your wisest investment is to use the best dog available for your bitch regardless of the cost; then you should wind up with more valuable puppies. Remember that it is equally costly to raise mediocre puppies as top ones, and your chances of financial return are better on the latter. To breed to the most excellent, most suitable stud dog you can find is the only sensible thing to do, and it is poor economy to quibble over the amount you are paying in stud fee.

It will be your decision which course you decide to follow when you breed your bitch, as there are three options: linebreeding, inbreeding, and outcrossing. Each of these methods has its supporters and its detractors! Linebreeding is breeding a bitch to a dog belonging originally to the same canine family, being descended from the same ancestors, such as half brother to half sister, grandsire to granddaughters, niece to uncle (and vice-versa) or cousin to cousin. Inbreeding is breeding father to daughter, mother to son, or full brother to sister. Outcross breeding is breeding a dog and a bitch with no or only a few mutual ancestors.

Linebreeding is probably the safest course, and the one most likely to bring results, for the novice breeder. The more sophisticated inbreeding should be left to the experienced, long-time breeders who thoroughly know and understand the risks and the possibilities involved with a particular line. It is usually done in an effort to intensify some ideal feature in that strain. Outcrossing is the reverse of inbreeding, an effort to introduce improvement in a specific feature needing correction, such as a shorter back, better movement, more correct head or coat, and so on.

It is the serious breeder's ambition to develop a strain or bloodline of their own, one strong in qualities for which their dogs will become distinguished. However, it must be realized that this will involve time, patience, and at least several generations before the achievement can be claimed. The safest way to embark on this plan, as we have mentioned, is by the selection and breeding of one or two bitches, the best you can buy and from top-producing kennels. In the beginning you do *not* really have to own a stud dog. In the long run it is less expensive and sounder judgment to pay a stud fee when you are ready to breed a bitch than to purchase a stud dog and feed him all year; a stud dog does not win any popularity contests with owners of bitches to be bred until he becomes a champion, has been successfully Specialed for awhile, and has been at least moderately advertised, all of which adds up to a quite healthy expenditure.

The wisest course for the inexperienced breeder just starting out in dogs is outlined above. Keep the best bitch puppy from the first several litters. After that you may wish to consider keeping your own stud dog if there has been a particularly handsome male in one of your litters that you feel has great potential or if you know where there is one available that you are interested in, with the feeling that he would work in nicely with the breeding program on which you have embarked. By this time, with several litters already born, your eye should have developed to a point enabling you to make a wise choice, either from one of your own litters or from among dogs you have seen that appear suitable.

The greatest care should be taken in the selection of your own stud dog. He must be of true type and highest quality as he may be responsible for siring many puppies each year, and he should come from a line of excellent dogs on both sides of his pedigree which themselves are, and which are descended from, successful producers. This dog should have no glaring faults in conformation; he should be of such quality that he can hold his own in keenest competition within his breed. He should be in good health, be virile and be a keen stud dog, a proven sire able to transmit his correct qualities to his puppies. Need it be said that such a dog will be enormously expensive unless you have the good fortune to produce him in one of your own litters? To buy and use a lesser stud dog, however, is downgrading your breeding program unnecessarily since there are so many dogs fitting the description of a fine stud whose services can be used on payment of a stud fee.

The very famous Ch. Gunhill's Mesa Maverick was a big winner, including all breed Bests in Show, National and local Specialties, and Sporting Group wins and placements during the mid-1970's. Bred and owned by P. Carl Tuttle, Gunhill Shorthairs, Hague, Virginia.

You should *never* breed to an unsound dog or one with any serious standard or disqualifying faults. Not all champions by any means pass along their best features; and by the same token, occasionally you will find a great one who can pass along his best features but never gained his championship title due to some unusual circumstances. The information you need about a stud dog is what type of puppies he has produced and with what bloodlines and whether or not he possesses the bloodlines and attributes considered characteristic of the best in your breed.

If you go out to buy a stud dog, obviously he will not be a puppy but rather a fully mature and proven male with as many of the best attributes as possible. True, he will be an expensive investment, but if you choose and make his selection with care and forethought, he may well prove to be one of the best investments you have ever made.

Of course, the most exciting of all is when a young male you have decided to keep from one of your litters due to his tremendous show potential turns out to be a stud dog such as we have described. In this case he should be managed with care, for he is a valuable property that can contribute inestimably to his breed as a whole and to your own kennel specifically.

Do not permit your stud dog to be used until he is about a year old, and even then he should be bred to a mature, proven matron accustomed to breeding who will make his first experience pleasant and easy. A young dog can be put off forever by a maiden bitch who fights and resists his advances. Never allow this to happen. Always start a stud dog out with a bitch who is mature, has been bred previously, and is of even temperament. The first breeding should be performed in

Well on the way to Australian Championship, Canawindra Teera was bred by M.J. and F.L. Park and is owned by W. and H. Stone, Australia.

Ch. Fieldfine's Ribbons, owned by Joyce Oesch and Kathleen Plotts taking Best of Breed, handled by Dot Vooris, at Suffolk County 1981 as her litter sister Ch. Fieldfine's Rocky River takes Best of Winners. These littermates are by Ch. Fieldfine's Rocky Run ex Am. and Can. Ch. Fieldfine's River Shannon, thus are Rambard granddaughters.

quiet surroundings with only you and one other person to hold the bitch. Do not make it a circus, as the experience will determine the dog's outlook about future stud work. If he does not enjoy the first experience or associates it with any unpleasantness, you may well have a problem in the future.

Your young stud must permit help with the breeding, as later there will be bitches who will not be cooperative. If right from the beginning you are there helping him and praising him whether or not your assistance is actually needed, he will expect and accept this as a matter of course when a difficult bitch comes along.

Things to have handy before introducing your dog and the bitch are K-Y jelly (the only lubricant which should be used) and a length of gauze with which to muzzle the bitch should it be necessary to keep

At the Eastern Specialty, under judge Anne Rogers Clark. Another good day for Fieldfines Shorthairs as Fieldfine's Maxmillion takes Winners Dog; Fieldfine's Meadow takes Reserve Winners Dog; Fieldfine's Summer Breeze takes Winners Bitch; and Fieldfine's Foxey Lady takes Reserve Winners Bitch.

her from biting you or the dog. Some bitches put up a fight; others are calm. It is best to be prepared.

At the time of the breeding the stud fee comes due, and it is expected that it will be paid promptly. Normally a return service is offered in case the bitch misses or fails to produce one live puppy. Conditions of the service are what the stud dog's owner makes them, and there are no standard rules covering this. The stud fee is paid for the act, not the result. If the bitch fails to conceive, it is customary for the owner of the stud to offer a free return service; but this is a courtesy and not to be considered a right, particularly in the case of a proven stud who is siring consistently and whose fault the failure obviously is *not*. Stud dog owners are always anxious to see their clients get good value and to have in the ring winning young stock by their dog; therefore, very few refuse to mate the second time. It is wise, however, for both parties to have the terms of the transaction clearly understood at the time of the breeding.

If the return service has been provided and the bitch has missed a second time, that is considered to be the end of the matter and the owner would be expected to pay a further fee if it is felt that the bitch should be given a third chance with the stud dog. The management of a stud dog and his visiting bitches is quite a task, and a stud fee has usually been well earned when one service has been achieved, let alone by repeated visits from the same bitch.

The accepted litter is one live puppy. It is wise to have printed a breeding certificate which the owner of the stud dog and the owner of the bitch both sign. This should list in detail the conditions of the breeding as well as the dates of the mating.

Upon occasion, arrangements other than a stud fee in cash are made for a breeding, such as the owner of the stud taking a pick-of-the-litter puppy in lieu of money. This should be clearly specified on the breeding certificate along with the terms of the age at which the stud's owner will select the puppy, whether it is to be a specific sex, or whether it is to be the pick of the entire litter.

The price of a stud fee varies according to circumstances. Usually, to prove a young stud dog, his owner will allow the first breeding to be quite inexpensive. Then, once a bitch has become pregnant by him, he becomes a "proven stud" and the fee rises accordingly for bitches that follow. The sire of championship-quality puppies will bring a stud fee of at least the purchase price of one show puppy as the accepted "rule-of-thumb." Until at least one champion by your stud dog has finished, the fee will remain equal to the price of one pet puppy. When his list of champions starts to grow, so does the amount of the stud fee. For a top-producing sire of champions, the stud fee will rise accordingly.

Almost invariably it is the bitch who comes to the stud dog for the breeding. Immediately upon having selected the stud dog you wish to use, discuss the possibility with the owner of that dog. It is the stud dog owner's prerogative to refuse to breed any bitch deemed unsuitable for his dog. Stud fee and method of payment should be stated at this time, and a decision reached on whether it is to be a full cash transaction at the time of the mating or a pick-of-the-litter puppy, usually at eight weeks of age.

If the owner of the stud dog must travel to an airport to meet the bitch and ship her for the flight home, an additional charge will be made for time, tolls, and gasoline based on the stud owner's proximity

to the airport. The stud fee includes board for the day of the bitch's arrival through two days for breeding, with a day in between. If it is necessary that the bitch remain longer, it is very likely that additional board will be charged at the normal per-day rate for the breed.

Be sure to advise the stud's owner as soon as you know that your bitch is in season so that the stud dog will be available. This is especially important because if he is a dog being shown, he and his owner may be unavailable owing to the dog's absence from home.

As the owner of a stud dog being offered to the public, it is essential that you have proper facilities for the care of visiting bitches. Nothing can be worse than a bitch being insecurely housed and slipping out to become lost or bred by the wrong dog. If you are taking people's valued bitches into your kennel or home, it is imperative that you provide them with comfortable, secure housing and good care while they are your responsibility.

There is no dog more valuable than the proven sire of champions, Group winners, and Best in Show dogs. Once you have such an animal, guard his reputation well and do *not* permit him to be bred to just any bitch that comes along. It takes two to make the puppies; even the most dominant stud can not do it all himself, so never permit him to breed a bitch you consider unworthy. Remember that when the puppies arrive, it will be your stud dog who will be blamed for any lack of quality, while the bitch's shortcomings will be quickly and conveniently overlooked.

Going into the actual management of the mating is a bit superfluous here. If you have had previous experience in breeding a dog and bitch you will know how the mating is done. If you do not have such experience, you should not attempt to follow directions given in a book but should have a veterinarian, breeder friend, or handler there to help you the first few times. You do not just turn the dog and bitch loose together and await developments, as too many things can go wrong and you may altogether miss getting the bitch bred. Someone should hold the dog and the bitch (one person each) until the "tie" is made and these two people should stay with them during the entire act.

If you get a complete tie, probably only the one mating is absolutely necessary. However, especially with a maiden bitch or one that has come a long distance for this breeding, we prefer following up with a second breeding, leaving one day in between the two matings. In this way there will be little or no chance of the bitch missing.

Once the tie has been completed and the dogs release, be certain that the male's penis goes completely back within its sheath. He should be allowed a drink of water and a short walk, and then he should be put into his crate or somewhere alone where he can settle down. Do not allow him to be with other dogs for a while as they will notice the odor of the bitch on him, and particularly with other males present, he may become involved in a fight.

Left to right, Dual Ch. Waldwinkels Painted Lady and Field Ch. Moescaard's Judy. Examples of beautiful Shorthair heads and the difference in type and expression of these two lovely bitches, who represent the Big Island and the Moesgaard lines respectively. Note one is dark-eyed and soft, the other lighter-eyed and very intense. Photo and comment courtesy of Helen B. Shelley.

Pregnancy, Whelping, and the Litter

Once the bitch has been bred and is back at home, remember to keep an ever watchful eye that no other male gets to her until at least the twenty-second day of her season has passed. Until then, it will still be possible for an unwanted breeding to take place, which at this point would be catastrophic. Remember that she actually can have two separate litters by two different dogs, so take care.

In other ways, she should be treated normally. Controlled exercise is good, and necessary for the bitch throughout her pregnancy, tapering it off to just several short walks daily, preferably on lead, as she reaches about her seventh week. As her time grows close, be careful about her jumping or playing too roughly.

The theory that a bitch should be overstuffed with food when pregnant is a poor one. A fat bitch is never an easy whelper, so the overfeeding you consider good for her may well turn out to be the exact opposite. During the first few weeks of pregnancy, your bitch should be fed her normal diet. At four to five weeks along, calcium should be added to her food. At seven weeks her food may be increased if she seems to crave more than she is getting, and a meal of canned milk (mixed with an equal amount of water) should be introduced. If she is fed just once a day, add another meal rather than overload her with too much at one time. If twice a day is her schedule, then a bit more food can be added to each feeding.

A week before the pups are due, your bitch should be introduced to her whelping box so that she will be accustomed to it and feel at home there when the puppies arrive. She should be encouraged to sleep there but permitted to come and go as she wishes. The box should be roomy enough for her to lie down and stretch out but not too large lest the pups have more room than is needed in which to roam and possibly get chilled by going too far away from their mother. Be sure that the box has a "pig rail"; this will prevent the puppies from being crushed against the sides. The room in which the box is placed, either in your home or in the kennel, should be kept at about 70 degrees Fahrenheit. In winter it may be necessary to have an infrared lamp over the whelping box, in which case be careful not to place it too low or close to the puppies.

Newspapers will become a very important commodity, so start collecting them well in advance to have a big pile handy to the whelping box. With a litter of puppies, one never seems to have papers enough, so the higher the pile to start with, the better off you will be. Other necessities for whelping time are clean, soft turkish towels, scissors, and a bottle of alcohol.

You will know that her time is very near when your bitch becomes restless, wandering in and out of her box and of the room. She may refuse food, and at that point her temperature will start to drop. She will dig at and tear up the newspapers in her box, shiver, and generally look uncomfortable. Only you should be with your bitch at this time. She does not need spectators; and several people, even though they may be family members whom she knows, hanging over her may upset her to the point where she may harm the puppies. You should remain nearby, quietly watching, not fussing or hovering; speak calmly and frequently to her to instill confidence. Eventually she will settle down in her box and begin panting; contractions will follow. Soon thereafter a puppy will start to emerge, sliding out with the contractions. The mother immediately should open the sac, sever the cord with her teeth, and then clean up the puppy. She will also eat the placenta, which you should permit. Once the puppy is cleaned, it should be placed next to the bitch unless she is showing signs of having the next one immediately. Almost at once the puppy will start looking for a nipple on which to nurse, and you should ascertain that it is able to latch on successfully.

If the puppy is a breech (*i.e.,* born feet first), you must watch carefully for it to be completely delivered as quickly as possible and the sac removed quickly so that the puppy does not drown. Sometimes even a normally positioned birth will seem extremely slow in coming. Should this occur, you might take a clean towel and, as the bitch contracts, pull the puppy out, doing so gently and with utmost care. If, once the puppy is delivered, it shows little signs of life, take a rough turkish towel and massage the puppy's chest by rubbing quite briskly back and forth. Continue this for about fifteen minutes, and be sure that the mouth is free from liquid. It may be necessary to try mouth-to-mouth breathing, which is done by pressing the puppy's jaws open and, using a finger, depressing the tongue which may be stuck to the roof of the mouth. Then place your mouth against the puppy's and blow hard down the puppy's throat. Bubbles may pop out of its nose, but keep on blowing. Rub the puppy's chest with the towel again and try artificial respiration, pressing the sides of the chest together slowly and rhythmically—in and out, in and out. Keep trying one method or the other for at least twenty minutes before giving up. You may be rewarded with a live puppy who otherwise would not have made it.

If you are successful in bringing the puppy around, do not immediately put it back with the mother as it should be kept extra warm. Put it in a cardboard box on an electric heating pad or, if it is the time of year when your heat is running, near a radiator or near the fireplace or stove. As soon as the rest of the litter has been born it then can join the others.

An hour or more may elapse between puppies, which is fine so long as the bitch seems comfortable and is neither straining nor contracting. She should not be permitted to remain unassisted for more than an hour if she does continue to contract. This is when you should get her to your veterinarian, whom you should already have alerted to the possibility of a problem existing. He should examine her and perhaps give her a shot of Pituitrin. In some cases the veterinarian may find that a Caesarean section is necessary due to a puppy being lodged in a manner making normal delivery impossible. Sometimes this is caused by an abnormally large puppy, or it may just be that the puppy is simply turned in the wrong position. If the bitch does require a Caesarean section, the puppies already born must be kept warm in their cardboard box with a heating pad under the box.

Three-week-old German Wirehaired puppies by Ch. Laurwyn's Banner ex Northwest Anji's Mathilda. Photo courtesy of Laura Myles.

Ch. Hilltop Honey's Beau Brummel, sire of 22 champions including two Best in Show winners, a well-known Top Producer bred and owned by Charles and Betty Stroh, Hilltop Farm, Suffield, CT.

Once the section is done, get the bitch and the puppies home. Do not attempt to put the puppies in with the bitch until she has regained consciousness as she may unknowingly hurt them. But do get them back to her as soon as possible for them to start nursing.

Should the mother lack milk at this time, the puppies must be fed by hand, kept very warm, and held onto the mother's teats several times a day in order to stimulate and encourage the secretion of milk, which should start shortly.

Assuming that there has been no problem and that the bitch has whelped naturally, you should insist that she go out to exercise, staying just long enough to make herself comfortable. She can be offered a bowl of milk and a biscuit, but then she should settle down with her family. Freshen the whelping box for her with fresh newspapers while she is taking this respite so that she and the puppies will have a clean bed.

Ch. Desert Mill's Ilda V Landhaus, the foundation bitch at Lieben-waid Kennels, Diana L. Nordrum, Maple Valley, Washington; with one of her litters at lunch time.

Unless some problem arises, there is little you must do about the puppies until they become three to four weeks old. Keep the box clean and supplied with fresh newspapers the first few days, but then turkish towels should be tacked down to the bottom of the box so that the puppies will have traction as they move about.

If the bitch has difficulties with her milk supply, or if you should be so unfortunate as to lose her, then you must be prepared to either hand-feed or tube-feed the puppies if they are to survive. We personally prefer tube-feeding as it is so much faster and easier. If the bitch is available, it is best that she continues to clean and care for the puppies in the normal manner excepting for the food supplements you will provide. If it is impossible for her to do this, then after every feeding you must gently rub each puppy's abdomen with wet cotton to make it urinate, and the rectum should be gently rubbed to open the bowels.

Newborn puppies must be fed every three to four hours around the clock. The puppies must be kept warm during this time. Have your veterinarian teach you how to tube-feed. You will find that it is really quite simple.

After a normal whelping, the bitch will require additional food to enable her to produce sufficient milk. In addition to being fed twice daily, she should be given some canned milk several times each day.

When the puppies are two weeks old, their nails should be clipped, as they are needle sharp at this age and can hurt or damage the mother's teats and stomach as the pups hold on to nurse.

Between three and four weeks of age, the puppies should begin to be weaned. Scraped beef (prepared by scraping it off slices of beef with a spoon so that none of the gristle is included) may be offered in very small quantities a couple of times daily for the first few days. Then by the third day you can mix puppy chow with warm water as directed on the package, offering it four times daily. By now the mother should be kept away from the puppies and out of the box for several hours at a time so that when they have reached five weeks of age she is left in with them only overnight. By the time the puppies are six weeks old, they should be entirely weaned and receiving only occasional visits from their mother.

Most veterinarians recommend a temporary DHL (distemper, hepatitis, leptospirosis) shot when the puppies are six weeks of age. This remains effective for about two weeks. Then at eight weeks of age, the puppies should receive the series of permanent shots for DHL protection. It is also a good idea to discuss with your vet the advisability of having your puppies inoculated against the dreaded parvovirus at the same time. Each time the pups go to the vet for shots, you should bring stool samples so that they can be examined for worms. Worms go through various stages of development and may be present in a stool sample even though the sample does not test positive in every checkup. So do not neglect to keep careful watch on this.

The puppies should be fed four times daily until they are three months old. Then you can cut back to three feedings daily. By the time the puppies are six months of age, two meals daily are sufficient. Some people feed their dogs twice daily throughout their lifetime; others go to one meal daily when the puppy becomes one year of age.

The ideal age for puppies to go to their new homes is between eight and twelve weeks, although some puppies successfully adjust to a new home when they are six weeks old. Be sure that they go to their new owners accompanied by a description of the diet you've been feeding them and a schedule of the shots they have already received and those they still need. These should be included with the registration application and a copy of the pedigree.

The notable German Shorthair, Ch. Robin Crest Chip, winning Best in Show at Greenwich Kennel Club in 1962. The judge is Mrs. M. Hartley Dodge, owner of Giralda Farms. John Remondi handling. Chip co-owned by Rita and John Remondi, who also bred him.

Chapter 16

Traveling with Your Dog

When you travel with your dog, to shows or on vacation or wherever, remember that everyone does not share our enthusiasm or love for dogs and that those who do not, strange creatures though they seem to us, have their rights, too. These rights, on which we should not encroach, include not being disturbed, annoyed, or made uncomfortable by the presence and behavior of other people's pets. Your dog should be kept on lead in public places and should recognize and promptly obey the commands "Down," "Come," "Sit," and "Stay."

Take along his crate if you are going any distance with your dog. And keep him in it when riding in the car. A crated dog has a far better chance of escaping injury than one riding loose in the car should an accident occur or an emergency arise. If you do permit your dog to ride loose, never allow him to hang out a window, ears blowing in the breeze. An injury to his eyes could occur in this manner. He could also become overly excited by something he sees and jump out, or he could lose his balance and fall out.

Never, ever under any circumstances, should a dog be permitted to ride loose in the back of a pick-up truck. It is horrible that some people do transport dogs in this manner, and I think it cruel and shocking. How easily such a dog can be thrown out of the truck by sudden jolts or an impact! That many dogs have jumped out at the sight of something exciting along the way is certain. Some unthinking individuals tie the dog, probably not realizing that were he to jump under those circumstances, his neck would be broken, he could be dragged alongside the vehicle, or he could be hit by another vehicle. If

The German Wirehaired Pointer Dual and Amateur Field Ch. Lutz Zur Cadenburg, C.D., T.D., at Westminster at ten years of age. Owned by Silke Alberts, Cadenberg Wirehaireds, Vallejo, California. Handled by Marge Mares.

you are for any reason taking your dog in an open back truck, please have sufficient regard for that dog to at least provide a crate for him, and then remember that, in or out of a crate, a dog riding under the direct rays of the sun in hot weather can suffer and have his life endangered by the heat.

If you are staying at a hotel or motel with your dog, exercise him somewhere other than in the flower beds and parking lot of the property. People walking to and from their cars really are not thrilled at "stepping in something" left by your dog. Should an accident occur, pick it up with a tissue or a paper towel and deposit it in a proper receptacle; do not just walk off leaving it to remain there. Usually there are grassy areas on the sides of and behind motels where dogs can be exercised. Use them rather than the more conspicuous, usually carefully tended, front areas or those close to the rooms. If you are becoming a dog show enthusiast, you will eventually need an exercise pen to take with you to the show. Exercise pens are ideal to use when staying at motels, too, as they permit you to limit the dog's roaming space and to pick up after him more easily.

Never leave your dog unattended in the room of a motel unless you are absolutely, positively certain that he will stay there quietly and not damage or destroy anything. You do not want a long list of complaints from irate guests, caused by the annoying barking or whining of a lonesome dog in strange surroundings or an overzealous watch dog barking furiously each time a footstep passes the door or he hears a sound from an adjoining room. And you certainly do not want to return to torn curtains or bedspreads, soiled rugs, or other embarrassing evidence of the fact that your dog is not really house-reliable after all.

If yours is a dog accustomed to traveling with you and you are positive that his behavior will be acceptable when left alone, that is fine. But if the slightest uncertainty exists, the wise course is to leave him in the car while you go to dinner or elsewhere; then bring him into the room when you are ready to retire for the night.

When you travel with a dog, it is often simpler to take along from home the food and water he will need rather than buying food and looking for water while you travel. In this way he will have the rations to which he is accustomed and which you know agree with him, and there will be no fear of problems due to different drinking water. Feeding on the road is quite easy now, at least for short trips, with all the splendid dry prepared foods and high-quality canned meats available. A variety of lightweight, refillable water containers can be bought at many types of stores.

If you are going to another country, you will need a health certificate from your veterinarian for each dog you are taking with you, certifying that each has had rabies shots within the required time preceding your visit.

Be careful always to leave sufficient openings to ventilate your car when the dog will be alone in it. Remember that during the summer, the rays of the sun can make an inferno of a closed car within only a few minutes, so leave enough window space open to provide air circulation. Again, if your dog is in a crate, this can be done quite safely. The fact that you have left the car in a shady spot is not always a guarantee that you will find conditions the same when you return. Don't forget that the position of the sun changes in a matter of minutes, and the car you left nicely shaded half an hour ago can be getting full sunlight far more quickly than you may realize. So, if you leave a dog in the car, make sure there is sufficient ventilation and check back frequently to ascertain that all is well.

Ch. Robin Crest Chip steps smartly around the ring handled by breeder-owner
John Remondi.

Chapter 17

Responsibilities of Breeders and Owners

The first responsibility of any person breeding dogs is to do so with care, forethought, and deliberation. It is inexcusable to breed more litters than you need to carry on your show program or to perpetuate your bloodlines. A responsible breeder should not cause a litter to be born without definite plans for the safe and happy disposition of the puppies.

A responsible dog breeder makes absolutely certain, so far as is humanly possible, that the home to which one of his puppies will go is a good home, one that offers proper care and an enthusiastic owner. To be admired are those people who insist on visiting (although doing so is not always feasible) the prospective owners of their puppies, to see if they have suitable facilities for keeping a dog, that they understand the responsibility involved, and that all members of the household are in accord regarding the desirability of owning one. All breeders should carefully check out the credentials of prospective purchasers to be sure that the puppy is being placed in responsible hands.

Certainly no breeder ever wants a puppy or grown dog he has raised to wind up in an animal shelter, in an experimental laboratory, or as a victim of a speeding car. While complete control of such a situation may be impossible, it is at least our responsibility to make every effort to turn over dogs to responsible people. When selling a puppy, it is a good idea to do so with the understanding that should it become necessary to place the dog in other hands, the purchaser will first contact you, the breeder. You may want to help in some way, possibly by buying or taking back the dog or placing it elsewhere. It is not fair just to sell our puppies and then never again give a thought to their welfare. Family problems arise, people may be forced to move where dogs are prohibited, or people just plain grow bored with a dog and its care. Thus the dog becomes a victim. You, as the dog's breeder, should concern yourself with the welfare of each of your dogs and see to it that the dog remains in good hands.

The final obligation every dog owner shares, be there just one dog or an entire kennel involved, is that of making detailed, explicit plans for the future of our dearly loved animals in the event of the owner's death. Far too many of us are apt to procrastinate and leave this very important matter unattended to, feeling that everything will work out or that "someone will see to them." The latter is not too likely, at least not to the benefit of the dogs, unless you have done some advance planning which will assure their future well-being.

Life is filled with the unexpected, and even the youngest, healthiest, most robust of us may be the victim of a fatal accident or sudden illness. The fate of our dogs, so entirely in our hands, should never be left to chance. If you have not already done so, please get together with your lawyer and set up a clause in your will specifying what you want done with each of your dogs, to whom they will be entrusted (after first making absolutely certain that the person selected is willing and able to assume the responsibility), and telling the locations of all registration papers, pedigrees, and kennel records. Just think of the possibilities which might happen otherwise! If there is another family member who shares your love of the dogs, that is good and you have less to worry about. But if your heirs are not dog-oriented, they will hardly know how to proceed or how to cope with the dogs themselves, and they may wind up disposing of or caring for your dogs in a manner that would break your heart were you around to know about it.

In our family, we have specific instructions in each of our wills for each of our dogs. A friend, also a dog person who regards her own dogs with the same concern and esteem as we do ours, has agreed to take over their care until they can be placed accordingly and will make certain that all will work out as we have planned. We have this person's name and phone number prominently displayed in our van and car and in our wallets. Our lawyer is aware of this fact. It is all spelled out in our wills. The friend has a signed check of ours to be used in case of an emergency or accident when we are traveling with the dogs; this check will be used to cover her expense to come and take

Ch. Gretchenhof Moonsong with Joyce Shellenbarger.

over the care of our dogs should anything happen to make it impossible for us to do so. This, we feel, is the least any dog owner should do in preparation for the time our dogs suddenly find themselves without us. There have been so many sad cases of dogs unprovided for by their loving owners, left to heirs who couldn't care less and who disposed of them in any way at all to get rid of them, or left to heirs who kept and neglected them under the misguided idea that they were providing them "a fine home with lots of freedom." All of us *must* prevent any of these misfortunes befalling our own dogs who have meant so much to us!

Index